I0575339

Andrew Reid

Vox clamantium

The Gospel of the People

Andrew Reid

Vox clamantium
The Gospel of the People

ISBN/EAN: 9783337280475

Printed in Europe, USA, Canada, Australia, Japan

Cover: Foto ©Lupo / pixelio.de

More available books at **www.hansebooks.com**

VOX CLAMA NTIVM

The Gospel

of

The People

by

Writers, Preachers & Workers

Brought together by Andrew Reid

London

A. D. Innes & Co.

Bedford Street

1894

Go and sell that thou hast, and give to the poor, and thou shalt have treasure in heaven.

Many that are first shall be last, and the last shall be first.

Thou shalt not covet : but Tradition
Approves all forms of Competition.

A. H. CLOUGH.

PREFACE.

———✦———

THE writers in this volume represent varying schools of thought, often very far apart. Each is responsible solely for his own contribution, and is in no way committed to special doctrines laid down by any of his associates.

In certain cases, the articles were written under the expectation that the volume would be called "Preaching unto the Preachers;" hence they were more directly addressed to the Clergy.

But there is one central principle common to all— that to every one, but most of all to those who call themselves Christians, the precepts of the Sermon on the Mount have not passed away, and belong no less to public than to private life. For this reason, the title of "Vox" rather than "Voces" Clamantium has been adopted.

ANDREW REID.

CONTENTS.

Contents.

VOX CLAMANTIUM

How long, O Lord, how long!

From the bosom of God, where Thou re-
posest, look down on the world where Thou
didst walk as a man. Didst Thou not teach us
to pray, "Thy kingdom come"? Didst Thou
not say that Thy kingdom was near, that some
who stood with Thee should not taste of death
till they had seen it come with power, that when
it came the poor should be blessed, the hungry
should be filled, the blind should see, the heavy-
laden should find rest, and the will of Thy
Father should be done on earth even as it is
done in heaven? With that promise didst Thou
not leave us for a little while, and in that hope
didst Thou not go in meekness to Thy death—
betrayed, belied, mocked, smitten, and cursed?

B

But nigh upon two thousand years have gone, O Lord, and Thy kingdom hath not come. Still receiveth the rich man his good things, and likewise Lazarus his evil things. Still doth the unjust steward who cannot dig, and to beg is ashamed, make to himself friends of the mammon of unrighteousness. Was Thy promise vain, and Thy hope in death a dream? From Thy heavenly place hast Thou seen Thy people watch and wait, and heard the cry of their despair? When, out of the darkness of the ninth hour on Calvary, at Thy triumphant shout "It is finished!" Thou enterest Paradise with the hand of the malefactor in Thy hand, didst Thou hear the awful voice of God proclaim, "Vain, vain, all is vain"?

Look down, O Lord, look down. Are the centuries a waste? Nigh upon two thousand years have gone since Thou didst walk the world, and the face of things is not unchanged.

In *Thy* Name now doth the Pharisee give alms in the street to the sound of a trumpet going before him. In Thy Name now doth the Levite pass by on the other side when a man hath fallen among thieves. In Thy Name now doth the lawyer lay on the poor burdens grievous to be borne. In Thy Name now doth the priest buy and sell the glad tidings of the kingdom, giving for the gospel of God the commandments of men, living in rich men's houses, faring sumptuously every day, praying with his lips, "Give us this day our daily bread," but saying to his soul, "Soul, thou hast much goods laid up for many years : take thine ease, eat, drink, and be merry."

Do men gather grapes of thorns, or figs of thistles? Is it this Thy gospel that yields that Thy fruit? Then will the master of the vineyard come shortly and say, "Cut it down; why cumbereth it the ground?"

Yet, Jesus of Nazareth, son of Mary and of

Joseph, Thy heart was single, Thy path was
pure, Thy words were as a child's story, and the
common people heard Thee gladly.   Thou didst
preach Thy gospel to the poor.   Thou didst
show us Lazarus in Abraham's bosom, the good
Samaritan having mercy on the fallen of Israel,
the publican in the temple smiting his breast,
and crying, "God be merciful to me a sinner!"
Thou didst shame the hypocrites, and fear the
face of no man.   Thou didst forgive the guilty.
woman, and didst suffer the Magdalene to love
Thee.   Thou didst teach us to lay up our treasure
in heaven, to sell all and to give to the poor,
to go forth in Thy Name without purse or scrip
or second coat, trusting to our Father for our
food, even as the birds of the air, and for our
raiment, even as the flowers of the field.   Thou
didst walk the world as a man and didst not fall.
Thou hadst choice of the kingdoms of the world
and didst put the prince of it behind Thy back.

Thou wast poor as Thy children and true as Thy gospel. The foxes had holes and the birds of the air had nests; but Thou hadst not where to lay Thine head.

Thy words were simple, and brave, and beautiful; but we have made them strange, and a howling and dark.

Thy gospel was peace and mercy and love; but we have made it violence and opposition and hate.

Thy life was human and God-like and finished, but we have made it unlike a man's, unlike a God's, a fragment, a symbol, and a mystery.

Nigh upon two thousand years have gone, and the world is full of the rumour of Thy Name. On the tongues of men Thou art Saviour, Redeemer, and Christ. But is it from fear that Thou wouldst find no faith on the earth that Thy kingdom doth not come?

How long, O Lord, how long!

The Christian Church and the Problem of Poverty.

THAT poverty is an evil, to be minimized by all possible means, and to be got rid of if that be practicable, I take to be a statement upon which all Christians, and all earnest men, ought to be agreed. When the Master said, " The poor ye have always with you," it is clear, no less from the context than from the words themselves, that He was not uttering a prediction, but stating a fact, a fact of His own time, but not necessarily of all future time. The Church has always looked upon the relief of poverty as one of her primary duties ; the only question is as to the best and most useful methods by which relief may be given.

It is hardly necessary to spend space in an endeavour to define poverty, or to explain the sense in which it is used in this paper. Becky Sharp thought that she could have been a good woman on £5000 a year, and it may be presumed that in her view poverty meant something less than that sum. Not long since, a writer in one of the monthlies provoked some amusement by discussing the possibilities of living upon a yearly income of £800, and we are familiar with the little manuals, which profess to show us how we may live comfortably, with due provision for the rainy day, upon less than half of that amount.

It is not poverty such as this that we have here to discuss, but that which we all understand sufficiently well to be able to dispense with any other definition than is furnished by Mr. C. Booth's maps ; that awful state of degradation and misery which follows upon the want of life's necessaries, and in which tens of thousands of our fellow-Englishmen are existing at this moment, with no faintest hope of ever reaching anything better. Becky Sharp touched the fringe of a deep social truth in her famous saying, little as she thought it ; for poverty is not merely evil in that it brings misery and pain and death, but in that it is beyond question a grave hindrance to the development of all higher and nobler forms of human life. Board-school children, breakfastless and cold, are less capable of being taught than if they were properly fed and clad. Men, whose whole interest is inevitably absorbed in the ghastly struggle to find bread for themselves and their families, can scarcely be expected to think much of their intellectual culture or their moral and spiritual development. True, the life is more than meat ; man does not live by bread alone. But he cannot live without bread, and if he has not enough bread he cannot live in health of mind and spirit any more than of body. Too much bread—"fulness of bread"—has the same effect on him.

Most men are disposed to allow far too little, in considering these questions, for the influence of environment on character. If it is too much to say with some moderns that "environment makes character," it is barely sufficient to say that it has a very large share in the moulding and making of each one of us. Along with heredity, it is one of God's chiefest instruments in the education of man. A healthy environment, therefore, should be secured, so far as is possible, for every human being. It will not indeed of itself make him either good or wise. The soul, in Tennyson's " Palace of Art," surrounded herself with a perfect environment of culture and refinement; yet she nearly died of selfish despair. But a healthy environment can help, to an incalculable extent, in the making of good and wise men ; it can remove difficulties out of the path ; it can create as it were a climate and soil suitable for the growth of good seed of all kinds. An evil environment, on the other hand, is one of the worst misfortunes which can befall any man. For one who rises above

its influence and conquers his doom, thousands sink
deeper and deeper, handing on to their children a
heritage of character already fatally loaded in the scale
of evil, to be weighted yet more hopelessly by the
continued power of degrading surroundings. To expect that men will strive victoriously against such a
destiny is to expect them to show forth the virtues of
saint and hero at once. Could we ourselves do as
much under like conditions? A famous English
reformer once said as he watched a condemned criminal
led forth to die, "There, but for the grace of God, goes
John Bradford." What should we have been had our
own lives been environed as are the lives of nearly one
half the families of this country?

Poverty is thus an evil, not merely because it is the
fruitful source of misery, though that is bad enough;
but because it tends directly to promote the growth of
wickedness, and to hamper the advancement of wisdom
and righteousness. Even those, therefore, who would
contend that the Christian Church is not concerned
with the promotion of men's happiness, and the getting
rid of misery, in this world, will admit that she is, or
ought to be, very seriously concerned to lessen, or to
destroy, such a formidable obstacle in the way of the
work her Master has laid upon her, as His organized
society for warring with the evil and building up the right.

It may be urged that this is universally admitted, and that, as has been already said, the Church in all ages has looked upon it as a duty to relieve the poor. But that is not enough. It is her office to convert sinners, to snatch brands from the burning ; but the Church has more to do than that. She has to find out how and why they fell into the burning ; to make it as difficult as possible for others to fall in ; to quench, if it may be, the burning itself. The conquest of sin is her high mission, no less than the saving of individuals out of its power. Just so, the relief of the poor is but a part of the Church's work with regard to poverty. She must go on to inquire what influences have combined to make men poor, and how those influences should be dealt with.

It is just at this point that many of us feel our modern Church organization and work to be defective. We spend strength and money in saving individuals, while we are often forgetful of the larger and heavier task. We deal with the outward symptoms of social disease, while we fail to reach or to grapple with its inner causes. The scientific physician can never be satisfied until he has discovered and attacked the cause which produces the symptoms. Merely to drive the symptoms out of sight is to increase the virulence of the disease. As an illustration of what is meant, let us take the temperance movement. That movement has done very noble work, allowing for all qualifications and deductions. But it has concentrated attention and labour upon symptoms, and only in a much slighter degree recognized and done battle with causes. Intemperance is undoubtedly a cause of poverty as of crime ; but is not poverty also a cause of intemperance ? The miserable homes of so many, the uncertainty of employment, long hours of exhausting toil, bad and insufficient food, strain upon brain and nerves, want of wholesome recreation, the sense of hopelessness for the future ;—who shall say that these are not causes, far more frequently than fruits, of intemperance ? Hence, if the evil is to be adequately met, something more must be attempted than fervid personal appeal to individuals for conversion and amendment. The temperance organizations should direct their artillery against bad housing, overwork, and other causes which make for drunkenness, no less than upon the drunkards themselves.

Similarly in the case of all moral disease. I submit that poverty, and the conditions which make for poverty, are shown to be primary causes of an enormous proportion of the sin of London and England ; and that the Church cannot hope to deal with the sin without attacking the cause. If this be "secular work " then it

is such secular work as was her Master's healing of
physical disease. The physical is so closely linked with
the mental and spiritual, that they can scarcely be
treated apart. Physical evil stimulates the growth of
moral evil, and to do battle with the latter involves war
to the knife with the former. So Lord Shaftesbury
saw when he began his great work for the bettering of
the physical conditions under which women and
children laboured. It was not a "secular" work with
him. To him, as he said in his first speech on the
Factory Acts, in 1833, it was "a great religious
question." The good earl has gone to his own place,
full of years and honours. It is for us to take up the
work in which he nobly showed the way, in his own
spirit. The struggle against poverty and the powers
which make for poverty, is a great religious question.

But even admitting the existence of an appalling
mass of poverty and misery, it is urged that all this is
really people's own fault ; that the drunken, thriftless
habits of the poor, their utter want of foresight and
prudence, are the true causes of social suffering ; and
that therefore the remedy lies in persuading them to
be provident and sober.

Unquestionably it is the fact that recklessness and
drunkenness will lead to suffering, just as debt and
gambling must entail their own bitter consequences ;

but although they aggravate the evils of poverty, it by no means follows that they are its chief causes. As has already been said, these vices are produced by poverty, at least as often as they produce it. And will it be contended seriously by any intelligent observer of the facts, that if we were all total abstainers we should thereby abolish poverty? Undoubtedly individuals would be happier and better off, but wages would not be raised, employment would not be one whit more certain. This "argument" always seems to me to resemble the assertion that because in a race a man with five yards' start has an advantage, it would be best to give everybody five yards' start. The evils caused by drink are horrible enough, and no one can deny them, or have any wish except to see them lessened, and help to do it. But, when that is done, you still have the problem to solve. You have been hitting out in the wrong place; at least for our present purpose.

So with thrift. Thrift is a good thing. But take the case of a workman who earns good wages, say thirty-five shillings a week. Allowing for rent, trade union payments, and necessaries, how much is left for saving? Nay, is it right for a man to save, if by so doing he deprives himself and his children of what they ought to have, say, in the way of wholesome recreation?

Moreover, if all workmen were as thrifty as some are, the result would inevitably be a reduction in wages. The "iron law" tends invariably to reduce wages to the living point, as every economist knows. If, therefore, the men earning thirty-five shillings a week made thirty shillings serve them for weekly expenses, wages would slowly but certainly sink to thirty shillings ; for the employer, ever on the alert to cut down his outgoings, would soon find that as a thrifty man could live on less than another, he could get him for less. Thrifty workmen would assuredly push out the others and take their places. But they would also take lower wages, and the only real gainer by the workman's increased thrift would be the employer. It will be seen how this argument can also be applied, *mutatis mutandis*, to the case of the teetotal workman. Clearly we have not got at the causes of the trouble in drink and thriftlessness. They are among the saddest incidents of poverty, but they are not its sources. If we could cure them at a blow the ghost would come again. It would never really have gone. The evils exist in countries and districts where workers are sober and prudent, no less than in London, where they often are not.

It is, I think, unfair to assert that well-to-do people are, as a rule, indifferent to the evils which exist. There

are far too many who try not to see them, like the
Quaker who is recorded to have driven from London
to Plymouth with the blinds of his carriage carefully
drawn down all the time, and there are some—more
I fear than we commonly think—who see and know
something of the facts, and who coldly leave them
alone with a cynical shrug and a murmured *après moi
le déluge*. But these are the minority, a large minority
perhaps, but a minority still. The bulk of the upper
and middle classes are painfully alive to the miseries
of the poor, and are ready to help, if only they knew
how to help effectively and well. That, however, is just
what they do not know. They are overwhelmed by the
complexity and difficulty of the problem. They hesitate about giving money, for they have been warned
so incessantly of the evils of indiscriminate alms, that
they have ceased to give as they used to do, for fear
of doing harm instead of good. If they formerly gave
not wisely but too well, they have now reversed the
process, and give not well, but too wisely. For myself
I confess that of two evils, I prefer the former error to
the latter. Better a warm heart, with all its faults and
risks, than a cold one. Better charity which forgets
prudence, than prudence which forgets charity. I had
rather run the risk of giving to an impostor or a
drunkard, than the risk of refusing to help a man in

need, the Charity Organization Society notwithstanding. I do not mean that we should make no inquiries, and take no pains to follow up a "case." I do mean that in probably the majority of such cases there is some doubt as to genuineness; the record is not spotless. Well, let the benefit of the doubt be given in favour of the "case," rather than, as is too usual, against it. Let us cease to use the Charity Organization Society as a convenient means for finding reasons why we should not help the poor. Let us remember that the "case" is a human being in want and suffering. Let us bear in mind that if we make it a rule "never to give to beggars," there are ways enough and to spare in which money may be employed for relieving the poor, apart from the evils of "pauperizing" and encouraging imposture or carelessness.

But, when all is said and done, private charity cannot solve the problem. It can only help individuals. It does not touch the *causes* of the distress; and so long as those causes are allowed to exist and develop unchecked, we might as well try to fill a sieve with water. If some one invents a machine for making match-boxes, and a company is floated to work the patent, the result would probably be that while the shareholders and directors made fortunes, Bryant and May's match-girls would be thrown in hundreds and thousands out of employment, so flooding the women's labour market, and reducing wages all round. Is private subscription the wisest, most effectual, and most reasonable method of meeting a difficulty which ought to be prevented, surely, rather than need to be remedied? Let the answer be given by those who know the inner history of the Mansion House Funds.

The Christian Church might do much to bring us nearer to the abolition of poverty if her preachers would speak out fearlessly upon social questions. But it must be observed that even then there are large numbers who lie outside the range of such an appeal. Preachers can only reach those who come to hear them preach. What of the selfish and wicked, who either would not come, or, if they come, would not listen or heed? What of the still larger number who are indifferent? What of the masses of the men who, like the liberated Israelites, are so dulled and blunted by slavery that they prefer Egypt to the efforts and responsibilities of freedom? The voice of the most dogmatic and earnest preacher cannot reach these and such as these. Personal appeal can do something, but not all, or anything like all. It can bring Christians face to face with the fact that our modern social organization is not in harmony with the New Testament; but it cannot touch those larger classes who, for one reason or another, are

C

insensible to such appeals, or do not recognize the authority upon which the appeal is founded. Moreover, an earnest man, trying to carry the principle of the Christian life into his social and commercial relations, will find himself hampered and thwarted at every turn by the conditions under which his business must needs be carried on. Over and over again I have been told, alike by employers and employed, "You can't be a Christian in business. You can't be honest and truthful. You would be ruined if you tried it."

Admitting, for the sake of argument, that this is saying too much, it must be granted that the cynical motto, "The golden rule must not come outside the Churches," prevails so widely in business and in social politics, that a man who will not bow the knee to this Baal stands small chance of success. The conditions and influences of his environment will be too much for him. He is caught in a great machine, and he must either go round with it, or be torn to pieces in struggling to go the other way.

I think I am understating rather than exaggerating the facts of the case. Browning's famous line—

"How very hard it is to be a Christian,"

might well be the despairing cry of a man who had striven to carry his Christianity into his trade and social relations.

It seems clear, then, that the earnest man must be helped to do what is right, and the selfish man hindered in doing what is wrong. This can only be carried out by one power, the State ; and by one means, legislation. The spirit of the New Testament must be breathed into our laws and their administration. For all our "national Christianity" this is not now the fact, although we are moving towards it more and more quickly. Take a single example. The rights of property are held so sacred among us, that offences against the person are punished more lightly than offences against the purse. Interference with property is still looked upon with the greatest jealousy and dislike. Yet the teaching of our Master is not of this sort. As one of the most judicially minded and calmly impartial of writers has said, "The whole strain of the teaching of Christ runs counter to the glorification of private ownership, and of the right of every one to do what he will with his own." *

Again, in the New Testament it is clear that idleness is a sin, and that every man ought to work, as a condition of life. "If any man will not work, neither let him eat." Yet among ourselves the existence of an idle class who "toil not, neither do they spin," is not regarded as an anomaly. Those who belong to it are

* Mr. Llewellyn Davies on "Property" in his "Social Questions."

rather envied than pitied ; they consume the fruits of
other men's labour, giving back nothing in return—
producing nothing.

It may be urged that legislation cannot alter human
hearts, and that selfish and greedy men will not be
made unselfish by Act of Parliament. Most true ; but
they can be prevented by legislation from selfishly
growing rich at the expense of their fellow-creatures.
Lord Shaftesbury did this when, in the teeth of the
opposition of the manufacturing interests, he carried
the Factory Acts. Since then we have had Mines
Regulation Acts, Truck Acts, Adulteration Acts, Land
Acts ; all of them movements in the right direction—
all efforts (however inadequate and incomplete) to prevent the oppression and exploitation of the workers at
the hands of selfish employers. Lord Shaftesbury
recognized that his work was a religious one, and he
was neither afraid, nor ashamed, of being called what
he really was—a Christian Socialist.

The right of the individual is subordinate to the
right of the community. It is not lawful for any man
to do what he will with his own, if in so doing he
wrongs his brethren. Nor is the wrong less because
it is done in a manner permitted, or at least not prevented, by the law as it stands. Slavery is not less
wrong from the Christian point of view in countries

where it is allowed by law than in countries where it is forbidden. It must be recognized that it is wrong, although not at present prevented by law, for wealthy railway companies to work their signalmen eighteen hours or more at a stretch, rather than lessen their dividends by employing more men and so thinning the ranks of the unemployed. The property of the shareholders is of more importance, apparently, than the lives of the passengers, the health and strength of the signalmen, and the starvation of men out of work.

The Christian Fathers were emphatic, not to say vehement, upon the iniquity of the rule of Mammon.* "The rich man is a thief," says St. Basil the Great. "The rich are robbers: a kind of equality must be effected by making gifts out of their abundance." "Better all things were in common" (St. Chrysostom). "Wealth is always the product of theft, committed, if not by the actual possessor, by his ancestors" (St. Jerome). "Nature created community; private property is the offspring of usurpation" (St. Ambrose). "In strict justice, everything should belong to all. Iniquity alone has created private property" (St. Clement).

These words read like the ravings of some street orator of to-day. Yet they could easily be paralleled

---

* These extracts are quoted from Lavaleye's "Socialism of To-day," Introd., p. xix,

from the great divines and preachers of a later day,
and from the sermons of our English bishops and
parish priests. The Reformation pulpit was singularly
outspoken on the burning questions of land and
property, as the most casual reader of Latimer or
Pilkington will remember.

Are we to carry on this tradition, or to look upon
these matters as none of ours? If we leave them alone
we shall lose the greatest opportunity a Church ever
had. Whether we like it or not, the progress of the
nation tends in a Socialistic direction. It is for us to
say whether its basis shall be Christian or not.

I have no hesitation in urging that the State should
be called upon to interfere : (a) to protect the helpless ;
(b) to prevent the greedy and selfish from enriching
themselves at the expense of others. This seems to
me to be the plain duty of a Christian nation. It is
simply the principle of Christian brotherhood and love
applied to social legislation and to commercial life.
The stock reply that this sort of thing is " sentimental "
and " unpractical," may be brushed upon one side
without much ado. A little more sentiment is just
what we want ; and some of us have come to loathe
the very word " practical," owing to its misuse in such
a connection as this. If it be indeed " sentimental " to
maintain that a Christian nation should be Christian in

its care of the poor, and in its commercial ideals, then
Christ Himself is open to the same criticism. He gave
us the true test of a nation's greatness, the crucial point
upon which every nation shall be judged of God, in
the "parable of the nations," known as the parable of
the sheep and the goats. When the Son of man shall
sit upon the throne of His glory, and before Him shall
be gathered all the nations, what is the one question put
to them—the single test, according to which they are
separated as sheep or goats, on right hand or on left?
Not wealth, or conquest, or capacity for rule; but care
of the needy, the poor, the oppressed. "Inasmuch as
ye did it unto one of My brethren, even these least, ye
did it unto Me," is His word to a Christian nation, not
to a charitable individual.

Nor is it of any greater force to talk of interference
with "personal liberty," or to repeat stale gibes about
"grandmotherly legislation." This is only the old
laissez faire argument over again, which, as we have
seen, has been blown out of the water long ago. There
is no such thing as personal liberty in this sense.
Liberty is not freedom to do what you like; but freedom to do what you ought. Moreover, "freedom of
contract" does not exist between a wealthy capitalist
and an unemployed workman. The former can impose
his own terms; the latter must needs accept them, or

starve. It is merest mockery to tell the workman that
he has any "freedom" in such a choice. Freedom to
go hungry is at best a doubtful blessing.

"Independence" is another of the fine words with
which objectors to State interference make much play.
It is nothing but a name, a false and rotten idol, which
needs only one bold blow—like that of the soldier who
overthrew the image of Serapis, and sent its inhabitant
rats flying in all directions—to dethrone it for ever.
Which of us is *independent* in any real or intelligible
sense? We are dependent upon each other, dependent
upon the State, dependent upon God, at every moment
and in every action and relation of life. As Maurice
was never tired of saying, "No man is really free until
he has discovered his own absolute dependence."

Further, it happens that we have ready to our hand
a striking illustration of the inadequacy of voluntary
effort to meet present needs, and the necessity of falling
back upon the State. The Early Closing Association
for a long time set its face against any demand for
legislation in favour of shorter hours in shops. It confined its endeavours to "moral suasion," like Artemus
Ward in the case of the historic kangaroo. But this
admirable weapon was as powerless in the hands of the
association as in those of the showman. After infinite
labour, the secretaries and officers would succeed in

persuading, say, the drapers of Camberwell to close early on one evening in the week. All would consent with a single cantankerous exception. This worthy would refuse to do any such thing; and, as a consequence, he would secure all the late customers and—as we say in the West—would "sloke them away" from the other shops. This was putting a premium upon late closing; the other drapers could not afford to lose custom to this extent; it was a weapon in the competitive war which would ruin them. So, unwillingly, they gradually yielded, and ceased to close early. This sort of thing happened over and over again, until at last, the Early Closing Association, pressed by a younger society, gave up its reliance upon voluntary effort, and declared that only legislation could meet the need.

More than mere legislation is wanted. Sir John Lubbock's Shop Hours Regulation Act was carried through Parliament, but no means for enforcing it were provided, and unless a small committee of determined men had taken up the matter, found the funds, and instituted prosecutions, the Act would have been a dead letter, and would not have been renewed when it expired, while all the sweaters and exploiters would have exclaimed in jubilant chorus that no young persons were overworked in English shops, and that employers were the most beneficent and unselfish of men!

Granting, then, that the true remedy for poverty is to be looked for in the Christianizing of methods of government, and the direct interference of the State or the municipality to protect the poor, and to prevent the exploitation of labour, in what directions and to what definite ends should this principle be applied ?

It will necessarily be directed towards finding temporary remedies for poverty in the first place, and permanent remedies in the second ; or, to put it in another way, it will endeavour to mitigate the *results* of poverty, while at the same time it traces and strikes at the *causes*. I will confine myself at present to temporary remedies, some of which may very possibly be found to apply, in some degree, when we pass on to consider permanent remedies.

Emigration and one or two other proposals, which we refuse to accept as remedies, may fairly claim to be regarded as temporary means of relief.   I believe, however, that they can only be successful, even within this limited sphere, if they are directed by the State, or the local organ of the State.   Otherwise there may be isolated experiments which succeed ; but, like the many efforts to promote co-operative farms or factories, they will sooner or later languish and fail, as General Booth's much-vaunted scheme is surely doomed to do.

Let me mention three practical methods by which, as

it seems to me, the Government or the local authorities may seek to give temporary relief to the poverty of to-day.

I. Useful relief works in town and country. Here, once more, we have practical examples at hand. During the distress in Lancashire which followed upon the cotton famine, Mr., now Sir Robert Rawlinson, was sent down as commissioner with considerable powers to provide relief works. He organized the starving operatives and set them to road-making, with results that were successful from every point of view. Let any who wish to look into the matter be at the pains to disinter Sir R. Rawlinson's report, and they will cease to question the practicability of relief works. What was done then can be done again. There are acres and miles of sand and marsh, which unskilled labour, properly controlled and organized, could reclaim from the sea. There are places upon our coast—I know more than one such spot among the iron-bound rocks of North Cornwall — where blasting the cliffs and throwing them into the sea would be almost all that is needed to make a harbour of refuge, and to save thousands of lives year by year. England could spend her millions to put down black slavery. Can she not spare a few thousands to put down white poverty ? *

* On the whole question of the unemployed, see Mr. John Burns' "Fabian Tract," and Mr. Llewelyn Smith's very able "Report to the Board of Trade."

Again, in the winter of 1886, the vestry of Chelsea, anxious to deal with the unemployed of the district, gave large powers to their able and kindly surveyor, Mr. Strachan. He opened a registry for the unemployed, sifted them carefully, and set them to work to pave King's Road. The experiment was a brilliant success ; the work was done thoroughly well at a reasonable cost, and two thousand hungry men, skilled and unskilled, with their families, were employed and fed. Are there no other districts of the metropolis where roads need relaying or other necessary and useful work wants doing ? Why should it not be done by the local authority, without the intervention of a contractor, into whose pocket all the profit is pretty sure to find its way ?

II. Let the Government look into their own contracts and see that proper wages are paid—the trade-union rate at least. As a matter of fact, Government contract work is almost the last refuge of the hard-driven and destitute, so hard is it, and so ill paid. Readers of the " Bitter Cry of Outcast London " will remember the pathetic description there given of the making of policemen's overcoats. Surely, with all the wealth of the wealthiest of nations behind it, the English Government need not give out their work to the lowest bidder, and so really become the most gigantic and unrelenting of sweaters !

III. One free meal daily in Board Schools, where needed. This is, I believe, an absolutely imperative necessity; indeed, it might well be considered a permanent rather than a temporary measure. How can children be taught when they are faint with hunger? The stunted bodies and pale faces of average Londoners are admitted to be a consequence of semi-starvation during the years of growth. Voluntary effort cannot overtake the need. It must be done by the community. What argument against State provision of food is not equally valid against State provision of mental nutriment? Why, if I pay a rate to provide the children of my poorer neighbours with knowledge, should I not be rated to provide them with a yet more elementary necessity—the food, for want of which what I now pay is frequently thrown away? " Overpressure is but another name for underfeeding ? "

I think it is certain that in dealing with so vast a problem many experiments will have to be tried, and many failures and disappointments recorded, before a final solution is found. But I believe that there is very strong reason to look with high hope upon the results of efforts made in these directions. Temporary measures are of course, however, insufficient by them-selves. They are merely makeshifts and stopgaps. We have been too long content with administering temporary relief in times of acute distress, and laying the flattering unction to our souls that we have done our duty as Christians, and subscribed largely in charity. The people, and the workers, are not asking for charity now, in the limited and narrow sense to which we have accustomed them. They are asking for *justice*. They declare that labour does not receive the proper proportion of its own products ; that unjust and inequitable social arrangements have created poverty, and keep the great mass of the workers inevitably poor. " The husbandman that laboureth must be the first to partake of the fruits," is the apostolic, the Christian rule. We have made him the last, and have denied him even his fair share. " He that will not work, neither let him eat," is the New Testament precept. We have exactly reversed it, and the class that does the least work is the class that has the most to eat and drink.

The causes of poverty, according to the best modern economists, are to be found in the results of free competition for profit, and the monopoly of land and the means of production. The worker cannot so much as get to his work until he has made terms with the landlord and the capitalist. He has nothing but his labour-force, and he must sell it to an employer in order to live. The employer competes with other em-

ployers, in order to make his profit, and, for the same
reason, he buys his labour-force in the cheapest market.
He has to buy as much labour as possible for the
smallest wage. The workman competes with other
workmen for the right to work, which means for the
right to live. The man who is beaten in this fierce
struggle, in which every one's hand is against his
brother, must go to the wall, crushed and trodden
under the fighters' feet. He can starve, or he can
go to the workhouse, never afterwards to lose the
taint of pauperism, or to be able to find regular
employment.

　　Even the workman who succeeds, and who is
allowed to work for his living, must work on his employer's terms. The hours may be long, the wages
low, the labour hard, the conditions unhealthy; no
matter, he must take it or leave it. The employers
can fill his place in a moment if he leaves; the vast
army of unemployed only loses—and gains—a man.
True, in certain trades the workers have, to some
extent, protected themselves by their unions. But
as yet the unions only represent a minority of the
workers, and those less the sufferers from poverty than
the aristocracy of labour. Nor can they thoroughly
protect even the proportion of workmen belonging to
them. As in the case of temporary remedies, so here,

the State is the only power which can adequately deal with the vast and complex problem.

I. The first step is in the extension of the principle of Lord Shaftesbury's Factory Acts, and of Sir John Lubbock's Shop Hours Regulation Acts. These laws represent the interference of the State with employers, in order to prevent them from making profits by over-working women and children. They are Acts for the shortening of the hours of labour.

We have seen that adults need this protection quite as much as children. An unskilled non-unionist work-man is helpless in the employer's hands. Signalmen, tramcar-men, and many other classes less known to the public, are now cruelly and scandalously over-worked, in order that railway and omnibus companies may continue to pay large dividends to the share-holders. I say that the State ought to interfere in the name of the God of right and justice, and of Him who warned us that we cannot serve God and Mammon, to prevent such an exercise of the " rights " of property as this, and to make it punishable by law.

This can be done by legal prohibition of the exaction of more than a certain number of hours' work in a week from the labourer. Eight hours' work a day is enough for any man. Let all Government employments reduce their hours to this limit; let the exaction of more than forty-eight hours a week be prohibited, and the prohibition enforced by inspectors, as in the Factory Acts. The shareholders might certainly lose a proportion of their profits; but I say boldly that they ought to lose them, if they are not ashamed of making them out of the misery and degradation of their brethren. When I see the shareholders of wealthy railway and omnibus companies a little more anxious about the well-being of the men whose labour makes their dividends, and a little less anxious about getting high interest without asking ugly questions as to where it comes from, it will be time to talk about "robbery." As things are, they themselves might conceivably be called by some hard names, if He who denounced the devourers of the poor were face to face with them.

Reduction of the hours of labour would undoubtedly provide work for the unemployed, and result in better work being done by more vigorous workers, more interested, and more thorough in their work, as all experience goes to show. Nor would it reduce wages, because the main force which keeps wages down is the eagerness of the unemployed to take work on any terms. When the pressure upon the labour market is lightened, as it would be by this proposed measure, this force will cease to be effective, and the more un-

D

scrupulous employers will be deprived of the weapon which now they use with such terrible effect.

II. There is no doubt that this measure must be accompanied by an international labour law, or by the regulation of the immigration of foreign labourers, or both, in order to prevent the employers from flooding the market with cheap foreign labour. If it is possible for nations to come to agreement as to methods of warfare—*e.g.* as to the Red Cross, and the non-use of explosive bullets—surely it is possible for them to agree upon labour questions. There is a strong feeling in favour of international legislation in not a few European countries whose competition might be formidable, and · if a nation or nations should refuse reasonable terms, the democracy will not hesitate to adopt other measures.

III. The Poor Law must be reformed. In the principles which lie at the root of it, the Poor Law is entirely sound. Every man has the right to live ; the State has the right to exact an equivalent of work from him. But the workhouse system, and the general administration of the law, are admitted on all hands to be unsatisfactory. Mr. Herbert Mills' book, " Poverty and the State," has much interesting information, and many valuable suggestions, upon this matter, especially in regard to the workhouse system of Holland, from which much may be learned.

It will be convenient here to contrast the different systems prevailing in America and this country. In the United States there is no poor law and workhouse as such. Workshops are provided by the State, in which destitute persons are found employment at their several trades or callings, for which labour they receive a fair equivalent, according to the measure of their skill. The contract is a mutual one, and they retain all the rights of citizenship, so that, in point of fact, a person so helped to-day may, *cæteris paribus*, become President of the Republic in half a dozen years. In fact, it is a matter of common knowledge that in more cases than one, the rise of the President has been as creditable and as marked as that of Pope Adrian IV. from an English gutter.

In this country, the unfortunate "casual," who may have paid rates to the poor himself for years, and whom misfortune alone may have rendered destitute, seeks relief at the workhouse—truly no misnomer. For the two blankets and a board which courtesy calls a bed, some "skilly" for supper, and the same with a little bread for breakfast, he is compelled to break some hundredweights of stones—if a woman, to pick a given quantity of oakum—which occupies several hours, and entirely prevents the "casual" seeking employment that day. If he be physically incapable of performing this task, from want of strength or knowledge, he may be hauled before the nearest magistrate and—since poor Montagu Williams is dead—will almost inevitably receive *seven days' hard labour ;* while, to add insult to injury, after earning his scanty accommodation ten times over, he is still branded a "pauper," and loses all civil rights. If the poor starving family receive only a loaf or two, half a crown, or even medical aid by way of "outdoor relief," the same applies. Some attempt is being made in some parishes to improve upon this state of things ; but still the exception proves the rule.

IV. At the Wolverhampton Church Congress of 1887, Mr. Stanley Leighton, M.P., in his paper on Socialism, uttered the following striking sentence : "Much is required from him who has received much, little from him who has received little. The Christian carries out this principle in practice when he maintains the revolutionary doctrine, which he has preached for centuries, that if any class habitually uses functions guaranteed to it by the State, not for the public service, but against the interests of the community, then the legal conditions of the guarantee should be readjusted. Reform is always a Christian duty ; Revolution may be."

The time has come for Christians and Church-folk

to inquire whether the legal conditions which guarantee the holding of land by a few persons for their own private benefit should not be readjusted. In theory, the land of England belongs to the whole people, and the legal conditions which govern its possession should be adjusted, without injustice or wrong to any, so as to make the land more serviceable to the whole community than it is now. In the country the decay of the old system has divorced the labourer from the land to which it bound him. The result we have seen—depopulation of country districts, congestion in the towns. The labourer must be brought back to the land, not by peasant proprietorship, which cannot succeed, but by some wider, equitable, well-considered measure, through which the State, or the municipality, may gradually resume the possession of the soil, to be used for the advantage of the whole community. In the same way, ground-rents in towns, which are simply created by the industry of the community, should be employed for the benefit of the community, instead of the enrichment of a few.

V. Finally, a progressive income-tax upon all incomes, say, above £500 a year. This proposal receives powerful support from so capable an economist as Professor Symes, and is already within the sphere of practical politics. It is simply the taxation of those

who can best afford it, for the benefit of the State as
a whole; and if such a task should operate in the
direction of lessening the number of millionaires, and
people generally who have too much money, I venture
to think that little harm will be done.

"The last triumph of Christianity," said Channing,
"will be a triumph over competition." Or, as Maurice
independently put it, "Society must be reconstituted,
not on the basis of competition, which is Mammon's
law of selfishness, but on the basis of Christ's law of
brotherhood."

That great triumph can never be won until we
realize that there is something more sacred than private
property, viz. public right; and that, when the former
is found to encroach upon the latter, the State is bound
to step in and do justice.

Added to these permanent remedies should be not
only elementary education without fee, but free technical education to follow; and finally, higher-grade
education, even up to the universities themselves, will
be as free to all alike as now to the fortunate holders
of many scholarships—scholarships founded for the
children of the poor in the days of unenlightened
ecclesiasticism, but which, in our glorious era of
"liberal" progress, have been handed over by university reformers to the sons of men who can afford to

pay a first-rate coach. Such is the beauty of "free competition," in which the battle is always to the rich. Only gratuitous education can afford equal opportunity for all. The Church, which in other days did so much for the free teaching of the poor, should be the last to oppose it now.

I have, finally, to endeavour to give some suggestions by way of answer to the question, "What can I do personally to remedy poverty?"

I. The first thing is to recognize, once for all, that poverty is not a mysterious dispensation of Providence, which, for some inscrutable reason, is the stern lot of the majority of our race; but an evil brought about by causes which can be remedied, an evil to be fought against, and ultimately destroyed. When this is once clearly seen, the sincere and faithful Christian can no longer rest satisfied with private charity, the relief of individual distress. He will feel himself in duty bound to throw his influence as a citizen, his power as a man, into some organized effort for the study of the causes and the cure of poverty. He will press upon his county councillors, his M.P., his local authorities generally, that the supreme question of the day is the condition-of-England question. Unfortunately, very little can be got out of a body of men elected for a term of years, unless you make yourself a nuisance. They are ready enough to make promises before an election; afterwards they are equally ready to forget, or to postpone them until an election is coming round again. Like the unjust judge, they must be importuned and worried into doing their duty. If every parish clergyman were a tribune of the people, watching every sidelong attempt to rob them of their commons, to extend their hours of work, to impose harder conditions of labour, and then fearlessly exposing it in the public press, bringing it before proper authorities, regardless of personal conse- quences, he would do more for the cause of Christ and His Church among the working classes than all the Apologies that ever were written, and most of the sermons that ever were preached. Let the Christian laity who are stirred in conscience on these matters, move their clergy to become leaders in this new crusade, and then stand by them. Let them insist that right shall be done and promises kept. Parliament would soon find time to consider useful measures for the benefit of the poor if the Christian people of England insisted that it should be done, and "turned the world upside down" until it was attempted. I think, then, that my first duty in this matter is to make myself such a nuisance to all those whom I can reach, who are in a position to do something and don't do it, that, for very weariness, they will yield to keep me quiet; and even then I mean not to be kept quiet, nor bamboozled with fair words and promises, but to keep persistently working on towards the one great end.

II. We naturally wish to get our clothes, our food, our goods generally, as cheaply as possible; and I should suppose that if we find that we can get, say, our printing done cheaper at Smith's than at Brown's, we shall go eagerly to Smith's, and chuckle over our saved halfpence. Now, does it ever occur to us to ask how it is that Smith can do the same work for a less sum than Brown? It may be, of course, that the quality of the type or paper may account for the difference in the price. But it may be, and it probably is, the fact that Smith pays lower prices, works his people harder, or employs boys and women to do men's work, which enables him to sell his goods at less cost. In these days when competition is so keen, and profits are cut so fine it may, as a rule, be taken for granted that the cheap work is done by cutting down wages, or cutting down quality.

Now, I contend that we cannot rightly put the thing off by saying that it is not our business whether Smith pays fair wages or not. It *is* our business. For our saving has really come out of the extra hour's labour wrung from that pale, stunted man at the compositor's frame, or from the meat meal which would have given nourishment to his harassed wife, but which,

with his docked wages, he cannot afford.   It is the price
of that meal which has gone into our pockets, and over
which we are exulting.

The rage for cheapness is responsible for much of
the scamped work, bad conditions of labour, clipped
wages, and the like. Let us see clearly what we are
doing when we go to the cheap shop. Better pay a
few shillings more than have the blood of sweated
workmen on our hands. To be sure it is a difficult
thing to make certain whether your tradesmen pay
proper wages or not. The high-class honourable men
will make no difficulty about showing you their books,
and their time sheet ; but here of course it is easy for
an outsider to make mistakes or to be taken in. Nor
can we always be confident, even if we do not go to
cheap shops on principle, that the extra prices go into
the right pockets. With ordinary care and persever-
ance, however, this can be done, and we ought to do it
ourselves, and get our people to do it. "Go without
rather than buy cheap goods," unless you *know* that their
cheapness involves neither nastiness nor knavery.
Never deal at a house which does not pay at least the
trade-union rate of wages, or where the hours are more
than ten daily, at the very utmost. Rigorously shun
any business which pays large dividends to its shareholders and grinds its workers.

III. You have some money placed in safe invest-
ments, and it brings you in a tidy little income.
Perhaps they are shares in a company. Have you
ever thought that you are a partner in that company,
responsible for its acts, and profiting by its methods of
management ? The company's servants are *your*
servants; *their* labour produces *your* dividends; has
it ever occurred to you to inquire into the conditions
and circumstances of their labour? what wages they
receive for what hours of work? Your gas shares are
profitable ; how about the workmen who get no
Sundays, and slave for twelve hours then as on other
days, to enrich you? Your money was put into a
Limited Liability Company. You don't know much
about it, except that it has the name of a great
clothier's establishment, and that the dividends are
regularly paid. You were profoundly moved when you
read in the newspaper of that poor seamstress; a girl of
seventeen, who laid her head down upon her work and
died, after stitching sixteen hours a day at *three
farthings an hour* for days and months together.
That seamstress worked for the man to whom the
manager of your company gave out his work. She
worked for *you*, and your dividends went up when her
pay was cut down, and she had to work an extra hour
per day.

You have house property. Who lives in your houses, and for what purposes are they let? Your agent or your lawyer sees to it all, and pays you the rent regularly. Are you sure that your houses are not employed for the very vilest purposes? Are you sure that they are not among those crowded and unhealthy dwellings where the poor of our great cities herd like beasts? The best-paying property in London is of this sort. Surely, we should not be satisfied with asking whether our property is *safe;* we should ask if it is being rightly used, meaning by "rightly" something more than "legally."

It is no compensation, when we have allowed our money to be used for oppression and guilt, to spend upon good works what we do not spend upon ourselves. We should think at the very outset of others, when we have money to invest; and be content to be poorer, that our hands may be clear of our brothers' and sisters' blood. It is little enough, after all, that we can do. Let us, at least, do what we can to make this world better than we found it, by helping to brighten and purify our own little corner of it; and by seeing to it that our carelessness and want of thought does not lead to more harm, than our charity can result in good, while we labour steadfastly at the great task of discovering and doing battle with the causes of poverty.

Why should we teach people to be contented with evil conditions and grinding toil? "The first step towards social improvement," says Mr. Walter Besant, in one of his novels, "is to make people discontented with things as they are, so long as things are not what they ought to be."

A great subject—the greatest problem of our time—cannot be exhausted in a comparatively short essay. I know how much I have left unsaid, how lightly I have touched even those points I have raised, how many objections may be urged against the remedies suggested. Of one thing I am sure, that the gospel of Jesus Christ is the only power that can cast out the devils that oppress our society; and that of the unsolved social problems which perplex us all, *the Church still holds the key.* If this is to be a Christian Socialist —and I think it is—then I am not ashamed of the name.

H. C. SHUTTLEWORTH.

NOTE ON RELIEF WORKS.

Essex Side of Thames.

1. Reclaim Essex marshes, and turn into pasture or other land.
2. East Tilbury, past Hole Haven, etc., into Sea Reach.
3. From Benfleet to Leigh.
4. One mile below Leigh, to a point two miles below Southend—say,

four and a half miles and one wide, dredge and remove sand and mud, letting in the sea, build sea wall, breakwaters, etc., improving the fishing grounds and the district. Local authorities would pay largely to this.

5. Reclaim part of the Foulness Sand and entrances of the rivers Crouch, Blackwater, Colne, and build sea walls.

6. Reclaim lands at intervals, including sea walls and dykes, stretches of sometimes four and five miles long by two or three wide at Clacton, Walton, Ramsey, Dovercourt, estuaries of Stour and Orwell, Felixstowe, Southwold, Lowestoft, Yarmouth, right down to, and including the Wash, and along the Yorkshire and Northumbrian coast.

Kent Side.

1. Plumstead marshes from just beyond Woolwich right down to Belvedere.

2. One mile and a half below Gravesend to beyond Francis' Works at Cliffe, and Chalk, and well down into Sea Reach.

3. Approaches to the Medway, Port Victoria, and Sheerness, and part of Sheppey.

4. Whitstable Flats, and part of Herne Bay.

5. Beyond Folkestone, Sandwich, Sandgate, Romney Marsh, Dunchurch, Lydd, and Dungeness, two miles wide, and build sea walls, construct dykes for overflow, etc., right on to Sussex.

Harbours of Refuge all round coast, including Ireland, Wales, and Scotland, thereby saving thousands of lives per year, particularly among our hardy and noble fishermen. Present loss entails poverty to the community.

7. Improve and set up the Irish fisheries, which alone could furnish food for all England.

This is *coast* work only.

There are millions on millions of acres lying idle in bog land and moorland, in Yorkshire, Derby, and Wilts.

In all relief works on a large scale, there is likely to be trouble with the loafer class, who would rather do anything than a day's work. Drastic and summary measures of treatment are necessary.

In the Matter of Incubus and Co.

THIRTY years ago Carronbrae feared God. A year ago it feared the Incubus Coal and Iron Company. To-day the fear of the Lord is getting a second chance. The originator of the Incubus Company was a far-seeing German analyst from Dusseldorf, who, upon departing this life for parts unknown, left his daughter to the senior of the present partners in the business, and his Latinized name to the great concern which had grown up at Carronbrae in the Scottish westlands.

It was thirty years since Carronbrae entered upon its present career of prosperity. Mining contracts were made. Royalties were arranged ; the railway brought to the works ; and the tall stagings, with the swiftly spinning wheels, were set up on the hillside, where for generations only the gowan had bloomed.

McKill and Grindlay were the sole partners in the Incubus Coal and Iron Company. It was Hector McKill who had wedded Sophia, the serious-minded daughter of Fritz Inkob, the Dusseldorf chemist, and

settled himself down to rule Carronbrae with a firm
but indubitably pious hand. Grindlay, on the other
hand, was an unmarried man who attended to the
worldly side of the connection, and did the swearing
in the office. He was a red-faced man with a massive
watch-chain of shining gold, and was not particularly
attached to any of the Carronbrae kirks. But he was
known at every drinking-bar within fifty miles of the
pithead.

Hector McKill was ruling elder in the Kirk of the
Valley, and a great hand at all the prayer-meetings.
Indeed, it may be said, he kept them up; for if his
foremen did not come out to hear their ruling elder
and master jerking petitions out of himself much as
though he were working a ship's pump, they might
discover some fine morning that at the works of
Incubus and Company, there was no further use for
their services.

The Valley Kirk was not the fashionable kirk of
Carronbrae. The county families did not frequent it,
and perhaps that was one reason why it seemed to offer
fairer scope for the peculiar talents of Hector McKill
than the Kirk of the Hill. For one thing, the Kirk of
the Hill did not believe in prayer-meetings. But it
had an admirable and eminently aristocratic Primrose
League attached to it, and the minister was said to be

shaping for candles on the altar and the eastward position. Also most of its elders were better judges of whisky-toddy than of prayer-meetings. Grindlay, for instance, was a member of the Hill Kirk, for he was a man of no pretensions to religion, and he found himself at home there. But Hector McKill wrought the piety end of the business to perfection. It does not do, in a thriving business, to overman any department.

Yet in the Incubus pits this division of labour wrought well. If it were desired to get rid of a man who belonged to the Valley Kirk, and was a regular attendant at the prayer-meetings, Partner Grindlay dismissed him. He had been taking up with ranters, to the neglect of his proper business. If the man attended the High Kirk (or, what was very much the same thing, if he attended no kirk at all), Partner Hector McKill called him into his office, wrestled with him in the spirit, prayed with him for his soul's good—and then dismissed him without a character. The men on the whole preferred Grindlay's rough "We've no use for you. Get out of this!" to the suaver methods of Hector McKill.

Now, so long as the Reverend Silas Sleekman was the minister of the Valley Kirk of Carronbrae, all things went according to the will of Hector McKill. Incubus and Company had the rule all its own way. The

Valley Kirk, with a splendid history of protest against
the oppression of king and state, had become only the
ecclesiastical arm of Incubus and Company.

McKill was indeed not so imperious and autocratic
in the pits of the Carronbrae hillside as he was in the
session of the Valley Kirk. The minister, Mr. Sleekman, was an admirable man of unblemished character,
a great authority upon the typology of the Book of
Numbers—in his way, both a gentleman and a scholar.
But he was so thoroughly under control of the blatant
personality of Hector McKill, that at all meetings he
confined himself to saying, "I think what our dear
friend has proposed will be best!" The rest of the
session murmured and abode their time, for they were
not men to be thus set aside. The congregation
seethed in silent and helpless discontent. But there
was no mistake that the arm of Incubus and Company
reached far in Carronbrae, and the man who openly
opposed it in the long run went to the wall.

Yet somehow Incubus and Company, with all their
graspings, did not seem very greatly to prosper. They
paid the poorest wages, and, as a consequence, they
had only good men in the most indispensable situations. But there was no manner of doubt that in
Job Henderson, their underground manager, they had
an excellent man. He was firm with the men under

him, and, in consequence, at first he was not over-well liked. But as the men of the Carronbrae pits grew to know Job Henderson, they found how often his calm, mild strength came between them and the wrath of the partners of Incubus and Company.

It was at this time that the Act of Parliament was passed requiring all pits whatsoever to provide themselves with a second exit within a certain time, under pains and penalties to be enforced by the newly appointed Government inspectors. Job Henderson openly rejoiced, and started the construction of the spare shaft at once. McKill and Grindlay were not often down the workings, and it was some time before Hector McKill knew that the work was proceeding. But as soon as he heard of the matter, he ordered such nonsense to be stopped at once. It was a waste of money. Besides, there had never been any accident in the Carronbrae pits, and the whole thing was wholly unnecessary and uncalled for. Surely a pit which was under the protection of the prayers of so noted a vessel as Hector McKill could come to no harm. The ruling elder of the Valley Kirk did not put this last into words, but his whole manner inferred it. Job Henderson went to lay the matter before the junior partner, Walter Grindlay. He found him at the bar of the Royal, telling a sultry story, which was causing uproarious laughter.

To him he stated the necessity, and what had been
ordered. Grindlay, in a very brief manner, condemned
the expense.

"But the Government inspector?" said the underground manager.

"Leave him to me. I know how to work such
cattle," said Walter Grindlay, returning to the bar.

So Job Henderson went back to the works and
wrote out his resignation. He was a man with a
family, and he did it painfully. But he could not
consent to play with the lives of men. He stated the
reasons for his resignation in his letter to the firm of
Incubus and Company. Walter Grindlay laughed as
he read it.

"Risk to the lives of men," he said. "Well, I
suppose we pay them for taking the risk, and they
know it as well as we do. I never did read such cant."

But the senior partner spoke seriously of it at his
prayer-meeting. He had been that day, he remarked,
wounded in his tenderest feelings by one whom he had
trusted—a serpent whom he had taken from the gutter,
and warmed in his bosom. Yet he was eminently sus-
tained in his affliction, and enabled to bear it all meekly.

So the spare shaft was stopped on the morrow, and
a new manager came to the pit whose conditions of
service were that he obeyed orders without question,

made no complaint, cut down the working expenses, and increased the profits. He was a good man, this new manager, according to his lights; but his lights were the conditions of his managership, and the continued good-will and favour of Incubus and Company.

The shifts came and went with great regularity. The pit filled and emptied, and the narrow twin air-shaft, which ran alongside the main incline or "dook," was half filled with steam-pipes; for it was, according to Incubus and Company, a great pity to have an empty space which could be filled with what was useful. But one or two men who spent their lives down there in the deeps of the earth tightened their lips, and said a prayer for wife and bairns that had little in common with the laboured paragraphs of which, on the evenings of the prayer-meeting, the senior partner delivered himself before going home to arrange for cutting down his men's wages ten per cent. all round.

Then came the Government inspector. The men had heard of his coming, and looked for great things. The obstructions were cleared away from the bottom of the abortive second exit, which had been carried so far and then abandoned at the end of the rule of Job Henderson.

But Mr. Grindlay had the inspector well in hand. He had treated him generously before he came, and

Grindlay was the best of good company, and made himself liked when he chose. The inspector descended, admiring, as he did so, the perfect working of the cage, and feeling the strong draft of air. He walked along the working faces ; he saw the men at their tasks. He passed the end of the partially constructed tunnel, which Grindlay indicated with a wave of his hand.

"Our new exit," he explained generally.

"Ah, indeed ; that is right !" said the Government inspector, for who could look too narrowly into the affairs of so pleasant and hospitable a man of the world as the junior partner of the great firm of Incubus and Company ?

Alas that there was none to tell him that the tunnel ran up to within a hundred yards of the surface, and there stopped where, on the day of Job Henderson's resignation, the last hole had been driven, and the work dropped to cut down working expenses !

"Now," said Mr. Walter Grindlay, hospitably, "we had better go up to dinner. It is hot and stuffy here ; and I told them to ice the champagne. You are to dine with me, of course ; I arranged that. Our old man is a teetotaler, and I thought you would prefer it."

And the Government inspector did prefer it.

This was all that the inspection of the Carronbrae pits accomplished, and the report was enough to certify that there was no health-resort in Britain so entirely salubrious in climate and appliances as the pits of Incubus and Company.

But, in the mean time, the senior partner was having trouble considerable in his ecclesiastical relations. The Reverend Silas Sleekman was laid quietly away to rest from his labours in the graveyard in the valley, and there was a vacancy in "McKill's kirk," as the commonalty named it irreverently. This meant the preaching of candidates, and an exceeding interest among all the members in the election. But it was generally thought—indeed, taken for granted—that, though patronage had been abolished, Hector McKill would get in his man. Mrs. McKill (*née* Incubus), for her own part, meant to have a young man with at least some tendencies to ritual. Hector did not much care one way or the other, but he was resolved like iron to have a man who would do as he was bidden, and who knew his place. In fact, he had found the very man. Providence had brought him to hand.

There was yet another Sleekman, and it was thought that the people would like a second of the breed— one of the same meekness and ineffectiveness as that Silas who had recently laid himself down to rest from labours which apparently ought not to have tired him very much.

The Reverend Alexander Sleekman was a pro-
bationer of some standing, meaning thereby that he
had been out of college several years without finding
a resting-place for his foot in kirk or manse. But he
had preached several times for his relative during the
summer holidays ; and Mr. Hector McKill, with that
interest in the young for which he was famous, had
sounded the lad, and found him of a very adaptive
and facile disposition. The senior partner thought
that this would be most suitable in a minister of the
Valley Kirk, who, above all men, ought to be a model
of humility. Mr. McKill liked all his sermons from
the Old Testament, and especially rejoiced in denunciations of the wicked—which, being interpreted, meant
those who did not agree with Hector McKill. On the
other hand, Mrs. McKill loved expositions of " the little
horn," and the settling of the exact year and day of
the end of the world. She subscribed to the *Prophetic
Herald,* and questioned all young preachers as to their
views on the literal fulfilment of prophecy.

So the Reverend Alexander Sleekman satisfied
both the chief inhabitants of Gripp Castle, which stood
among sprouting larches over the hill out of sight of
the pits. He was asked there to lunch. He stood with
his hat in his hand on the gravel walk when he spoke
to Hector McKill, and he expressed the most lively

delight at finding a copy of the *Prophetic Herald*, " my favourite journal," on the drawing-room table.

Mr. Sleekman did not mean to miss the good things of this life if he could help it.

He was altogether a suitable young man, and Hector McKill said, " He'll do fine ! "

Now, the senior partner in the great firm of Incubus and Company had not the least doubt that he should be able to carry the congregation of the Valley Kirk along with him. Indeed, that was a factor which he had not so much as considered. Were not most of the members his own employees ? Hector loved the word. He was their employer, their master ; and it would be a strange thing if he could not hire them to think as he thought as well as to do as he bade them.

Yet it will hardly be believed that there was rank treason and rebellion against so good a master being freely mooted in the pits themselves, and preparation was being made for the congregational meeting, with a view to disappointing his earnest and just expectations. This was a matter to which it is eminently painful to allude. We hardly like to enter into the depths which are to be found in human nature. · Hector McKill made it a matter of public prayer that he should get his own way, and Mrs. McKill frequently consulted the *Prophetic Herald.* Who would dare to gainsay two such single-minded and powerful Christians ?

Now, in the Presbyterian Kirk of Scotland, a selected number of those who have been proposed as candidates for the pastorate have to preach on one or more Sabbaths before the congregation, so that the people may judge as to the merits and popular gifts of the man whom they elect to rule over them in spiritual things.

Accordingly, the Reverend Alexander Sleekman preached first. He had a plaintive and monotonous voice, and he selected his text from the Prophet Daniel to please Mrs. McKill. But he was far from pleasing the rank and file of the free and independent members of the congregation. They complained that he whined whenever he did not snivel.

" That craitur can never preach. He can only peep and mutter ! " said Angus Gilruth, gardener and theologian.

" That piece o' machinery wadna work bena (except) when Hector McKill turned the handle ! " said Sandy McClymont. And so the word ran through the congregation.

But Hector went about the next day, saying to every member and adherent he met, " You were at the kirk yesterday, John. Wasna yon a grand sermon ? "

And John thought that it was, having regard to the
fact that he was speaking to his master. But he relieved
himself when he sat on his hunkers at the pit-bottom,
waiting for the cage.

But there was one of those who came to preach
whose name was David Oliphant. He certainly did
not peep and mutter. He had a message to deliver,
and, at least, he stood and gave it forth like a man.
He had long been wrestling with a poor district, where
sin was the handmaid of poverty, and where prayer was
not so divorced from the brotherhood of helping as it
was﹞ in the theology of Hector McLean. He prayed
with the people in the evening, and saw that they got
milk for their babes in the morning.

In the Valley Kirk he preached on the address of
Paul to the men of Athens, from the Hill of Mars.

" This agitator," he called him, " this inciter of the
populace, this socialistic lecturer, proclaimed his
message, and the Athenians listlessly hearkened. ' For
God hath made of one blood all the nations of men that
are upon the face of the earth.' And the citizens smiled
at one another as they heard the new doctrine. Did the
little swarthy Jew think himself of the same race as
themselves ? And the Roman centurion smiled behind
his hand like a stalwart British policeman in his pride
of place. The slave-owner shrugged his shoulders and

turned away. But on the skirts of the crowd, here and there, one listened and set his head nearer to catch every word. The helot heard a new thing. 'Of the same blood ; equal in the new faith; neither Jew nor Greek, male nor female, bond nor free ;—all free and equal in Jesus Christ the new Prophet.' Swart Ethiopian and flaxen-haired Goth, they paused ere they went to their task, hearing of 'a new burden and easier yoke,' a brotherhood of man ! There was hope for them in the new faith. No wonder the common people heard him gladly, and the rich and increased in goods passed him by, for it was a helot's faith, this of the Nazarene, and once more to the poor the gospel was preached."

David Oliphant's words rang through the Valley Kirk like the accents of a new inspired prophet. Such things had never so been spoken there. The workers had been dulled into apathy. Use and wont alone took them to their accustomed places on the morning of the Sabbath day ; but the words of the preacher had fallen dully on their ear as something with no possible bearing upon their daily life.

And as the kirk emptied itself, there were many who whispered one to the other, " We have heard a new thing to-day ! "

But they said little aloud, for Hector McKill was condemning the unhallowed doctrine in no measured tones. He would write to the officers of the Kirk about the men whom they sent out to preach to vacant congregations. He never had heard the pulpit so prostituted before. It was all he could do to keep still in his place. There was not a word of spirituality in the whole discourse. The young man was a disgrace to the presbytery that licensed him.

" But he'll no get off with the like of that ! " said Hector McKill.

Yet he took him over the hill to Gripp Castle for dinner, and tried to overwhelm him with his importance. But David Oliphant was not overwhelmed. He had not met the great ones of the earth in vain, and he could give a reason for the faith that was in him. He told Mrs. McKill several things about Christ and his religion which considerably astonished Hector. More than that, he had the passages at the end of his tongue to bear out his doctrine.

" He said to me in the smoking-room," said Hector to his astonished wife, " that there was no doubt that Jesus was a working-man, and His followers Socialists."

" But you surely did not sit and listen to such doctrine ? " queried his wife, aghast.

Hector McKill looked uneasy. He shrugged his shoulders and played with his watch-chain.

"But, Sophia, in a manner he proved it—that was the awkward thing."

"Nonsense," said Sophia, sharply; "I wish I had had him through my hands. I would puzzle him with the 'little horn,' and the 'time and a time and half a time.'"

Which indeed was likely enough, for David Oliphant devoted most of his attention to the vials of wrath which were being poured on the earth at the present time, and the horn that he was interested in was mostly to be found on the palms of the workers with whom he consorted, and in the hearts of such firms as Incubus and Company, whose employees they were.

So it was decided at Gripp Castle that Alexander Sleekman was to be their minister, and that Hector McKill should write to all the vacant churches, and warn their committee against the life and doctrine of David Oliphant.

"I owed this duty to the Church at large," said Hector; "such a wolf ought not to be allowed to masquerade in fleecy clothing among the silly sheep."

But at the congregational meeting a sharp and horrid surprise was waiting for this worthy and notable follower of the apostles. He proposed the Reverend Alexander Sleekman. He lauded his likeness to his worthy predecessor. He called him "a chip off the old

block " (an irreverent person in the back benches inter-
jected the syllable "head" at this point, which raised
a laugh among the unthinking). Hector McKill
repeated his observation with greater emphasis, and
again the objectionable syllable came from the back of
the church. Then he went on to advert to the excellent
doctrine which they had heard in the discourses of
Mr. Sleekman, and the admirable manner in which the
preacher had settled disputed points in the prophetic
interpretation of Daniel. It would be a blessing of no
ordinary calibre if they were privileged in the Valley
Kirk to listen Sabbath after Sabbath to such teaching.
For his part (Hector McKill's part), he asked nothing
better than an eternity of such Sabbaths. He concluded
by proposing the name of Mr. Sleekman, and he said
that, were Mr. Sleekman elected, he should personally
make it his business to give him all the assistance and
advice in his power in fulfilling his onerous ministerial
functions in their midst.

It will hardly be believed, yet it is a fact that at
this point a deliberate wink was observed to pass round
the congregation. Hector McKill caught Sandy
McClymont in the act, and Sandy coughed and pretended that some obstruction in his throat was bringing
the water to his eye. Man is by nature depraved.

Then there was a pause in the proceedings, till one

of the firemen at the Carronbrae pits seconded his master's motion, as he had been ordered that morning to do. He kept his head down, and appeared very unhappy. But he had ten of a family, and was two quarters back with his rent.

Then, without note or comment, Angus Gilruth stood up and moved the election of David Oliphant. A member at the back of the hall, believed to be another of the pit firemen—an unmarried man—swiftly seconded the motion. The worthy moderator, who was minister of a neighbouring church, all innocent of the complication of interests, rose to put the matter to the vote; but Hector McKill, choking with anger, was before him. He fell upon David Oliphant, his character and doctrine, with tooth and nail. His doctrine was unspeakably bad. His opposition to constituted authority showed what manner of man he was better than anything else. His character, also, was more than doubtful. He would be a disgrace to the parish, and, for one, Hector McKill would give no support to a congregation which would call such a man to rule over them.

"I and my wife," said Hector, speaking after his manner, "have had opportunities of diagnosing his character denied to the others here present, and we can vouch that our impressions were not favourable."

Mrs. McKill nodded her head violently. David

In the Matter of Incubus and Co. 65

Oliphant's views on the "little horn" had been very unsatisfactory indeed.

"But I do not doubt that this factious opposition to such an admirable man as Mr. Sleekman, against whose character and doctrine there is no breath of suspicion, is confined to one or two irresponsible persons of no particular standing."

Mr. McKill paused for a reply.

The people did not reply; but every man and woman made ready to vote.

Yet when the election proceeded, and a show of hands called for of those favourable to the candidature of the Reverend Alexander Sleekman, only eleven could be counted ; and there was even a considerable uncertainty about some of these, for as soon as Hector McKill took his eyes off several of those who voted for his candidate, strangely enough their hands instantly dropped to their sides. These were all married men with large families and in the upper places about the Carronbrae pits. The moderator, indeed, declared that he could only count seven at any one time.

Then came the vote on behalf of David Oliphant. A whole forest of hands arose. The moderator thought there were about two hundred. Hector McKill was on his feet all the time, turning round like a teetotum, trying to focus his attention upon those of his em-

F

ployees as were voting against him ; but it is a strange thing that for every one of these whom he really got his eye upon, and by dint of frowning prevailed upon to keep his hands beneath the pew, at least two others who were not so focussed held up their hands, so that the moderator could not in any way make the numbers of those voting for David Oliphant less than two hundred and ten. He rose to give his decision, and was interrupted by Hector McKill. But the moderator was not under the thumb of Incubus and Company. He lived in another parish, and so he made short shrift of the ruling elder, who only managed to say that he washed his hands of the responsibility of bringing such a man into their midst.

When David Oliphant came to Carronbrae, he was welcomed with a great assembly in the Valley Kirk to do him honour, and down in the pits and along the working faces there was joy which did not readily find expression. And, what pleased these swarthy miners as much as anything, their owner, the senior partner in the great firm of Incubus and Company, was explosively indignant, and refused to have anything to do with the ceremony. This was a capital introduction to the confidence of the workers of Carronbrae, and there was a larger contingent of them at church on Sabbath than had ever been there before. But the McKills' pew was empty, and the congregation whispered to each other that Hector McKill, lord of Gripp Castle, and of the serfs of the Carronbrae pits, had left the Valley Kirk, and betaken himself to the Kirk on the Hill. The "little horn" went with him.

But this was not yet decided. Hector and his wife were that day deep in debate as to their future action. Should he secede forthwith, or remain to be a thorn in the side of the new minister? He could not hope to have the same authority in the Kirk of the Hill. On the other hand, the Reverend Septimus Easiman was ready to have any views or none upon the "little horn," and he was entirely sound on the question of the rights of employers; so that it was finally decided by the conclave at the Castle that immediate withdrawal from the tainted and disgraced Valley Kirk was abso- lutely necessary. So Hector McKill "lifted his lines" and removed his Bibles during the week.

Then, being without employment for his facility in petitioning, he started a prayer-meeting at the offices of the company, and invited those who attended to send in notices of requests for prayer. But the notes received showed the evil minds of the senders. One stated that the sepulchres of the neighbourhood stood much in need of a new coat of whitewash, and urgent prayers were asked for the same. Another remarked upon the tattered condition of the hypocrites' cloaks, and suggested a fresh supply. Another referred to the " second exit " at the Carronbrae pit as a subject for Mr. McKill's petitions ; while yet another suggested a rise of ten per cent., and an examination of the insanitary condition of the company's houses. The proposed prophetical prayer-meeting in Mrs. McKill's drawing-room was abandoned, and in the town of Carronbrae all things went on as they had done before.

The Government inspector came every three months, and strolled along the mains of the pit accompanied by the junior (drinking) partner. The senior (whitewashed) partner kept out of the way. Then at a certain fixed point Walter Grindlay proposed a return to the surface in time for dinner. So, with a magnum of champagne before him, the inspector rested from his labours and found all things very good.

And David Oliphant, cleared of Incubus and Company and all their works, preached the gospel as it was given to him, and instructed his people, among other things, that the fatherhood of God meant the brotherhood of man.

But on a day unforgotten in Carronbrae, swift and unexpected as lightning, fell the terror of great darkness.

At Carronbrae pit No. 1, the day shift had turned

out at six in the morning, stolidly taking its way to the pit to do the day's darg. In the little red houses the men and boys breakfasted mostly with little said; and as silently rose to go, each with his dinner-can along with him, into the still sunshiny morning.

The men went to labour. The women abode at home, worked, and waited. The laddies followed their fathers as soon as it was time for them to leave school and go to work.

"Weel, I'm awa'!" was the more effusive greeting heard as the men shut to the doors. Yet some of the younger of them took a look at wives and bairns ere they went forth, for to all who win the coal from the deeps of the mine, there is the grim risk that they who go forth in the morning with head erect, may be brought home before ever evening come with drooping head and feet that are carried first through the door.

So in scattered groups, fathers with their boys walking manfully by their side, sometimes running a few steps to keep up, and single men in silent companionship with their mates, they took their way up the hill to the pit-mouth.

The wheels spun round opposite ways on the tall scaffolding. The cage sank and rose. The engineman pulled his levers and tested his throttle-valves. Down to the bottom of the long dark shaft and diagonally

along the "incline," the parties of men and boys sped
to their work. Tools clinked as the men lifted them to
their shoulders.

Fifteen hundred feet beneath the yellow cornfields,
fifteen hundred feet beneath the great house of Gripp
Castle, where Hector McKill, senior partner in the firm
of Incubus and Company, was not yet out of bed, lay
the workings where the picks began to play a merry
tune. The pony-boys brought the waggons quickly
along the dark underground ways. Here and there the
lamps glimmered and danced over the mounds of
rubbish. From the abandoned workings there came
strange faint smells, and the lamp-flame sometimes
forsook the centre wick and seemed to cling strangely
to the wire of the Davy frame.

Few of the men in that great pit remembered as
they wrought that the yellow sunshine of the autumn
day slept above them. For the pit hummed like a
hive, and there was little enough time for thought.
The door-boys heard the whistle of the men running
the coal-trucks through the dark passages, and threw
back their doors. Then with a yell and a gust of
wind, a long line of cars rushed through the open door-
way. Sometimes one of the men upon them would
wave a hand kindly to the lonely boy, left by himself
in the darkness. And the flames of their hat-lamps

streamed back like the smoke-track behind a railway engine.

Suddenly that day in August, as the boys were bringing their loads of coal to the bottom of the "dook," John Roy, the "bottomer," looking upward, saw thick volumes of smoke pouring down the shaft of the long incline.

"The pit's afire!" was his quick and terrible cry. There was but one way to the surface ; but one to the outer air, and the flame had gripped it, as John Roy well knew when he saw the red glow in the heart of the smoke.

Now, doubtless it was his duty to bide by his signals, for the bottomer is the man at the helm, and only he can communicate up that long incline, nearly a third of a mile in length, with the men in the engine-house on the surface, whose levers and wire ropes control in turn the movements of the cage by which alone safety can be reached. But John Roy had little time to think. Bewildered, stunned, not knowing which way to turn for the blinding downpour of smoke and the crackling of the deadly fire among the timbers of the pit, he leapt into the cage, and stood with his hand on the bell-lever.

But before he "belled himself away," he called to the three boys who stood beneath with their loads ready for the trucks.

" The pit's afire, lads ; come away with me ! "

Then these three lads, whose names deserve to be written in golden letters, though no more than boys in years, returned to the bottomer the answer of brave men. They said—

" No ; we will gang and warn the men."

John Roy jerked the lever thrice, and was whisked through the smoke and fire just in time, leaving the hundred men below to their fate.

But the three boys sped on their way. The weight of many men's lives was on their boyish hearts. Breathing deep to give them vigour, they ran through the gathering smother, which, instead of feeding the great pit with pure air, was carrying down the deadly smoke along all the faces of the pit. They raced with bent backs under the black archways. Every moment they were risking their own lives to warn their comrades.

" The pit's afire ; run, men, run ! " they cried, and at the word each man and boy dropped his tools and ran for the bottom of the incline.

But when they arrived there they found only the red fire glowing down from above on the dull waters of the " sump," and the cage gone, which ought to have been there to take them to safety. Some started for the air-shaft ; but it was blocked with steam-pipes, and no man could climb thirty yards up it. The legal second exit had, as we know, never been driven, and a hundred yards of solid rock lay between. So down there men and boys were penned, with the great fire roaring in their only exit. They were no better than rats caught in the trap set for them by Incubus and Company, and baited with thirty shillings a week. But the senior partner was a pious man, and had often prayed for them—only he had not finished the second exit. The thought must have been a comfort to them at that moment.

But on the plans of the pit, approved and passed by the Government inspectors, there were splendid exits, wide and clear. All was completely arranged on paper. It is a pity that men cannot escape on paper.

And above in the sunlight women wailed and wept, and watched and waited. Through the long and anxious August night the women-folk, many of them with their babies, stood about the pit-head. Hector McKill, in a white waistcoat, moved among them, telling them that they had better go home; they could do their men no good.

Suddenly a woman broke down, and the weird, unforgettable sound of the Irish "keen" went out on the air. It nearly broke the hearts of those that heard it. Grief among the Scottish women was quieter—more patient, stiller.

But when the dead-carts began to rumble, and the bodies were brought home, the women broke loose from all restraint, and clambered on the waggons, crying for their husbands. Then David Oliphant, who had gone from house to house, ran along to meet each cart, and, reverently laying the cloth aside, he identified the poor clay, and so drove the husband home to his wife's fireside, which he had left sound and well that morning.

Yes, the boys had warned the men! The three heroes who thought of no Victoria Cross had done their deed, and now they lay quiet—one in his father's house, with the deadly reek oozing stilly out of his nostrils ; another as quiet, the only son of his mother, and she a widow. But one lay at the bottom of the black water of the "sump," so deep that even the ruddy fire scarce glimmered down upon him.

But the boys had warned the men.

On a quiet Scottish Sabbath they were laid in their resting-graves on a breezy hilltop, looking down on the place that had been their death-trap. The fields over them were yellow with the corn, but under the sheaves fifty men lay buried in a deep common grave. They had a service on the green, and the lift of the widowed and orphaned voices as they sang their psalm almost broke our hearts.

"Yea, though I walk through death's dark vale,
  Yet will I fear none ill ;
  For Thou art with me, and Thy rod
  And staff me comfort still."

And at the open-air service, behind the rows of
weeping women, the children played upon Carronbrae
Green, or stood staring open-eyed as at a show, with
never a father among them all.

But Hector McKill went to the church with a conscience void of offence. He had subscribed a hundred
pounds to the relief fund.

Now David Oliphant had a word to say, and he said
it. "I do not stand here to apportion blame or to
decide legal quibbles ; but I say that the men who are
responsible for failing to provide a way of escape for
these men are responsible for the loss of these hundred
lives, and one day shall have to answer for the murder
before the bar of God."

Two mornings after David Oliphant found on his
table a legal letter from the solicitor of Incubus and
Company. The letter informed him that he had laid
himself open to an action for libel, and requested the
name of his solicitor. David Oliphant had no solicitor ;
but he had an answer, and his answer ran thus:

"I specially declared in my address that I had
nothing to do with apportioning blame before human

tribunals; and I shall rejoice to meet your clients at the bar which I mentioned, on the great day when the secrets of all hearts shall be revealed, when all wrong shall be righted, and all evil punished."

David Oliphant's faith was simple; but, like many simple things, it wore well and carried him through. He heard no more of the action for libel.

* * * * *

The water had filled the mine. It was seven months before it was again pumped out of the flooded pit. Then once more the explorers enter the dread place where the smoke choked, the fire burned, and the water drowned so many lives that were bright and young. They are again at the pit-bottom. They pass along the dripping passages, from which the great pump has sucked the water. They clamber over falls of rock which have thundered down from the roof. They shade their eyes and hold up their lamps as they go down the slope.

"Stop! what is that?"

This is what they see—dark shapes, leaning against the wall, some sitting as if in thought, some resting at ease as if asleep, some lying prone on their faces.

"I declare," said one of the searchers, "they were sitting there, after seven months under water, as if they were waiting for the oversman to call the next shift!"

He was right. The Great Oversman *had* called the

next shift, and every man had answered to his name. One little lad had run upon the first alarm to find his father. The men who lifted him had strong arms, but the tears ran down their cheeks upon their grimy hands. And well they might, for the boy lay lovingly and confidingly with his head upon his father's knee. He had found his father. Perhaps so had they all. At any rate, it was better to die with them than to live with Hector McKill.

Incubus and Company still survives, but does not greatly prosper, though Hector's white waistcoat is broader and whiter than ever.

But, though he got clear in the Government inquiry, the Great Court of Appeal has not done with him yet. There is a certain white throne to be set up ; and even if there be no hell, as the new-fangled folk say, God is going to set about making one specially for Hector McKill.

S. R. CROCKETT.

Social Aspects of the Gospel.

WHEN we speak of "the gospel," we mean the message of good news which God has sent to this earth by Jesus Christ. But the gospel is usually taught as dealing with individual men as individuals only. Each man by himself is said to be able to be forgiven, able to be nurtured, able to be changed, able to be saved, *i.e.* made a spiritually healthy being, a son of God.

But the question we are asking in these days is this : "Is the gospel no more than this ? " Has not God sent a message to men, as well as to each man, to society at large, for the great body of mankind to adopt and assimilate? Does not God look for a "saved society," as well as a number of isolated "saved souls "? Is there no "social gospel " ?

I venture to think that there is such a gospel : not a separate gospel from the other, but one great message which acts in a similar though not identical way, both on society at large, and on individuals in particular.

Individuals sin, and God can save them. Society sins, and God can save it. A man is morally deficient; God can supply his weakness. Society is degenerating; God can regenerate it. Moreover, the two workings of this one gospel interlace one another. Often, as we can see, it is only by the saving of an individual, or of a number of individuals, that society can be saved; often, on the other hand, it is by the saving of society, as, for example, by the practical adoption of a new social principle, that individuals can save their own souls.

We are, however, chiefly concerned now with the gospel in its social aspect; that is to say, with the gospel as delivered to, and to be applied by, great bodies of men, by nations, corporations, classes, masses, societies, neighbourhoods.

Firstly, the Englishman, with his great love of the Bible, asks, "Is this scriptural?" Most assuredly, "Yes." The most righteous book in the world reveals to us the characteristic working of God, the "ways of the Lord." And what are His ways? In the Old Testament, His ways are shown to be most clearly national, social, world-wide. He chooses out a nation, that He may exhibit to the whole world the picture of a perfect State, governed by His merciful, loving laws; always happy and prosperous in obedience, and correspondingly miserable and disjointed and defeated at

every turn, when it separates itself from Him, and
prefers its own way to His. Then, when the fulness
of the time is come, He descends to this earth of ours,
and enters into human society Himself, in the form of
man, to rearrange the disordered mass, disordered just
because it refused to be ordered by Him. He goes in
and out among men, taking part in their ordinary
life. He chooses His twelve apostles, and imparts to
them His secret that they may go out and spread the
gospel. This gospel is about a kingdom ; a new way
of bringing men and women together in one great
united body under Himself, their King. All the
nations of the earth are to be invited to enter into
this kingdom ; not forced into it, but gently drawn by
love. This kingdom is to be set up at once upon the
earth ; His followers are to pray unceasingly for its
coming and its maintenance. The glorious ideal which
He puts before His followers is that of gradually
claiming the whole world for Him ; society is to be
reconstructed on a new basis, the basis of love and
brotherhood ; the kingdoms of this world are to
become the kingdoms of our Lord. The picture of
the perfect state, in the great unseen world, is that of
a city, the heavenly Jerusalem, compact and solid,
bright with righteousness, filled with an atmosphere of
holy prayers and aspirations—with injustice, sorrows,

miseries, swept away by the all-pervading essence of the holiness of God triumphant.

Surely this is a social gospel! Good news to mankind that there is a better way of organizing themselves. Let God be your King. God in His human nature, the God Who knows the sorrow and suffering, the perversity and selfishness of men, the God Who has submitted Himself to the discomfort of poverty and the humiliation of obedience, the God Who hates wrong and loves right, the God Who will have a new earth in which righteousness shall dwell.

II. Now, when we look back on the history of the world since the appearance of God on the earth, we read, it is true, a sorry story of violence and selfishness and lust. Does this mean that the social gospel has failed?

Certainly not. In the first place, the failure, if any, is not nearly so apparent in the case of the social gospel as it is in the case of the individual one. There are still millions of individual sinners on whose lives the gospel of Christ seems to have made but little effect, and yet we know that, underlying all that, the leaven of Christ has been gradually permeating the lump. The grain of seed dropped on Mount Calvary when Jesus' blood was shed by cruel men, has entered into the earth of men's consciences, and from it has sprung up that wonderful Tree which covers the whole

G

world with its greatness. There are amongst us—here there, and everywhere—men of gentleness, uprightness, love, and self-sacrifice, whose very life speaks of the living Spirit of Jesus. They are the leaves of that Tree, the fruitful branches of the True Vine.

So with society at large, with nations (at least with the nations of Europe and the new world). The broad result may seem to argue failure, and yet we know that great principles of love, justice, liberty, and brotherhood are gradually making their way into the heart of politics and social reconstruction. What are these but some of the foundation truths which Jesus taught?

" Still," you will say, " there is failure, terrible failure still—the kingdom of God is not a fact." That is, unfortunately, too true. It is not a fact in the world ; but neither is it a fact to any very large extent in the hearts and lives of individuals, yet we still preach and teach and minister grace ; we still organize Home and Foreign Missions.

The Christian Church has no right nor reason to despair. She must, however, in these days, take care not to subside into a state of fatalistic despondency and shirk three-quarters of her duty by confining herself to the conversion of individuals.

What, then, is her social duty?

The social duty of the Christian Church is twofold.

She has first to maintain herself as the living perpetual witness to the desirableness, the beauty, the reasonableness of united Christian living. She must keep her members together in holy living as the one united, brotherly body, the family of God, the society which moves along guided by the indwelling Spirit of Christ, nourished by the sacred Humanity of the Son of God, obedient to the laws and principles of Jesus. She is, potentially, the kingdom of God on earth, containing, alas! good and bad members, a field in which wheat and tares are growing; but pressing onward till she attains to that perfect society, the New Jerusalem, the city foursquare, with its triumphant enjoyment of social peace and good will, basking in the sunshine of God's love.

Secondly, she is to act upon the world at large by her example, her teaching, her persuasion. She is to strive to win the whole human race to herself. There is to be no limit to the sphere of her action, no department of human life which she is to shrink from or shirk. Industry, politics, home life, professional practice, the world of science and art, of literature and recreation —all of it is in the field where the Church must work.

She is a "City set on a hill," that cannot and must not be hid. Out from the watch-tower must shine the pure light of righteousness in the darkness of the world, seeming to say, "Come unto Me, all 'ye that labour and are heavy laden, and I will give you rest." Out, too, from the gates of the city, Christian men must go and mingle in the world below and persuade humanity that up on the hill is the true life, the true liberty, the true progress.

This, then, is briefly the twofold duty of the Christian Church : (1) to exist as a solid body of righteous men, living under Christ and His law, and utterly dependent on Him, believing in complete sincerity in Him as the King, the Lord, the Master; (2) to go out into the world and spread the knowledge of their Lord, entering deep into the woes and wants of humanity, and endeavouring, by example, by precept, by the infection of enthusiasm for Christ and His all-sufficiency, to draw the whole world after Him.

III. How shall we of the Christian Church do this, practically, in this nineteenth century of Christendom ?

First, let us make ourselves absolutely sure that it has got to be done. We are not unnaturally half-hearted about it. The Church has, in the course of ages, got so mixed up with the world that to talk of "existing as a solid body of righteous men " seems almost a mockery. So, too, to talk of acting upon the world from the outside as a "city set on a hill," seems almost impossible, in view of the fact that, as an organized body that can talk and act together, we can hardly be said to exist.

Despair, however, is a vice which, as a Church, we must never allow ourselves to be guilty of. It is at our peril that we recede by one hair's-breadth from the position that, somehow or other, Christ is to be made known as the King of the whole earth ; that, some-how or other, He is the Way out of social distress, " The true Light which lighteth every man that cometh into the world."

We must not, then, be fatalists, as Mr. Gore warned us at the Holborn Conference. We must say, "Here are these two duties which the Church is pledged to perform. Let us see to it that they are being done." Complete success will almost certainly not attend our efforts during our short lifetime, but that thought must not hold us back from the task.

Anything which tends to bring the Christian Church together into compact unity is good for the furthering of the social gospel. Without saying one word in disparagement of the Evangelical movement, which has done so much to impress individuals with an earnest love for the Person of Christ, I believe that the great Tractarian movement of the last fifty years has done m uch in this particular respect. It has made the Church of England realize herself as a visible society, with its regular orders of officers and members presided over by Christ. The same movement has also had its influence on the whole mass of Christians in this country. It has substituted the idea of social religion for mere individual devotion. The Broad-Church teachers, too, have done much to raise and widen the ideals of Christian men. "The kingdom of Christ" is felt now to be no mere form of words, but a thing for which Christian men must be looking and working. The age of successful hypocrisy and contentment with platitudes is passing away. Christians are feeling more and more that their religion must be carried out in their lives, if it is to be professed at all. The so-called secular Press often exercises a stimulating effect upon the Church by the steady exposure of Christian incon-sistencies, which is one of the features of the "New Journalism."

The increased attendance at and reception of the Holy Communion which, thank God, is the most con-spicuous glory of our modern Churchmanship, ought, it seems to me, to be issuing in a greater realization of the social character of Christianity. It is allowed on all hands that it was the Holy Eucharist, in the early days of the Church, which broke down the selfishness and individualism of the heathen world. Why is it that the modern revival is not having more of the same effect?

Is it not that we think too exclusively of the Sacrament as God's gift to each individual, and not enough of it as the great corporate act of the whole Church, and the great instrument of unification in Christ? We are members one of another, because we all partake of one loaf. The substitution of the expression "Our Communion" for the vulgar phrase "My Communion" would serve to bring about a better idea of the meaning of the Blessed Sacrament.

The circumstances, then, of the age, are in many respects advantageous for the practical extension of the Christian social gospel. Let us now consider the exact directions in which these two branches of social duty can be furthered.

(1) The inner life of the Christian society has to be carefully attended to. A process of edification must perpetually be going on. The social life of the Church must grow more and more into the likeness of the heavenly city. It has been pointed out by a thoughtful teacher that the distinctively Christian virtues are eminently social virtues.

Faith, Hope, Love—the three cardinal virtues—are not mere individual perfections; they are principles on which the fabric of the Christian society is to be built up. There must be social Faith, whether it be the faith of mutual confidence between the members of the Christian body, or the tenacious trust of confident believers in the promises of Christ and the power of His grace, or the concerted reliance on the foundation truths of the Christian religion, the facts of the Creed. There must be social Hope, an untiring sense of certainty that Christ holds the key of all complexities, that in time a way out will be found, if only the body remains true to the Head, and answers obediently to His guidance and control; that the Will of the Almighty Father is wholly on the side of right and justice; and that so far as there is wrong and wickedness, it is from a disregard of that all-just Will. There must be Love, not a mere sentimental affection, but a deep love, rooted in the innermost heart of the Christian body, and spreading itself out through all the nerves and fibres of the members, and issuing forth into the great world around. Christians must love their neighbours as themselves, and God with all their strength and wills. "For God and for Man" must be the real head and heart motto of the Church.

And these virtues must be allowed to grow up regardless of worldly consequences. At all costs, Christ's Will must be done. The works of the flesh, envy, hatred, and all uncharitableness, must be cast out of the society; they must form no part at all of its stock-in-trade. Now, it is these worldly consequences which at present check the growth of virtue in the Christian community. These are the fashions of society; the ordinary methods of business; the fear of Mrs. Grundy; the innate, blind conservatism of the vast mass of mankind, which increases with the acquisition of comfort. These, and a hundred things, spoil the free development of true Christian virtue in the Church. No one single person dares to make a fresh departure in ordinary, everyday practice. A single Christian landlord or employer of labour who fearlessly set himself to live on a very much higher plane of conduct, who dared, in fact, to let his righteousness "exceed the righteousness of the Scribes and Pharisees," would find himself in a very uncomfortable position. Our Lord Himself, knowing that this would be the case, organized His followers into a society that should have the inestimable strength and sustaining power which comes from union. They were of one heart and one soul; they continued steadfastly in the one fellowship. Hence it was no surprising thing when a Barnabas gave up all his possessions and laid them at the apostles' feet. What we want, then, nowadays, is for Christians to draw together, to live together more, to establish inner circles of religious friendship and mutual interchange of views, to study together in common how to apply the principles of Christ in ordinary conduct. This

drawing together of Christians would minimize the difficulty which, it would be foolish to deny, exists in
applying religion to life.*   Much of the failure of Christians to apply their religion to life arises from ignorance of the facts of life.   If, for example, we Christian
consumers could have it brought home to us vividly
how we are directly responsible for a great part of the
"sweating system": if we were to come into more real
contact with the lives of the victims of it, I do not
suppose we should rest content until we had amended
our ways.   Hence comes the great importance of the
"new philanthropy" which aims at getting knowledge
before giving assistance.   The University settlements
in East London ; the collection of statistics like Charles
Booth's ; the increasing desire to get at the truth about
social problems, which is witnessed to by the multipli-
cation of "inquiries," pamphlets, and books on the
social question, etc., are, all of them, the earnest of
good things to come.

But all this must be multiplied tenfold, if the Christian Church is to stand out separate as the righteous
society which God means it to be.   Shareholders must
find out what is done with their money ; employers

---

* I must acknowledge my indebtedness here and throughout this paper
to two writings by the Rev. Charles Gore, viz. "The Mission of the
Church" (Murray), and "The Social Doctrine of the Sermon on the
Mount" (Percival).

must find out the conditions of life and labour under which their work is done ; clergy must get to know the exact circumstances of the lives of the hearers to whom they preach. Above all, there must be much more frank recognition on the part of Christians of such truths as the Fatherhood of God, the brotherhood of man, the essential equality of all men in the sight of God, the need of justice to all men. The Christian Church has been wofully remiss in recognizing these truths, which are the very foundations on which Christ told us to build the Church. And this recognition must be something much more than a mere acknowledgment of the truth ; it must be coupled with a courageous determination to incur any risk in order to bring the truth into immediate relation to the facts and acts of life. It ought not to be such an extraordinary thing as it is for rich and poor to live together and share the pleasures and anxieties of life. Great acts of self-sacrifice ought not to be so rare as they are among those who call themselves the followers of the Crucified. At present, if a Catholic duke subscribes largely to Church work, and gives thousands instead of hundreds in alms, it is looked upon as a sort of desirable form of lunacy by his fellow-Christians. Correspondingly, there is little or no shock experienced by the Christian community on hearing that a rich fool has given two

hundred pounds for a single orchid. Great efforts are
made by one set of Christians to prevent another set
from worshipping an image, while all of us are, more
or less, tainted with the love of money, which St. Paul
tells us is the real idolatry of the later ages of the
world.

There should also be a much greater desire on the
part of Christians to help one another in leading the
Christian life. Are, for example, Christian employers
of labour anxious to enable those whom they employ to
live as God meant them to live? Do the masters and
mistresses of domestic servants assist them in leading a
Christian life? Do parents bring their children up on
really Christian principles? They teach them, perhaps,
one or two Christian precepts, and take care that they
are confirmed; but do they bring home to them early
in life that, as Christians, they have to live a different
life from that of worldly people? Do they teach them
that all men are brothers in a much more than conventional sense? Do they teach them that hard work is a
necessary part of Christianity? We are for ever priding
ourselves on the beauty and simplicity of our Prayer-
book, but it is questionable whether we have ever yet
fully and uncompromisingly taught the "duty towards
our neighbour" to rich and poor alike. Is it impressed
on the minds of our gilded youth at public schools, before

they are shovelled in by fifties and hundreds to the sacred ordinance of confirmation, that henceforth they are to "learn and labour truly to get their own living," to do their duty, to love others with all that devotion and attention which they obviously bestow upon themselves, to order themselves lowly and reverently—not to those who are more rich, but—to those who are more good than themselves, to be true and just in all their dealings ; especially to be careful of this if they are about to become stockbrokers, landlords, lawyers, or M.P.'s ? Why are children brought up to think that "to be able to do nothing " is rather a desideratum than otherwise ? As a Socialist has remarked somewhere, "if a young man comes into a fortune which enables him to live without working, or if he obtains an appointment to an office in which the hours are very short, he is immediately congratulated by his friends on his good fortune." Now, it would be far more Christian if such young men were condoled with, or, at any rate, were warned that it is very hard for a rich man to enter into the kingdom of God, or that an idle man is a curse to society.

Separation, then, not from the world itself, but from the spirit of the world, is what is needed if ever the Church is to perform her first social duty. Christian men and women must "come out of it," in the sense that there must be a clear understanding between them that they are bound by a higher law than other men; that their Master requires it of them that they should present before the eyes of mankind a visible union of those who hunger and thirst after righteousness, who are ready, at whatever sacrifice, to obey God rather than man in all the details of their private and public life. I frankly own that my judgment in this matter must include myself. I feel herein, and throughout this paper, that I am the chief of sinners. I must add that in my opinion "the whole body of the Church" will not advance much in this direction until the lead is given, as in the old times, by the Religious Orders. A revival of Community Life under the three Vows, in a form suited to our changed conditions, may be confidently looked for in the near future. May God, in His mercy, give us a St. Francis!

(2) And now as to the second branch of the Church's social duty. She is to act upon the world at large. Objections have lately been taken to the interference, or suggested interference, of the Church in these social questions. It has been said that Christianity is not to be forced upon the State; that God has not revealed to us what particular form of government or what particular organization of industry is right, and therefore that we have no right to go out into the world in the name of Christ, and call upon men to adopt this or that plan of

government or of commerce. This argument is partly true. It would not be right for Christians (at any rate, not with their present limited knowledge and experience) to call upon the State in the name of Christ at once to adopt "Collectivism" as the national industrial system. I say, advisedly, in the name of Christ. An individual Christian might think such a system right and best, and might move heaven and earth to get it adopted, but he has no right to say that Christ demands all nations to be Collectivist. So, in the same way, Christians are exceeding their rights in calling upon their fellow-Christians to oppose Disestablishment in the name of Christ. Such a formula as "God or Gladstone," a formula used, I believe, in the agitation of 1893, is grossly un-Christian and immoral, and no one has a right to use it.

But though to this extent it is true that the Church must not force on so-called reforms in the name of Christ, she may, and ought, to declare herself distinctly on a particular side where the point at issue is clearly a moral one. Where it is distinctly a matter of right and wrong, there the Church is bound to be openly and avowedly and actively on the side of right as against wrong, justice as against injustice. Now, here comes in the necessity of study and careful discussion of the points at issue. In so many cases the point at issue is not quite clear. But the Church is under a distinct obligation to try to find it out. What is wrong is for the Church to hold aloof. She who ought to guide the nation in all moral matters ought not to be standing aside where questions of morals are concerned. In almost every great trade dispute, for example, there is a question of right and wrong involved, and it is clearly the business of the Church, the moral guide of the people, to find out the right, and declare herself for it, and help forward what is a right and just object. Of course, there are many difficult cases in which the right course is not very clear. In such matters the Church should be at least found declaring · principles and advising peace, and recommending patience and justice. We have had splendid examples in such men as Dr. Westcott and Dr. Jayne of what bishops can do in this way, but they are almost by themselves. It is a great mistake to suppose that a clergyman can do nothing in a trade dispute unless he is prepared to offer himself as an actual arbitrator. Probably, as an arbitrator, he would be a failure; but he can do a great deal, and so can all Church-people, by educating public opinion. Professor Marshall, our leading political economist, says he hopes that "public opinion, based on sound economics and just morality, will become ever more and more the arbiter of the conditions of industry." If this is to be so—if, for example, we are going to have many more disputes settled, as the dock strike undoubtedly was, simply by force of public opinion—then it is most important that public opinion should be educated in a right way for its tremendous responsibilities. Now, I ask, who is the proper educator of public opinion, if not the Church of Jesus Christ?

But unfortunately the Church, to a great extent, wants educating herself. Her own conscience is terribly unenlightened. She has kept so much outside the national life so long that now she either cannot speak, or what she says is not listened to. The record of the social and industrial progress of this country during this century is notable for one thing, the almost entire absence of any corporate assistance on the part of the Church to the nation. With the exception of national education, I do not think much social progress could be attributed to the Church. Think of some great national reforms which have come to pass during the last hundred years—the abolition of the slave-trade ; the abolition of capital punishment for trivial offences ; the reform of prisons ; the repeal of the corn laws ; the Factory Acts ; the trades union movement ; the co-operative movement. In all these, grave moral questions were involved ; but, so far as I know, the Church

H

as a body remained practically silent and inactive while they were being effected.

Of course, great Christian men and women like Wilberforce, Howard, Elizabeth Fry, Lord Shaftesbury, John Bright, Frederick Denison Maurice, Charles Kingsley, and others, were prominently connected with these matters; but the Christian Church as a body did nothing. There was no social gospel at work.

But there was much excuse in those days, because the Church did not believe in herself or her Divine mission. Now there is no excuse, because she believes in both. The Catholic movement ought to issue in the Christian social movement, just because it is the Catholic movement which has, or ought to have, spiritualized the Church. She knows herself now to be God's own society, pledged to claim the world for Him, entrusted with His Divine grace by which the world can be regenerated. How can she dare, then, to stand aloof when questions of social reform are filling men's minds? She is bound by every claim she makes for herself as a Divine society, to be in the forefront where the question under consideration is the reform of God's own earth. But in order that the Church may be acceptable to men as their leader, the guide of their public opinion, she must have knowledge. She must be a body which men will not despise. Here, again,

Churchmen are lamentably deficient. They will not study the social problem; hence they have not the knowledge which commands respect. A business man said to me the other day that he was tired of hearing the clergy get up in the pulpit Sunday after Sunday and denounce business men without any real understanding of their sins or their temptations. So, again, in a trade dispute, unless Christians have some knowledge, their claims to leadership will be ignored. At the same time, I think there is a danger in the opposite direction of supposing that a very great deal of knowledge is needed. I think, probably, with just an elementary knowledge, much more might be done by Christians than is done at present.

All this time I have been speaking of cases where the moral issue is complicated and difficult to discover. But there are numberless cases where the moral issue is quite plain and on the surface; and here, too, I am afraid, Christians are quite as much in the background and afraid to act. I have lately been reading various reports on social matters, and I notice how again and again the remedy proposed is a moral one. Mr. Llewellyn Smith, in his admirable Blue Book lately published on the "unemployed," is in despair about all the modern agencies for dealing with the problem. Labour bureaux, labour colonies, charity organization municipal relief work, and all the rest, he says, only touch the fringe of the evil, they do not touch the heart of it. We must aim, he says, at "improving character and preventing men from sinking down." Moral reform is needed. The Royal Commissioners on the Sweating System lay the blame on the employers, who, they say, are regardless of moral considerations in allowing sub-contracting without inquiry into the conditions of those who do the work. The Report of the Lady Commissioners on Women's Work is practically unanimous about the immoral conditions under which those whom we call our sisters are being allowed to work. Examples of such are the cruelly long hours of shop-assistants and laundresses; the insanitary conditions of workshops; the bullying; the vexatious fines and dismissals; the want of decency; the dangerous employment in noxious trades, resulting in early death.

Only the other day, in the newspapers, we were told of a purely moral reform which the State is about to undertake. I allude to the Report of the Home Secretary's Committee on "White-Lead Poisoning." The deadly effects of lead are graphically described. The committee recommends total prohibition of women's labour as soon as possible.

But why could not the Church have found this out?

Why could not the Church make the recommendation and agitate till it was done?

These are only a few instances out of thousands where the moral issue in social problems is perfectly clear, and it seems to me criminal that the Church should be resting silent and inactive in the face of them.

IV. But it is not only by enlightening public opinion and declaring herself boldly on the side of right, that the Church is to preach her social gospel. There is at the present moment a great active movement going on in our midst in the direction of social reform, and it is the duty of the Church to go right into the midst of it, to sympathize with what is good in it, and to moderate or correct what is wrong, and to provide what it lacks. She should sympathize with what is good in it, and there is very much more good in it than Churchmen think. The comfortable Church lady, who scoffs at a trades union leader, and calls him a wretch who ought to be shot; the sleek business man or the idle aristocratic youth who use bad language about strikes and Socialism, only show their complete ignorance of what they are talking of, and, what is worse, their lamentable deficiency in the virtues of the religion they profess.

I do not believe there is any country in the world in which the social movement is in the hands of such good, honest, straightforward, earnest men as it is in

England, and I am proud to reckon many of them amongst my friends.

All clearly righteous movements, such as co-operation, women's unions, etc., might be heartily supported and furthered by Christians.

Moreover, the "Socialists," as they are carelessly and ignorantly called, are far ahead of many of us Churchmen in preaching what are distinctively Christian principles, such as some I have already mentioned, viz. the dignity of labour, the equality of men, the beauty of brotherhood, the necessity of work and the abomination of idleness, the duties of property, etc.

It is sad that the Church, instead of welcoming this, should be found in some cases opposing it. Let us take care lest haply we be found to be fighting against God.

But the chief work that the Christian Church has to do with the social movement is to guide it and to show how she can provide what it lacks. For though it says much and does much that is distinctly Christian, it is, I fear, to a great extent, avowedly non-Christian. This is partly due to the want of sympathy it has met with from Christians, but it is also very largely due to a failure to perceive what is really essential in social reform. The movement is too materialistic — the leaders do not yet understand that a man's life does not consist in the abundance of things that he possesses.

The "living wage," for instance, in most men's minds means a "feeding wage" only. Of course it is a disgrace to a Christian country that there should have to be all this agitation to prevent starvation and to provide men with food and clothing; it is also true that if we could secure to all a "feeding wage" we should have done much to make it possible for men to go on to those higher developments of their spiritual being which we Christians understand to be life in the truest sense. But, when all is said and done, a movement for social reform which leaves out the reformation of man's character is utterly inadequate, and I am always surprised that our labour leaders and others do not see this more clearly. There is not a single plan for social reform which can possibly succeed ultimately without some such moral force as Christianity proposes to supply. "Socialism," or "Communism," presupposes that men will love one another and will be willing to work hard.

Co-operation necessitates a large amount of un-selfishness. Trade unionism requires mutual confidence and trust. All our modern socialistic legislation, such as the Factory Acts, the Education Acts, the Employers' Liability Acts, the proposed Local Veto Bill, the Parish Councils Act, and such like, all demand a great amount of brotherly feeling and a steady growth of mutual love and fellowship, if they are not to be dead letters. All

our social evils are due to sin, to selfishness, unlove,
envy, class hatred, individualism, and unbridled competition. Consequently, to attempt social reform without moral reform of men's character is like building a
house on the sand.

The world will not be made better simply by re-
constructing an external paradise. It is no good having
a new paradise if you are going to people it with nine-
teenth-century Adams and Eves. Christianity offers a
new Adam, offers, that is, to regenerate man in Jesus
Christ, the Second Adam, and that is why Christianity
is the only true basis of reform. Jesus Christ is the
only Person who has ever dared to offer to mankind the
taking away of sin. He alone offers to make possible a
fresh ethical start, to provide a new standard of living,
and to give men the power to live it : to pay, in fact,
a real "living wage." It is sad, too, that many otherwise good social teachers are so anxious to discredit
the old Faith in the Divine Nature of our Blessed Lord,
and to reduce Him to the level of a mere Philosopher
and Philanthropist, thereby depriving Christianity of its
great right to be considered the instrument *par excellence*
of Social Reform. For if Christ be not Divine, He
certainly cannot change man's nature ; and if man's
nature remain unchanged, the world will remain pretty
much what it is for all that Parliaments may do. If

you want a New Jerusalem, you must have new Jews. This is the social gospel, and it remains for us who serve the Lord Jesus Christ to preach it and make it a fact in the world.

JAMES ADDERLEY.

Clergy and Laity.

PREACHING might be defined to be saying as distinct from doing. Cynical as the definition may sound, so, it is to be feared, would the world, which has been cynical from the beginning about its priests and Levites, define that particular form of gaining a livelihood which consists in pretending that you are ever so much better than everybody else, and yet acting like the rest of mankind; of promulgating ideals which you expect others to put into practice. The world is, after all, no fool, and it has long since observed that the men whose business it is to be saints are no more unselfish, no more heavenly-minded, than their poor struggling lay-brethren, buffeted by storms of trial and temptation to which "the fugitive and cloistered virtue" of their spiritual masters is never subjected. The simple truth, of course, is that the estate of the clergy is merely an ingeniously conceived engine of the land-grabbing aristocracy. It preaches the gospel of the poor in order to safeguard the pockets of the rich. Not con-

sciously, maybe ; and far be it from any one but vulgar
demagogues to deny the piety and loveliness of life
which are characteristic of many professional teachers
of religion. It is not the men, but the system to which
they belong that is most to blame. And what ironical
paradoxes does that system constantly present!
Clergymen with fat livings preaching the uses of
adversity, as they hand the eleemosynary loaf—a loaf,
too, not paid for by them, but provided for by the
endowment of ancient piety. It shows us poor half-
starved curates doing all the work, and the luxurious
rector taking nearly all the pay. On what Christian
principle, one wonders, does the rector justify *that?*
However, we must guard against seeming to imply that
the clergy are *worse* men than us laymen. All that it
is necessary to insist is that, as a body, they are no
better; or, at any rate, that the majority of them have
no such clear call to their high office as many a layman, whom the caprice of existence has also given the
wrong work to do. The whole secret of the failure of
the Churches is in the fact that the priesthood is a profession, a business, open to all men, like any other,
irrespective of fitness or inclination. We often laugh
in our careless way at the threadbare axiom which
destines the fool of the family to the most sacred and
momentous responsibilities allotted to men. Yet what

a melancholy, what a tragic jest! What a confession truly interpreted, of the immemorial futility of ecclesi-astical methods! The curate is not a recognized comedy type for nothing. Why does the world laugh at him? Why does it listen with mock deference to his platitudes, and yet never think of applying them in its daily life? How often have we heard the average hard-driven man of the world exclaim that it is all very nice and pretty for the Reverend Mr. So-and-so to talk, but he doesn't know the city. He lives in a charming fool's paradise of Dorcas societies and tea-parties on the rectory lawn. In short, the implication is that, though he may know a great deal of the life hereafter, he has no practical knowledge of the life here. He underestimates its difficulties, has no ex-perience of its temptations, and generally ignores its conditions.

What the average man wants is a religion that will help him on week-days. He wants a faith that is wise in doubt, a strength that understands weakness, a purity that has touched the pitch of life and not been defiled. He wants doctrine that lays stress on real and not merely fanciful sin. It has been the custom of the Church for centuries to denounce as sinful many pleasures which the heart of man has known all along to be proper to be enjoyed. Consequently man has drawn his conclusion that the Church is a somewhat fanciful institution, not adapted for everyday use. The true teacher—like Him whose messenger he is—" remembereth that we are dust." He is not a mere symbol of an impossible ideal : he is an elder brother who has gone through the mill of life before us, and he preaches of what he himself knows, of what in his own life he has made stern trial. If he talks of " conversion," of the mystical " second birth," it is not as the ecclesiastical parrot talks of these things ; and the peace that passes all understanding is to be found on his face as well as in his sermon. There is that convincing sincerity of experience about him which makes these transcendental matters seem no longer remote from humanity ; but, verily, as Christ intended them to be—practicable sustaining realities of daily experience.

If we take the central truth of Christianity to be what we variously call " conversion," " the second birth," that mysterious " change of heart," which is as undeniably a fact of hourly experience as the physical birth from which it is imaged, then we have this startling fact to face—that the majority of professional Christian teachers have never undergone that experience which they preach every Sunday as the first condition of the spiritual life. " Ye must be born again ! " From how many pulpits every Sunday is that

immortal message thundered and fluted by an uncomprehending parson to an uncomprehending world!
How many clergymen, one wonders, have anything
more than a theological understanding of its significance? The dilemma of the Christian Churches is put
into a nutshell, the secret of their failure understood
at once, when we realize that the majority of clergymen, and religious ministers of all kinds, have never
been "converted" themselves! How is it possible that
they can convince the world of truths which they have
not first realized for themselves? When one remembers
the system on which religious ministers are turned out,
there is nothing to surprise us in this. Just as there
are men in the legal profession with no "legal bias,"
men in the city without business instincts, painters and
musicians with no true imperative "gifts," so there are,
and must be, clergymen without any true vocation to
their high office. There is but one cure for this—the
abolition of the Church as a "learned profession." The
teacher should be a free-lance, like the artist, or the
literary man. He should be left to discover his own
message, and invent his own methods. So it has been
with those teachers who have caught the ears and
changed the hearts of men.

So much for the teachers. What of their teaching?
Have they taught the living gospel of the Galilean

or the dead letter of ingenious theological sophists? Who that has ever been to church or chapel can doubt the answer? Man cries out daily for the true bread of spiritual enlightenment, and the clergy diligently feed him with stones of dogma and symbol, with the east wind of mystical precepts. A sorry diet for any genuine hunger and thirst after righteousness. Either they thus send him empty away, or they lull him with the opiates of some such comfortable illusion as the mischievous doctrine of the Atonement, or the Life Hereafter. Instead of strengthening him to bear his own burdens, to fight his own battles, they teach him pusillanimously to leave them to be borne and fought by Another. Instead of encouraging him to make the best of this present life, by strength to wring out its sweetness, by courage to lay its fears, they feed him with dreams of a life to come, in which everything shall be exactly as his weakness desires it, and his sloth shall recline for ever on perpetual rest.

The wrong teachers, and the wrong teaching! What wonder that the kingdom of heaven should be so long in coming to pass! It has happened with Christianity as it happened with religions before it, as it happens to this day with every new message. The parabolic utterances of Christ, daring *aperçus* of spiritual intuition, early became the property of unspiritual men, without understanding of their symbolic significance. Superstition took the place of apprehension, and what had been living truth became dead letter, reverenced and enforced with all the fanaticism of superstitious ignorance. The old religion of rite and formula, the old monopolistic hierarchy, which Christ came especially to overthrow, gained, so to speak, a new lease of life, draining the blood of the new spiritual impulse to reanimate its failing organism. Paradoxically enough, the articles of the new faith soon insisted upon were not the new vital elements it had brought into the world (or, at any rate, brought before the world in a unity and with an urgency unapproached before), but the tags and remnants of that very pagan symbolism and philosophy it had come to displace. The Jewish type of the scapegoat, bearing the sins of the world; such originally "heathen" rites as baptism; such metaphysical symbols as the Trinity;—these, the misleading motley in which the message of Christ was soon to be clothed, not to say smothered, were the barren propositions by which men were taught to be saved or lost. The essential matters, the new law of love, the spiritual significance of man, the blessedness and sanctity of life—the clergy, having little or no apprehension of these things, educated only in the letter, uninitiated in the spirit, were unable to preach them with authority or conviction. The utmost they could do was to terrorize or bribe man into virtue, or the appearance of it, by "threats of hell, and hopes of paradise;" so that he remained virtually what he was before—the slave of a tyrannous and vengeful deity, whom it was his duty to appease as directed by the priests. It is idle to deny that this primitive dread of a Moloch and a Jah is still at the bottom of most of our church-going.

Given the right preachers, what, then, should they preach to us to-day? Two doctrines they should emphatically cease preaching: the doctrine of the Atonement, and the doctrine of the Hereafter, with its sordid corollaries of rewards and punishments. These two dogmas have, I believe, injured humanity, retarded its progress, more than any delusions that have from time to time dominated the world. They are utterly opposed to the ideal of unselfishness which is the chief corner-stone of Christ's teaching. As Christ taught them they were either parable, or—let us frankly face the possibility—they were delusion. Christ saves the world merely in so far as the nobility of His personality and the force of His words move men to grow like Him. Understood in any other way, the idea of " salvation " is a most dangerous fallacy, whereby men abandon

I

individual effort, in fact give themselves up to the unchecked impulses of their natures, on the reliance of a few misinterpreted texts. What the preachers must be bold to tell us, what, to do them justice, some of them are beginning to preach, is the more salutary gospel, that man must save himself if he is to be saved, and not weakly depend (surely an abhorrent idea to any manly soul !) on the ignoble dream that, " He hath borne our trangressions for us ; the burden of our iniquities is upon Him, and with His stripes we are healed."

Similarly, the dream of the hereafter—especially now that the dogma of eternal punishment is practically abandoned—is dangerous to man in that it diminishes the spiritual importance of the life here, distracts him from a determined cultivation of its opportunities, and gives him, so to speak, all eternity to procrastinate in. The idea of immortality is one to which the human heart must perforce cling with tenderness. To be eternally blotted out, to lose our beloved dead for ever, are possibilities that strike a chill into the bravest soul. But is it not better courageously to prepare for these possibilities than to shut our eyes to them and indulge in enervating dreams ? The life hereafter may be a blessed reality, but as yet it is nought but an eager perilous conjecture. Would it not be wiser, until we know it true of a certainty, not to place our reliance upon it, but rather to live this present life nobly, fully, as though sure we shall be given no other? What a heightened value is thus added to our mortal days, what a momentous significance to all our actions, what a poignant zest and responsibility to all our relations with our fellows! Then we should not wait for the hereafter to be kind to one another, or put off doing our best work from day to day; nor would we undervalue the solid blessedness of earth in dissatisfied dreaming of the shadowy joys of heaven. The blessedness of earth, of our present life, and the sacredness of it—that is to be the theme of our true preachers. The fanatic asceticism which has usurped the name of Christianity was no ideal of Christ's. Temperance in the joys of life, and an indulgence in them in no brutish way, but with a sense of their mysterious sacred significance, as symbols, maybe, of joys still more rare—Christ certainly taught us this, but this also is the teaching of all true epicureans. Here again we see how Christ's apostles have misapplied His teaching, and by an insistence upon the letter of one part of it, have destroyed the vitalizing harmony of the whole.

RICHARD LE GALLIENNE.

Christian Ethics and Practical Politics.

As the politics of the future will be more and more determined by ethical considerations, it is worth while inquiring whether Christian ethics and practical politics are reconcilable. Might not the occupants of the Treasury benches profitably seek to apply the doctrines of the Sermon on the Mount to the exigencies of statesmanship? In other words, is it possible to govern in accordance with the principles laid down by Jesus of Nazareth in that wonderful discourse? To most people, I should hope, it must be a matter for surprise that this question should ever have arisen in this country, where the State shows its profound respect for the apostles by appointing their professed descendants to offices with incomes rising to £15,000 a year, and where, according to the first article of our great and glorious constitution, it is impossible for the Government of the country to proceed without the permission of these heavily endowed, but, I trust, nevertheless humble followers of the Carpenter of Nazareth. It so happens, however, that it is one of these right reverend prelates who must be held responsible for having raised the question.

The late Archbishop Magee stated that if you attempt to govern in accordance with the principles of the Sermon on the Mount, society will tumble to pieces. I have always thought that was a remarkable statement to be made by one, who not only rose to one of the highest positions in the Church, presumably for the learning and piety with which he was able to defend those principles, but who, at the same time, was a member of the Upper House of the Legislature, and therefore helped " to shape the whisper of the throne." How could he reconcile the two positions? If by " society " the bishop meant that charmed circle composed of the British nobs, and worshipped by the British snobs ; if he meant that system of things under which the rich have every facility for plundering the poor; if he meant the system of social and political corruption which Thomas Carlyle described as a "damnable cesspool of lies, shoddies, and shams," then he was perfectly right. But, if by "society" he meant the domocracy of England, with all its hopes and aspirations after a higher life, then I say he was hopelessly and radically in the wrong. You can govern in accordance with the principles laid down by Jesus Christ in the Sermon on the Mount,—that charter of man's redemption, which He sealed with His blood— and it is only in so far as you honestly attempt to do so that you can hope to arrive at anything like a civilized order of things.

Of course, in the space at my disposal, it would be impossible to go through the whole of that discourse, and to grapple with its many difficulties and apparent contradictions. On the other hand, I have no desire to follow the example of the old Scotch Minister who, when he came to a difficult passage in the Scriptures, of which he could give no satisfactory explanation, remarked : " My friends, we will look this difficulty boldly in the face—and pass on." Now, before passing on, let us look at one of the greatest difficulties in this Sermon on the Mount, one which, no doubt the good bishop had in his mind when he came to the conclusion that Jesus was altogether a failure for serious politicians. I refer to that passage, " But I say unto you, That ye resist not evil : but whosoever shall smite thee on thy right cheek, turn to him the other also." I can imagine some of the sympathizers with the bishop asking me, " Do you really think it is possible to govern in accordance with that doctrine ? Do you really believe that those who are responsible for law and

order, can act up to that principle?" It would be well
if they tried to do so. That passage, however difficult
it may be for us as individuals, to carry it out literally,
yet, as applied to communities and societies of men,
embodies a principles far more dreaded by tyrants and
oppressors than all the armies and navies which you
can bring against them—the principle of passive resistance. It is to the dread of the application of this
principle—to the dread of the Government of a general
strike against the payment of taxes—that we owe some
of the greatest reforms of the century. It is to this
principle that labour owes all its triumphs in its conflicts
with capital. How was the great lock-out won by the
miners? Simply by taking this advice of Jesus Christ.
The mine-owners smote them on the one cheek, by
refusing them a substance wage, the miners turned to
them the other also, and said, " We will take no wages
at all ; we will not storm your offices, or organize
rebellion ; we will regard every man who attempts to
carry out a policy of violence as the worst enemy of
our cause; we will wait patiently trusting to public
sympathy and public opinion, for our cause is just."
They waited, and they won.

The leading principles of the Sermon on the Mount,
I imagine, are contained in the Beatitudes. Let us
take the first of them : " Blessed are the poor in spirit :

for theirs is the kingdom of heaven." The theologians
have, it seems to me, very inadequately treated this
passage. They have interpreted it in the light of the
narrowest possible individualism, whereas it is capable
of interpretation in the light of the widest possible
collectivism. This has been suggested by a French
Biblical critic quoted by Matthew Arnold. The
theologians tell us that what these words mean is that
poverty of spirit, self-abasement, is the first essential in
the process of working out our own salvation. Self-
abasement may be a very desirable virtue in these days
of self-assertion, but it was not of the salvation of any
individual or set of individuals that Jesus was thinking
about when He uttered these words. He was thinking
of the salvation of the whole human family—of the
conditions under which alone it was possible to establish
the new order of things which He came to introduce.
What the words mean therefore is this : Blessed are
they who are *with* the poor in spirit, who dare not
become rich by the robbery of the poor ; who if they
are rich, are willing to devote their wealth to the
betterment of the masses of the people : Blessed are
they whose sympathies are with the poor, for theirs is
the kingdom of heaven—not alone beyond the clouds
and beyond the tomb, but here in this world ; the
kingdom of heaven upon earth, the regenerated society

of the future, the new democracy, whose mission it would be, in the beautiful words of William Blake—

"To build Jerusalem
In England's green and pleasant land."

Interpreted in this light, these words appear to me to be the sublimest utterance that ever fell from human lips, the text to the greatest sermon that was ever preached, the keynote to the whole of Christ's ethical and economic system, the statement of the Divine principle of the brotherhood of man. "Blessed are the poor in spirit!" When we have realized the full meaning of that, the days of flunkeyism and of snobbery will be at an end, the poor man will come in for the rightful share of the wealth which he creates; we shall no longer be faced with the difficult problems arising out of the terrible contrast between poverty and wealth, which is the curse and the shame of this nation; nor shall we any longer find it necessary to pay archbishops £15,000 a year for holding out prospects of perdition to workers on fifteen shillings a week. The dear old archbishop and his colleagues in the House of Lords have not, it seems to me, made any desperate effort to realize the meaning of being poor in spirit. It seems to me they are far more eager to look after the interests of Dives, than to promote the welfare of Lazarus. They did their best to destroy two great

measures—the Employers' Liability Bill and the Parish
Councils Bill—passed by the House of Commons for
Lazarus's benefit. The descendants of the apostles
offered no protest even when the Lord of Hatfield gave
Lazarus a contemptuous kick, by telling him that if he
wanted to take part in parish meetings the proper
place for him is not the parish schoolroom, but the
public-house. Now, if these right reverend prelates
had been true to the traditions of their own Church they
would have welcomed the Parish Council not only to
the parish schoolroom, but, if need be, to the parish
church. These " old grey churches of our native land,".
crowning the wooded upland, or nestling in the valley,
and within whose shadows sleep the generations of our
fathers—these ancient temples were never intended to
be utilized by a mere sect; nor were they built for
devotional purposes only. They were originally not
only the parish churches but the parish town halls and
the parish theatres. I should like to see them restored
to their original purpose. It seems to me that if the
House of Lords cannot rise to the conception of the
meaning of this first Beatitude—if these proud patricians,
prelates, and " partridge breeders of a thousand years,"
cannot understand that Dives has had his day and that
the turn of Lazarus is coming, they will soon be sent
to swell the ranks of the unemployed.

Again, how can we reconcile with this first beatitude
the conduct of the archbishop and some of his colleagues
in advising their clergy not to interfere in labour disputes? They were asked to stand aloof, even when the
whole country was convulsed by the greatest industrial
struggle of this century—the great coal lock-out of
1893. We had then, on the one side, half a million of
men and women willing to face starvation and death
for the sake of an idea, for the sake of a principle, and
on the other a ring of capitalists who, in order to save
themselves from loss, or to increase profits, proposed
to degrade the worker by reducing his standard of
living. Yet, in a struggle of this kind, the clergy were
advised not to interfere! I am afraid the archbishop
must think that Aaron, priest of God, was very impru-
dent, made a great mistake, when he interfered to bring
about a very revolutionary settlement of a certain
labour question which arose among the brickmakers
in the land of Egypt in the days of Pharaoh the
king.

If the Church cannot understand the significance of
these important industrial questions, if it stands aside
at these great industrial crises, it appears to me that
its religion is a failure, that it has lost all faith in the
possibility of establishing the kingdom of heaven upon
earth. If the clergy have lost faith in that, let them

revise their Prayer-book, let them eliminate from it the best thing that is in it—namely, the Lord's Prayer. The first petition in that sweetest canticle ever heard on earth, is that earth may be made as heaven. The second petition suggests the first condition under which this can be brought about, namely, that every dweller upon earth shall have his "daily bread." There you have the principle of the living wage laid down by the highest authority. This young Workman of Nazareth was the greatest political economist that ever walked the earth. He not only insisted on this principle of the living wage, He showed us how it could be carried out in that wonderful parable of the lord of the vineyard, who, seeing the people standing idle in the market-place, took them into his vineyard, and when the day's work was over paid them all alike. You may think that was very unfair. The old unionists, the regular workers, grumbled that the men who came in at the eleventh hour should be paid at the same rate as those who had borne the heat and burden of the day. But possibly these poor fellows who came in at the finish had been out of work for a considerable time, and the lord of the vineyard was perfectly justified in giving them a fair start, and the other men were very un-gracious in grumbling about it. But what this parable really signifies is this: that you must have a fixed

minimum wage, below which there shall be no discussion. You may say that is contrary to the laws of
political economy. No; it is not. It is sound science,
and has been proved to be sound science by the greatest
political economist still living, John Ruskin, who founds
his economic philosophy upon this parable, and takes
from it the title to the greatest of all his works, " Unto
this Last." What says Ruskin?

" Pay good and bad workmen alike? Certainly.
The difference between one prelate's sermon and his
successor's, or between one physician's opinions and
another's, is far greater as respects the quality of mind
involved, and far more important in result to you
personally, than the difference between good and bad
laying of bricks. Yet you pay with equal fee, contentedly, the good and bad workman upon your soul,
and the good and bad workman upon your body; much
more may you pay contentedly, with equal fees, the
good and bad workman upon your house. Nay, but
I choose my physician and my clergyman, thus indicating my sense of the quality of their work. By all
means also choose your bricklayer. That is the proper
reward of a good workman—to be chosen. The natural
and right system respecting all labour is that it should
be paid for at a fixed rate, but the good workman
employed and the bad workman unemployed. The

false, unnatural, and destructive system is when the
bad workman is allowed to offer his work at half-price,
and either take the place of the good, or force him by
his competition to work for an inadequate sum."

Then there comes the question of what you are to
do with the men who cannot find work. Still follow
the advice of the Nazarene. Take them into your
vineyard. You have at the present moment twenty-six
million acres of land lying idle in the United Kingdom.
Professor Schlich, of the School of Forestry, Cooper's
Hill, tells us that, upon parts of these waste lands, we
might grow all the timber which we now import every
year from abroad, to the value of six millions of money.
The afforesting of our waste lands would employ, on
the professor's estimate, seventy thousand men for forty
years ; after which we should begin to get our crop,
when the number of men employed would be far greater.
This is one of the little schemes by which we might
solve this unemployed question, if the Government
would only face it honestly.

Let me pass on to the next Beatitude, " Blessed are
they that mourn : for they shall be comforted." Every
man who has thought seriously upon the problems of
government, every statesman with an element of moral
grandeur in his character, knows full well what that
means ; which is, that you never need despair of the

democracy, however dark and gloomy the prospect may lie before you. Perhaps the political significance of this second Beatitude was never more finely expressed than by John Bright, in a remarkable speech he delivered in the House of Commons in his old Radical days, on the occasion of the proposal of the Government of the day to suspend the Habeas Corpus Act in Ireland. After reviewing the efforts of successive Governments— Liberal, I regret to say, as well as Tory—to govern Ireland in accordance with principles which I do not think you will find in the Sermon on the Mount, he appealed to Ministers to know whether they could not find a more excellent way, and concluded a magnificent speech, which made a wonderful impression on the House, with that fine quotation from the sacred writer, "Unto the upright, there ariseth a light in the darkness." That is the meaning of "Blessed are they that mourn : for they shall be comforted," and that is what makes this Beatitude specially applicable to those who undertake the responsibility of governing a nation.

"Blessed are the meek: for they shall inherit the earth." Such is the state of education in this country, that meekness has come to be regarded with a kind of contempt. The meek man is looked upon as a weak man. Let us not run away with this notion. Meekness is not weakness; it is just the opposite. It is

moral strength, and has been characteristic of great
men in all ages ; of men great, not only by reason of
their learning, their genius, or their piety, but of men
great in action, of some even of our great naval and
military commanders—not your jingo generals and
pipe-clay field-marshals, not your gallant captains who
invade African villages with Maxim guns and seven-
pounders ; but your real fighting men, your Wolfs
and Nelsons, and Wellingtons and Outrams. Wolf
displayed the meekness of his character on the eve of
Quebec, when he repeated those wonderful lines from
" Gray's Elegy "—

> " The boast of heraldry, the pomp of power,
>   And all that beauty, all that wealth e'er gave,
>   Awaits alike the inevitable hour—
>   The paths of glory lead but to the grave."

" I would rather," said Wolf, " have written those four
lines than be the conqueror at Quebec." Nelson showed
that he possessed some of the meekness of a childish
nature in that pathetic moment of death and victory
at Trafalgar, when, looking up into the face of his
devoted attendant, he said with his last breath, " Kiss
me, Hardy." Wellington, the Iron Duke, also showed
that he had some element of meekness in his character,
when, on the plains of Waterloo, amid the groans of
the wounded and the dying, he gave utterance to that

remarkable expression, "There is nothing more awful than a victory, excepting a defeat."

I am sorry to say, however, that meekness has not been a remarkable characteristic of our sovereigns and statesmen. Swagger and arrogance, and an insolent disregard of the principles laid down by Jesus of Nazareth in the Sermon on the Mount, have been more in their line. Hence they have reversed the whole policy of Jesus on the land question. In the language of sovereignty and statesmanship, it is not, "Blessed are the meek," but "Blessed are the proud," "for they shall inherit the earth." Hence the greater part of the land of England, of Scotland, and of Ireland, is in the possession of a few aristocratic families who boast of their long descent—about the most foolish thing that any rational being can brag about! The late Mr. Spurgeon, notwithstanding his grim theology, had a redeeming sense of humour, and, preaching on one occasion on the subject of family pride, he said, "What a ridiculous thing this is, seeing that we are all descended from an old gardener, who was turned out of his Master's employment for stealing His apples!" If you prefer the scientific view of our origin, you will find that we have a still less reputable record; you will find, if you carry the inquiry far enough back, that you have some very near relatives in the Zoological

K

Gardens. When Sydney Smith was asked by a lady about his pedigree, he said he could only trace it back to his grandfather, who disappeared about the time of the assizes, and the family asked no questions. Now, with regard to the ancestors of some of our great landed proprietors, I am afraid it must be said that they *ought* to have disappeared about the time of the assizes; but, instead of putting in an appearance at an assize court, they managed somehow to turn up at the Court of Hampton, or Whitehall, or St. James, and so came in for a share of the plunder whenever the sovereign had a confiscation scheme on hand by which the people could be robbed.

But the English people are not going to submit to our present land system for ever. The fact that we have in the United Kingdom twenty-six million acres of land lying idle—crying out to the workless worker, as Carlyle said, "Come, and till us"—and many more millions of acres only partly cultivated, proves that our aristocratic system of ownership has broken down; and I believe the day is not far distant when the State will be forced to make provision for the inheritance of the earth by the meek—that is to say, by the general body of the industrious, peace-loving community. All the measures now before Parliament are but leading up to the one great measure which, I trust, will be settled before the century is out—the measure for securing the land for the people.

"Blessed are the peacemakers." I have just stated that Jesus preached the doctrine of passive resistance, which I am glad to say to-day is being emphasized with marvellous eloquence by him who, now that Lowell and Whitman are no more, now that Browning and Tennyson are gone, and Ruskin has ceased from active work, stands almost alone in his prophetic grandeur as a truly great living man of letters. I mean Count Tolstoi. Still I do not go the whole length with Tolstoi. I do not think that Jesus was for peace at any price. This Beatitude suggests a state of war. It seems to recognize the fact that for some inscrutable reason of Providence all animate life is a struggle for existence. One species of animals preys upon another, and man himself is a fighter from his birth. He comes into the world with his fists clenched, and I need not remind those who are fathers and mothers how desperate a pugilist the baby is in his cradle. These infant struggles are but the prelude to the great battle of life in which he must engage, until, as the poet says, the time comes when the clenched fists open wide at the kindly touch of death, and the struggle ends in the ineffable calm that settles on the dead man's brow. Seeing, then, that life is a constant struggle, how important is it that there should be peacemakers—peacemakers not only as regards the prevention of a policy of actual violence, but peacemakers as regards the modification or the abolition of that terrible system of competition in industry and trade by which not only the weakest, but sometimes the strongest—if they happen to be honest and honourable men—must go to the wall. Blessed are they who are seeking to abolish industrial warfare by the establishment of the principle of the living wage, without which there can be no peace.

Unfortunately, our statesmen have neglected none of the Beatitudes of Christ more shamefully and more wickedly than this. They, as a rule, have not been peacemakers, but war-makers. Hence they have piled up for us a national debt of hundreds of millions, which has already been paid three times over in interest, and which will continue to hang like a millstone round the nation's neck for generations yet unborn. This colossal debt has been piled up by the pursuit of a policy which can best be described as one of blunder and of crime.

It would be difficult to point to any single war in which England has been engaged, excepting that which resulted in the defeat of the Spanish Armada, which has been justified by the results. We boast of our military prowess; but, as a matter of fact, there is no nation on the face of the earth that has suffered greater military disasters than we have. Yet we seem rather proud of our military history—of so long life is Jingoism ! We teach our children in our schools to be proud of it. I am certainly very proud of the British soldier, of the man who will go anywhere and do anything; I am not proud of the policy that has hounded him on to the slaughter. Every schoolboy can tell you of the glories of the campaigns of the Third Edward, the Fifth Henry, and of Marlborough and Wellington. He can tell you of the glories of Cressy, and Poictiers, and Agincourt. But he cannot tell you, for he has perhaps never been taught, that these were but brilliant episodes in a ghastly drama played out for a period of a hundred years, and resulted, not in the triumph of the British arms, but in our being thrust out of France, bag and baggage, with the loss of every inch of territory we possessed there. We not only lost an empire in France, through militarism, we lost a far more splendid empire across the Atlantic; and we are threatened with the loss of another in the East, unless we modify the terrible military policy which is involving the Indian people in a burden of debt too grievous for them to bear.

I may be charged with want of patriotism ; but I

confess I am not particularly proud of our Indian
Empire as it is at present governed. I am not particularly proud of the fact that we have some two hundred
millions of our fellow-subjects there who are probably
the very poorest people on the face of the earth—whose
poverty is due to the exorbitant taxes we levy upon
them in order to maintain one of the costliest military
systems the world has ever known. India, it seems to
me, is governed by Englishmen to-day either in ignorance or in reckless neglect of the great warning uttered
by Jesus of Nazareth, " They that take the sword shall
perish by the sword." No truer or wiser words were
ever spoken, and their wisdom and their truth have
been amply illustrated in the history of all the military
empires of the past.

What is to be said of the latest of our little wars—
the war undertaken in the Queen's name by a chartered
company of Stock Exchange gamblers and land-grab-
bers, the war against the Matabele? It appears to me,
this beats the record of our national infamy. Yet,
strange to say, it has received the blessing of a bishop
of the English Church, who had the temerity to defend
the policy of Messrs. Rhodes and Co. in the national
pulpit in Westminster Abbey. It was afterwards discovered that this right reverend prelate, the Bishop of
Derry, was a shareholder in Mr. Rhodes's company.

A bishop booming the Chartered Company over the grave of David Livingstone in the national temple, was a sight for gods and men! The bishop defended the war on the ground that it was undertaken to protect the meek Mashonas against the cruel Matabele. But does any man in his senses imagine that the lust of gold had nothing to do with the invasion of poor Lobengula's territory? Because some of us raised our voices against the treatment which this cruelly wronged potentate received—because we cried shame upon the murder of his envoys and the slaughter of thousands of his brave men by Maxim guns and seven-pounders— we were charged with advocating a policy of cowardice. It seems to me the cowardice was all on the other side. Some people may think it heroic to violate the Queen's solemn word, and, in defiance of treaties, and without condescending to make a formal declaration of war, to invade with horse, foot, and artillery, the territories of a chief who did his best to be on friendly terms with us, and who could only defend himself, at fearful odds, by men untrained to modern warfare. If war, on the methods of the Chartered Company, is a necessity of our civilization, it is something for which we ought to put on sackcloth and ashes. It is certainly nothing to be proud of. I protest against the assumption that we, as a so-called civilized and Christian nation, have any right, prescriptive or otherwise, to exploit the territories of alien races on the ground that they are savages and barbarians. In many respects these native African races are far more civilized than we are. They have neither gaols, nor workhouses, nor gambling hells, nor other dens of infamy, which we consider necessary to our beautiful civilization. Moreover, they are collectivists to a man, and sink the interests of the individual in the interests of the tribe.

Then, I am told, that I am for a *little* England. No, I am for a *great* England; an England great in her peaceful commerce and her industrial enterprise; an England great in her literature and her art, and in the glory of her adventurous sons, her great navigators and explorers, of whom Franklin and Livingstone, and not Cecil Rhodes and Co., are the true types. I am for a great England—great as the mother of free communities beyond the sea; great in her loyalty to her old traditions as the land of religious liberty, the home of constitutional freedom; great, not by the extent of her military frontier, but in the strength of her moral position—in that righteousness which exalteth a nation; an England great for Christ and humanity. These are some of the principles, as I conceive them, of the Sermon on the Mount; and the man who tells me that you cannot govern in accordance with them, to him I say what Cobden said to the man who told him, with regard to his great agitation, "It can't be done." "Then," said Cobden, "if that is the only objection, the sooner we set about it the better."

A. E. FLETCHER.

The Wrongfulness of Riches.

"THERE must always be rich and poor," say the smug
middle-class optimists by their cosy firesides. "Of
course we are very sorry for our poorer brethren. We
send them to nice hospitals when they're ill or injured,
and we mete them out little doles of bread and blankets
at Christmas—a season at which some vague sentimental
recollection of Christian principles comes home to us for
a moment: but as to supposing we can ever get rid of
the fundamental distinctions of rich and poor, why, that's
all pure moonshine. The Lord has ordained it so. We,
who are well-to-do and warm and comfortable, mustn't
dare to quarrel with the Lord's ordaining."

If I thought like those unctuous hypocrites, I wouldn't
care to go on living. It is just the hope of seeing this
ancient wrong one day redressed—the belief in moral
progress as possible for humanity—that enables one to
live on in the world as we find it. Let us bear up and
be brave. Perhaps we may help to make it better. But
better it can never be so long as people suppose it is

naturally and necessarily divided into two classes, one of which must always live on the plunder, spoliation, and degradation of the other.

Acquiescence in the wrong is itself wrong-doing.

Let me put a little parallel. "The world," says the robber chief, "must always consist of the robbers and the robbed. Of course, I'm very sorry for my poor robbed brethren, whose fields I ravage, the fruit of whose harvests I seize and carry off, and whose cattle I drive away to my fortress in the mountains—to say nothing of their wives and daughters, whom I often take captive. But there! 'tis Heaven's will. There will always be robbed and robbers. Providence has chosen to make me one of the spoilers, not one of the spoiled ; and it would be crass ingratitude in me to complain of it. Not more than others I deserve—if indeed as much, since I never do anything for it—but Heaven (not unaided by my own good sword) has given me more. How thankful I ought to be that I was born a robber! Whene'er I take my walks abroad, how many robbed I see! and how vividly I realize the pious fact that 'tis I who have been graciously permitted to rob them! It is all very sad, I admit ; and we must all deplore—quite in the abstract, that is to say—that such distinctions of class and function should exist among us ; but as to supposing that a strong man, with a castle in the hills" (or a few

thousand acres of his own, or a factory by the river),
"could ever be induced to cease from robbing his neighbours, why, that's all pure Utopianism. And don't we
do our best, we robbers, for the good of the robbed ?
When seasons are bad, don't we often give them back,
as a special favour, some small percentage of the corn
and meat of which we robbed them before ? Don't we
help the poor devils with little presents of money, just
to tide them over bad times, and enable them to raise
a fresh crop for us next summer ? Oh yes, we do our
duty by the robbed, I can tell you. Depend upon it,
this is a very well-ordered world. We robbers don't
envy the robbed their easy life of growing crops and
beasts for us to steal. Why should they envy us our
castles in the hills, and our hard mental work in collect-
ing and eating it ?"

Change but a word, and it is the case of the rich
with the poor among us. Wealthy people think they
have done quite enough by their poorer neighbours
if they merely give "charity," as we absurdly call it ;
if they return to some few feeble members of the class
they have robbed some miserable fraction of the wealth
they have robbed them of. They seldom go back to
inquire with themselves where their wealth came from.
They seldom ask themselves, "Is it mine at all ? Who
made it ? Who produced it ? Why is it in my hands,

instead of in the hands of those who begot it? Why am I living in excessive comfort and in debilitating and effeminate luxury, while the people who make the wealth I use so ill are toiling underground in darkness and nakedness, are facing the stormy sea in cold and fog, are labouring long hours for dear life at whirring wheels, are tending endless sheep on dry Australian plains, are massacring helpless seals amid arctic icebergs?" The propertied classes never think these things. The conventional language of "capital and labour" blinds their eyes to the simple underlying human truths of the matter—that others have toiled, and that they, by dint of false and cruel social arrangements, have entered into their rest, doing nought in return for it.

It is *not* true that there must be always rich and poor. Rich and poor are made by deliberate human contrivance. It is *not* true that the rich have done their entire duty·when they have returned to the needy some small part of the wealth of which they have deprived them by means of man-made social arrangements. It is *not* true that tea-parties on lawns to "the deserving poor," and doles of flour or flannel at Christmas, and donations to infirmaries on Hospital Sunday, can redress the wrong inflicted on the workers by our wicked and immoral political economy. What is wanted is, not charity, but justice. We say to the rich man, not "Give half thy goods unto the poor," but, "Go and sin no more." People must wake up to the consciousness of the fact that to be rich is in itself a wrong thing; that no man has a right to monopolize to himself the product of many men's labour; and that the bare existence of poverty and destitution in our midst is a fatal blot upon the character of our civilization. Instead of saying, "There must always be rich and poor," we say boldly, "There need never be rich and poor." And what we aim at is such a reconstruction of society from its base as shall make the existence of poverty in our state an absolute impossibility.

Not the relief of poverty, but the abolition and prevention of poverty, is the end to be held in view. We look forward to a time when no man will be poor, because the conditions which produce either poverty or wealth have been deliberately and strenuously eliminated among us.

One man can only be rich by making many men poor. To say he is wealthy is merely another way of saying in one brief sentence that he has concentrated upon himself the wealth produced by many of his fellows. That is of the very essence of opulence. It springs from spoliation. Others have toiled and not enjoyed; the rich man has not toiled, neither has he spun; but he enjoys the product of all their labour.

Thoughtless people sometimes say, "How strange that where there is the greatest wealth there is often side by side with it the deepest poverty!" Poor innocent souls! They might as well say, "How strange that where there is a great despot there should often be side by side with him a number of slavish subjects!" Or, "How strange that where one person in a community gets too much, somebody else should frequently get too little!" Wealth means just that. Viewed from one aspect, it means that one man has juggled into his own hands almost all the wealth produced by many of his neighbours. Viewed from another aspect, it means that one man has obtained the practical right to command the labour of so many dozen or hundreds of his fellow-creatures. On the one hand, he is keeping so many toilers at work producing what we call an income for him alone; on the other hand, possession of that income gives him in turn the practical power to keep so many other men employed in producing the things which minister to his comfort, his whims, or his luxury.

And, one way or another, all this concentration of wealth, or of the power to command labour, into single hands, is the result of injustice. Wealth is always, or almost always, based upon wrong-doing. I say "almost always," because there are a few special cases (such, for example, as those of the great doctors) where it seems at first sight as if wealth had been well acquired, and where, so far as the individual is concerned, it has in all probability been blamelessly heaped up ; though even there we have to face in the end the wrongfulness of its employment for selfish purposes. But this wealth itself is only rendered possible in the last resort by the previous accumulation of excessive riches in the hands of capitalists and landowners, who are thus enabled to pay extravagant sums for the ablest professional attendance, and at the same time to divert it from the service of the men who are really doing the best work for the community. So again with the artist. His function ought to be to produce beautiful things for the enjoyment of his kind ; too often he is compelled to prostitute his genius to the task of painting or moulding useless and ugly things for the over-wealthy patron. Wealth thus earned may be a trifle less wrong in its origin than the wealth directly wrung from land or capital, but indirectly it springs from the same tainted source, and it bears upon it the curse of its unjust derivation.

Incidentally, I cannot help remarking how much nobler and happier the life of the artist of every sort would be in a free and equal community, where, instead of having to produce work which is often distasteful to him, in order to please the low and vulgarized tastes of a wealthy patron or a wealthy public, he would be able to deliver direct to a sympathetic world the message which his genius or his conscience imposes upon him.

But, directly or indirectly, in the last resort all wealth springs from some form of injustice. This truth, long perceived by the deeper thinkers and the higher natures, we have now, in this generation, to drive home to the souls and consciences of the wealthy. Already there are a few better types here and there among the opulent class who realize the fact about certain trades or certain forms of property. For instance, to take an extreme case, there were slaveholders (all honour to them!) before the American War, who refused to owe anything to the accursed thing, and who manumitted their slaves, in spite of the anger and rage of surrounding slaveowners. So, too, in our midst, there are a few men to-day who have inherited wealth connected with the hateful and degrading liquor-traffic, and who have declined to benefit by money which they believe to be ill-gotten and blood-stained. I can easily imagine, again, that a sensitive soul, coming into property derived from the iniquitous Chinese opium trade, might refuse to accept any share in wealth which had its origin in pandering to the hopeless corruption of a whole nation, and which had been forced upon the indignant authorities of

L

a heathen people by one of the vilest and wickedest wars in the history of Christendom. But as yet, very few people of the capitalist and landowning class have seen that the selfsame taint clings round all great wealth, from whatever source derived; that it has been acquired by what is, at bottom, essentially robbery ; and that to benefit by it is as wrong as to benefit by the profits of encouraging drunkenness, or debauchery, or opium-eating.

I say "very few," for there are already some ; and we may hope that in time, with strenuous preaching of the word, their numbers may increase ; that the conscience of the capitalist and landowning class may gradually wake up to the uselessness and wickedness of capitalism and landowning.

On one or other of these two, all great wealth is ultimately based. And of the two, landowning is perhaps the wickedest and most unjustifiable, though capitalism is now answerable for the larger part of the world's misery. For landowning has not a leg to stand upon, morally speaking. I do not remember ever to have heard or seen any one attempt to justify it on moral grounds. On grounds of what is called expediency, indeed, I have heard it defended, feebly and fatuously ; but on grounds of morality, never. No man could ever show a clear and certain title to the possession (or rather

to the monopoly) of land. Either he stole it himself,
like some extreme squatters in South Africa or elsewhere, in which case his criminality is obvious and
unconcealed; or else he inherited it from those who
stole it; or else he bought it from the thieves or their
representatives, who clearly could not give a title to that
which came to them as the result of rapine and plunder.
No matter how acquired by the individual holder, land
is always unjustly held; and no lapse of time or antiquity
of injustice can make that right which was wrong from
the beginning.

"But surely," many people will say, "if a man has
inherited vast landed estates from his father, and he
again from his, and so on *ad infinitum*, there can be no
great harm in his continuing to hold them; nobody in
particular is wronged, because nobody else has any
special claim to them. All the others were born landless, and inherited the landless condition from their
fathers." I beg your pardon. Somebody *is* wronged.
Everybody is wronged. The soil of the world belongs
by right of nature to the inhabitants. If you permit
one man to monopolize a large part of it—a larger part
than his own fair share, a part which he does not occupy
or cultivate himself, but which he lets out to others,
receiving and monopolizing the fruit of their labour—you
allow him to do an obvious injustice. For he is clearly

keeping all the rest of us out of it. He is tabooing soil he
did not and could not create himself, and he is preventing
any one else from enjoying his fair share of the gifts of
nature. Such a man is a malefactor ; and as a malefactor
he will be regarded in the society of the future. Men's
moral instincts are getting enlarged and purified ; before
very long all the world (with the exception of the male-
factors themselves) will feel that to live in idleness on
the toil of others is a shame and disgrace to any man.
The landowner and the capitalist will be scouted as
mean and vile creatures ; just as we scout nowadays the
grasping, usurious money-lender, or the keeper of a
gambling-hell like the tables at Monte Carlo.

For the political questions of the future will all be
moral questions. It will be the wrongfulness of opulence
in the midst of squalor that will engage attention.
People will be shocked at the callousness of the classes
who can amuse themselves with horse-racing, with
coursing, with vulgar ostentation, with hateful orgies,
while their fellows are starving. People will shrink from
contact with the rich as polluting and degrading, instead
of admiring and fawning upon them as the unenlightened
conscience too often does at present. For snobbery is
not, as most men imagine, a mere absurd little personal
weakness; it is a deep-seated index of acquiescence and
satisfaction in an essentially unjust and cruel social

system. It is a slavish adulation and admiration of those on whom we ought rather to look down with scorn from the conscious height of moral superiority.

The landowner does a wrong to every member of the community, in that he makes a personal claim to that which is the common property of us all, and compels us to pay for the use of what is really our own inheritance. But he is unjustest of all to the poorest and most helpless, whom he deprives of the bare means of earning a subsistence. Have you ever reflected with what equipment of rights the average citizen is born endowed in England? With the right of moving up and down the public roads till he drops from exhaustion. That is all. Literally and absolutely all. He has no more than that. He cannot even lay down his head to rest anywhere without paying rent for it. If he does, he is liable to be prosecuted as a rogue and vagabond. In town or country, there is nowhere he can pause for sleep or repose without being requested to "move on" by the paid representatives of the propertied classes. He cannot live at all without paying rent to some landlord for the pittance of ground he builds his hut upon. He cannot exert his industry upon any raw material without the landlords' leave. Every stick and stone, every rood of soil, every plant or herb, every mine and mineral, every fragment of coal, or wood, or iron, is

already monopolized. The citizen must pay rent for
leave to sleep on the bare, bare ground ; rent for every
mouthful of food he eats ; rent for every object on
which he can exert his intelligence or his capacity.
Nature does not exist for him ; she gives him nothing.
He may not till the soil, for that is another's. He may
not kill the wild beasts, for those are the landlords'.
He may not make anything to sell or exchange for
food or clothing, out of wood or metal, unless he can
satisfy the demand for blackmail on the part of the idle
man who taboos them. In every way, and at all times,
he is at the mercy of the robbers and their representatives. Coal and wood for his fire are theirs ; every
blade of grass, every grain of wheat, is theirs ; one thing
only can we landless ones claim as our own—the
public highway ; and along that we can but tramp
till we drop with fatigue ; when the propertied classes
carry us off to their jails to "learn us to be landless."

Is it not an appalling and horrible thought that the
vast majority of Britons have absolutely no legal right
to anything whatsoever on the soil of Britain ? That
they are in everything at the mercy of a handful of
landlords ? Does it not make us pause and ask in
horror whether these things are so ? Does it not give
us qualms of conscience to think we ourselves have

acquiesced so long and so tamely in so horrible a system of injustice and cruelty?

I suppose it is old use and wont alone that blinds most comfortable souls to the wickedness of permitting such a system to continue. But imagine for a moment there were a family in England which had possessed from the Plantagenet times onward the right, or rather the privilege, of cutting off the heads of any ten people they chose on Christmas morning. What should we think of anybody who defended their horrible claim like this? — "Well, you see, they've always had the right, and their fathers had it before them. It's worth them a good deal of money, because they threaten to kill well-to-do people ; and the threatened persons pay heavily to be let off from Christmas to Christmas. It's a vested interest, don't you see? and it's always dangerous to meddle with vested interests. Besides, all the rest of us have always been brought up with the knowledge that the privileged family—Grosvenors, or Hamiltons, or Stanleys, or somebody—might any day cut our heads off; so we're all accustomed to it. And the desire to have money to buy one's self off acts as an additional incentive to industry. Only the very poorest ever really get killed ; and nobody cares about *them* in a Christian country!"

Now, is it not just as bad to starve people to death

as to kill them suddenly? Is it not just as cruel to cut
off their food as to cut off their heads? Is it not just
as deadly to keep a whole people in poverty, misery,
and degradation, as to murder a few of them annually?
The argument, which is absurd when applied to the one
form of wrong-doing, is equally absurd when applied to
the other. What is unjust in its inception becomes no
more just by long prescription. On the contrary, the
longer the injustice continues, the wider do its effects
spread and multiply on every side. Landowning,
which was a comparatively small evil two hundred
years ago, is now in effect a criminal system only com-
parable in its horrors with American slavery.

The element of ethical wrongfulness in capitalism is
less immediately evident than the same element in
landowning; but it is there all the same, in a less hateful manner. For the capitalist does seem, at first sight,
to have contributed something towards the production
of the wealth he possesses and monopolizes. Often,
indeed, he even deceives himself; he says, and really
believes, he made it all by his own exertions. He does
not see that no one man can ever be truly entitled to
more than the product of one man's labour. What he
calls "making" money is really the power of cleverly
juggling into his own hands the product of the labour
of many other workers. Capitalism is at bottom

identical with slave-owning. It has in it the same
ethically hateful principle. The sooner people clearly
see and recognize this fact, the better for our consciences.
The slave-owner has many slaves, to whom he renders
out of the fruit of their toil the bare necessaries of life
—food, clothing, fuel, a hut to shelter them: all the
surplus product of their labour he keeps for himself,
that he may live in luxury in his own great house,
while they live in penury in their wattled shanties.
The capitalist employs many operatives, or "hands," as
he contemptuously calls them ; like the slave-owner, he
gives them, in the form of wages, what is necessary to
sustain them in the barest requisites of life: the remainder of the product of their united labour he keeps
for himself, that he may live in luxury in his splendid
mansion, while they fester and pullulate in the noisome
slums to which landlordism relegates them. The difference is but slight. The slave-owner pays in kind: the
capitalist generally pays in money. The slave-owner
allows his slave some site for a cabin ; the capitalist
lets him make his own bargain for himself with the
grasping and stingy urban landlord. The slave-owner
can dispose of his slave outright ; the capitalist allows
him the privilege of being dismissed when trade is bad,
and of finding a place for himself, if he can, with some
other capitalist. The free labourer has an advantage

over the slave, in that he can strike for higher wages, can to some extent improve his class standard of comfort, and can refuse to work for an exceptionally hard or cruel master. But the slave, on the other hand, has security of tenure. Industrialism is the form of slavery which immediately succeeds the condition of serfdom. It is slavery still in all its essentials. The labourer still labours, not for himself and his family, but for the benefit of his master. The master, doing nothing himself, still absorbs the surplus product of the labourer's industry. A state of moral feeling which permits and condones such injustice as this is a very low one. We must outgrow it in time: we are now outgrowing it.

Slavery was a greater evil than industrialism. I do not deny it; I admit it freely. The labourer has conquered on some points of importance. He has gained the right to his own person; the right to preserve intact his family relations; the right to locomotion, migration, free choice (so far as it goes) of masters. But in some ways what he has lost partially counterbalances what he has gained. For the slave was always found in work, and in food and clothing, no matter what happened. Hard times never threw him out of employment, or drove him into starvation. He was not forced into a cut-throat competition with his neighbour workman. He was not driven into the vilest slums, the most undesirable quarters of towns and cities. In sickness and old age he was often well tended. The spectre of no-work-to-do did not loom continually before his mental vision. Industrialism has failed ; our mass of unemployed, our East-end dens, the poverty and misery of so many of our people, are the confessions of its failure. It has got to be changed. Our consciences must be roused to a knowledge of the fact that we have to deal to-day with an evil in some ways as great as slavery, and, in the squalor and wretchedness which accompany its developments in our northern climates, perhaps even more terrible. For poverty with us means cold as well as hunger—means homes more wretched than southern climates with their warmth and sunshine can ever emulate.

It is the callous selfishness of the wealthy class that has brought these evils upon us. And we have now reached the point where even the wealthy are beginning to be ashamed of themselves. As yet, indeed, I do not see much sign that they are ashamed of their wealth, or of the dubious means by which they have acquired it. They do not seem to realize that it has all been piled up in their hands partly by chance opportunity, partly by an exceptional knack in manœuvring against others, partly by unscrupulousness or hardness of heart or selfish determination to get as much as they can

into their own pockets. There is little or no remorse
as yet about the acquisition of wealth ; there is beginning to be some remorse about the mode of its employment. Rich people still continue to suck up like
sponges all they can absorb of the earnings of the
community, but they are beginning to be uneasy about
what they do with it. It is the position of the slave-
owner who still believes in and upholds slavery, but
whose conscience is pricked by a nascent sense that he
ought to do something for his slaves with his money.
So far as it goes, this is a step in advance. It is well
that the wealthy, while the wealthy exist, should use
their wealth for public or unselfish purposes. But it
would be better to get rid of the wealthy altogether.

Still, we have taken a first step in the right direction
if we have shamed the opulent into feeling that they
owe something to the public in return for all that the
public does for them. This point we have now begun
to reach. The wealthy are groping their way dimly
towards some vague conception of what the world
expects of them—that they shall devote at least some
portion of their useless wealth to unselfish objects of
general utility. Hence the greater frequency at the
present day of the rich philanthropist. If men are to
be rich at all, the least they can do, if they pretend to
possess a sense of right and wrong, is to render to the

people a little of what they owe to the people, and not to spend what was never truly theirs on the merest selfish and personal amusements. "Property has its duties as well as rights," was the high-water mark of public opinion on these questions a generation since ; " Property has its duties, whether it has rights or not," is the watchword the present generation must attain to.

Most rich men, however, still use their wealth, no matter how acquired, for nothing but the most selfish and often the vilest purposes. Unthinking observers are astonished at this ; they wonder the rich do not wish to use their riches better. How could it well be otherwise ? They are rich, for the most part, just in virtue of this very selfishness in themselves or their ancestors. People of fine moral fibre are hardly likely to grow rich. They think too much of the rights and claims of others ; they are not perpetually occupied with the one pressing question of how they can feather their own nests at all hazards. They are more anxious to do good in the world than to make money. The people who make money are, as a rule (I do not say always), the most selfishly calculating, the coldest, the hardest-hearted among us. They get their labour at the cheapest possible rate ; and, provided they have got it, and got their pound of flesh out of it, they care nothing for its comfort, its convenience, its decency.

As long as we are organized on a system of unrestrained competition, this is almost inevitably so; for if a man does not beat down his unskilled labour to the lowest possible figure, and does not grind out of it the largest possible amount of work, some other man, less scrupulous and more cruel, will do so and undersell him ; and the public will buy the cheapest goods in the market, however produced, irrespective of the producer. Hence it happens that wealth is for the most part concentrated in the hands of the sternest and cruelest people in the community, who use it entirely for their own bad purposes.

The actual first founder of a wealthy family is almost necessarily a bad man, judged by any high moral standard. His wife is pretty sure to be a woman of low aims and no moral beauty of character, who has been attracted to such a man by his excessive wealth, and who has attracted him in return by the way she appeals to his sensuous passions. The offspring of such people are hardly likely, on the ordinary principles of heredity, to possess or develop much moral elevation ; and so it results that even in the second generation, to reverse Tennyson's saying, "the rich in the lump are bad." Furthermore, children brought up in the enjoyment of extreme and luxurious wealth, while they see their fellow-creatures wanting for everything around them, are prone to grow callous to the sufferings of others, as we observe habitually among the wealthy classes; they are prone to look upon the grades of society beneath them as altogether outside the pale of their sympathy, and to be only seriously affected by the misfortunes or pains of the small fraction of humanity which they call their equals. Hence it comes about that the hereditarily wealthy are often less actively cruel, but more passively callous, than the first generation of wealthy people.

"But all rich men are not so bad." No; some few are better, and an insignificant number are really helpful. The action of heredity is to some extent fitful and incalculable. Moral qualities, in particular, sometimes crop up unexpectedly; and even among the rich the occasional influence of a good mother, imported as by chance into the opulent class, may here and there do wonders. Among the Quakers, for example, and to a less degree among the Unitarians, the accumulation or inheritance of wealth has not entirely killed out all moral impulse. Even the landowning caste, as a rule the most selfish and cruel of any, sometimes produces by exception some *lusus naturæ* of a real philanthropist. But at best the possessor of extreme wealth can but use with reasonable consideration the money he has taken from other people. What is wanted is rather a

resolute determination not to be rich one's self, and not
to tolerate the possession of riches in others.

At the present day, indeed, this is for every one of
us the one really great and pressing moral question.
Are you or are you not on the side of progress? Are
you for the rich or the poor, for the oppressed or the
oppressor? Are you trying to set these social injustices
right, or are you trying to perpetuate them? Do you
wish to get wealthy yourself at all hazards, or do you
wish to see others enjoying the fruits of their own
labour? Most people treat these as political questions.
They are nothing of the sort; they are moral questions.
Political questions are mere questions of policy, and
belong to the *régime* of the selfish classes, who care
only for policy, and not at all for principle. But these
are moral questions—questions of right and wrong;
and according as a man answers them one way or
the other is he on the side of good or on the side of
evil.

There is no other effective test of high morality at
the present day save this. If you are on the side of
the spoilers, then you are a bad man. If you are on
the side of social justice, then you are a good one.

Critics of the middle-class type often exclaim, of
reasoning like this, "What on earth makes him say
it? What has *he* to gain by talking in that way?

What does he expect to get by it?" So bound up
are they in the idea of self-interest as the one motive
of action that they never even seem to conceive of
honest conviction as a ground for speaking out the
truth that is in one. To such critics I would answer,
"The reason why I write all this is because I profoundly
believe it. I believe the poor are being kept out of
their own. I believe the rich are for the most part
selfish and despicable. I believe wealth has been
generally piled up by cruel and unworthy means. I
believe it is wrong in us to acquiesce in the wicked
inequalities of our existing social state, instead of trying
our utmost to bring about another, where right would
be done to all, and where poverty would be impossible.
I believe such a system is perfectly practicable, and
that nothing stands in its way save the selfish fears
and prejudices of individuals. And I believe that even
those craven fears and narrow prejudices are wholly
mistaken; that everybody, including the rich themselves, would be infinitely happier in a world where
no poverty existed, where no hateful sights and sounds
met the eye at every turn, where all slums were swept
away, and where everybody had their just and even
share of pleasures and refinements in a free and equal
community."

GRANT ALLEN.

M

England to Her Own Rescue.

OH, what avails thee, England fair,
   Thy hoard of toil-wrung gold,
If, 'midst thy wealth, ill-clad they fare—
   Thy children hungry, cold ?

Oh, what avail thy sea-girt shores,
   Thy fleets beyond the foam,
If direst foes are at thy doors,
   And ravage hearth and home ?

Oh, what avails thy empire's pride,
   Thy banner world-wide spread,
If greed and cunning it doth hide,
   To mock thy heroes dead ?

What boots it, all thy gilded spoil
   Of commerce, east and west,
If still, at home, tax-burdened Toil
   Is joyless, and none rest ?

Hast struck the fetters from the slave
    To bind thy factory hand?
How may thy faith the heathen save
    While unredeemed thy land?

Of what avail to teach life's laws,
    Cram brain, with heart unfed,
With stones of knowledge at the Board,
    While children cry for bread?

Why raise for Beauty still a plea,
    And praise Art's flower and fruit,
If yet for gain ye sell the tree,
    Or sap it at the root?

What home-fed virtue sweet atones,
    Or spotless flocks in fold,
While in thy streets thy fairest ones
    For vice are bought and sold?

Shall Britons e'er be slaves, or lose
    Liberty, while lions ramp?
The landless Briton still may choose
    To trespass or to tramp.

Let England to herself be true,
   And, rising in her might,
Lift up the lamp—the beacon new
   That soon shall pierce the night.

Strike down the coiling worm of greed,
   With poison-breath that blights
The country-side with bitter need,
   And steals the common rights.

Let honest labour win the right
   To work in joy and health ;
Let England's brain and hand unite
   To build the Commonwealth.

With words of comfort and good-will,
   Forgetting caste and creed,
The fallen raise, the hungry fill—
   Help each and all at need.

Dear country, then, to see thee freed,
   Should each true heart be glad,
From wolves of want, and hounds of greed,
   Thy fields with plenty clad.

England to her own Rescue.

O England, could this be thy state—
United, joyful, free,
My country should indeed be great,
Though small her borders be.

February, 1894.   WALTER CRANE.

Economic and Social Justice.

DURING many past centuries of oppression and wrong there has been an ever-present but rarely expressed cry for redress, for some small instalment of justice to the down-trodden workers. It has been the aspiration alike of the peasant and the philosopher, of the poet and the saint. But the rule of the lords of the soil has ever been so hard, and supported by power so overwhelming and punishment so severe, that the born thralls or serfs have rarely dared to do more than humbly petition for some partial relief; or, if roused to rebel by unbearable misery and wrongs, they have soon been crushed by the power of mailed knights and armed retainers. The peasant revolt at the end of the fourteenth century was to gain relief from the oppressive serfdom that was enforced after the black death had diminished the number of workers. John Ball then preached Socialism for the first time. "By what right," he said, "are they whom we call lords greater folk than we? Why do they hold us in

serfage? . . . They are clothed in velvet, while we are
covered with rags. They have wine and spices and
fair bread; and we oat-cake and straw, and water to
drink. They have leisure and fine houses; we have
pain and labour, the rain and the wind in the fields.
And yet it is of us and our toil that these men hold
their state." John Ball and Wat Tyler lived five
hundred years too soon. To-day the very same claims
are made by men who, having got political power,
cannot be so easily suppressed.

A century passed, and the great martyr of freedom,
Sir Thomas More, powerfully set forth the wrongs of
the workers and the crimes of their rulers in his ever-
memorable "Utopia." Near the end of this work he
thus summarizes the governments of his time in words
that will apply almost, if not quite, as accurately to-
day: "Is not that government both unjust and
ungrateful that is so prodigal of its favours to those
that are called gentlemen, or such others who are idle,
or live either by flattery or by contriving the arts of
vain pleasure, and, on the other hand, takes no care
of those of a meaner sort, such as ploughmen, colliers,
and smiths, without whom we could not subsist? But
after the public has reaped all the advantage of their
service, and they come to be oppressed with age, sickness, and want, all their labours and the good they

have done is forgotten, and all the recompense given
them is that they are left to die in great misery. The
richer sort are often endeavouring to bring the hire of
labourers lower—not only by their fraudulent practices,
but by the laws which they procure to be made to that
effect ; so that though it is a thing most unjust in itself
to give such small rewards to those who deserve so
well of the public, yet they have given those hardships
the name and colour of justice, by procuring laws to
be made for regulating them.

"Therefore I must say that, as I hope for mercy,
I can have no other notion of all the governments that
I see or know than that they are a conspiracy of the
rich, who, on pretence of managing the public, only
pursue their private ends, and devise all the ways and
arts they can find out; first, that they may, without
danger, preserve all that they have so ill acquired, and
then that they may engage the poor to toil and labour
for them at as low rates as possible, and oppress them
as much as they please." *

Here we have a stern demand for justice to the
workers who produce all the wealth of the rich, as
clearly and as forcibly expressed as by any of our
modern socialists. Sir Thomas More might, in fact,
be well taken as the hero and patron-saint of Socialism.

* Cassell's National Library—"Utopia," p. 17.

A century passed away before Bacon in England, and Campanelli in Italy, again set forth schemes of social regeneration. Bacon's "New Atalantis" supposed that the desired improvement would come from man's increased command over the powers of nature, which would give wealth enough for all. We have, however, obtained this result to a far greater extent than Bacon could possibly have anticipated; yet its chief social effect has been the increase of luxury and the widening of the gulf between rich and poor. Although material wealth, reckoned not in money but in things, has increased perhaps twenty or thirty fold in the last century while the population has little more than doubled, yet millions of our people still live in the most wretched penury the whole vast increase of wealth having gone to increase the luxury and waste of the rich and the comfort of the middle classes. Campanelli, more far-sighted than Bacon, saw the need of social justice as well as increased knowledge, and proposed a system of refined communism. But all these ideas were but as dreams of a golden age, and had no influence whatever in ameliorating the condition of the workers, which, with minor fluctuations, and having due regard to the progress of material civilization, may be said to have remained practically unchanged for the last three centuries. When one-fourth of all the deaths in London occur in workhouses and hospitals, notwithstanding that four millions are spent there annually in public charity, while untold thousands die in their wretched cellars and attics from the direct or indirect effects of starvation, cold, and unhealthy surroundings ; and while all these terrible facts are repeated proportionately in all our great manufacturing towns, it is simply impossible that, within the time I have mentioned, the condition of the workers as a whole can have been much, if any, worse than it is now.

At the end of the seventeenth, and during the eighteenth century, a new school of reformers arose, of whom Locke, Rousseau, and Turgot were representatives. They saw the necessity of a fundamental justice, especially as regards land the source of all wealth. Locke declared that labour gave the only just title to land ; while Rousseau was the author of the maxim, that the produce of the land belongs to all men, the land itself to no one. The first Englishman, however, who saw clearly the vast importance of the land question, and who laid down those principles with regard to it which are now becoming widely accepted, was an obscure Newcastle schoolmaster, Thomas Spence, who in 1775 gave a lecture before the Philosophical Society of that town, which was so much in

advance of the age that when he printed his lecture the
society expelled him, and he was soon afterwards
obliged to leave the town. He maintained the sound
doctrine that the land of any country or district justly
belongs to those who live upon it, not to any individuals
to the exclusion of the rest ; and he points out, as did
Herbert Spencer at a later period, the logical result of
admitting private property in land. He says, "And
any one of them (the landlords) still can, by laws of
their own making, oblige every living creature to
remove off his property (which, to the great distress of
mankind, is too often put in execution) ; so, of consequence, were all the landholders to be of one mind,
and determined to take their properties into their own
hands, all the rest of mankind might go to heaven if
they would, for there would be no place found for them
here. Thus men may not live in any part of this
world, not even where they are born, but as strangers,
and by the permission of the pretender to the property
thereof." He maintained that every parish should have
possession of its own land, to be let out to the inhabitants, and that each parish should govern itself and be
interfered with as little as possible by the central
government, thus anticipating the views as to local
self-government which we are now beginning to put
into practice.

A few years later, in 1782, Professor Ogilvie published anonymously, "An Essay on the Right of
Property in Land, with respect to its foundation in the
Law of Nature, its present establishment by the Municipal Laws of Europe, and the Regulations by which it
might be rendered more beneficial to the Lower Ranks
of Mankind." This small work contains an elaborate
and well-reasoned exposition of the whole land question,
anticipating the arguments of Herbert Spencer in
"Social Statics," of Mill, and of the most advanced
modern land-reformers. But all these ideas were
before their time, and produced little or no effect on
public opinion. The workers were too ignorant, too
much oppressed by the struggle for bare existence,
while the middle classes were too short-sighted to be
influenced by theoretical views which even to this day
many of the most liberal thinkers seem unable fully to
appreciate. But the chief cause that prevented the
development of sound views on the vital problems of
the land and of social justice, was, undoubtedly, that
men's minds were forcibly directed towards the great
struggles for political freedom then in progress. The
success of the American revolutionists and the establishment of a republic founded on a Declaration of
the Rights of Man, followed by the great French
Revolution and the Napoleonic wars, entirely obscured

all lesser questions, and also led to a temporary and fictitious prosperity, founded on a gigantic debt the burden of which still oppresses us. These great events irresistibly led to the discussion of questions of political and personal freedom rather than to those deeper problems of social justice of which we are now only beginning to perceive the full importance. The rapid growth of the use of steam-power, the vast extension of our manufactures, and the rise of our factory system with its attendant horrors of woman and infant labour, crowded populations, spread of disease, and increase of mortality, loudly cried for palliation and restrictive legislation, and thus occupied much of the attention of philanthropists and politicians.

Owing to this combination of events, the nineteenth century has been almost wholly devoted to two classes of legislation—the one directed to reform and popularize the machinery of government itself, the other to neutralize or palliate the evils arising from the unchecked powers of landlords and capitalists in their continual efforts to increase their wealth while almost wholly regardless of the life-shortening labour, the unsanitary surroundings, and the hopeless misery of the great body of the workers. To the first class belong the successive Reform Bills, the adoption of the ballot in elections for members of Parliament, household and lodger suffrage,

improved registration, and the repression of bribery.
To the second, restriction of children's and women's
labour in factories and mines ; Government inspection
of these industries ; attempts to diminish the dangers of
unhealthy employments and to check the ever-increasing
pollution of rivers ; the new poor law, casual wards, and
other attempts to cope with pauperism ; while various
fiscal reforms, such as the abolition of the corn laws
and the extension of free trade, though advocated in
the supposed interest of the wage-earners were really
carried by the efforts of great capitalists and manu-
facturers as a means of extending their foreign trade.
Later on came the Elementary Education Act of 1870,
which was thought by many to be the crowning of the
edifice, and to complete all that could be done by legislation to bring about the well-being of the workers, and,
through them, of the whole community.

Now that we have had nearly a century of the two
classes of legislation here referred to, it may be well
briefly to take stock of its general outcome, and see how
far it has secured—what all such legislation aims at
securing—a fair share to all the workers of the mass of
wealth they annually produce, a sufficiency of food,
clothing, house-room and fuel, healthy surroundings,
and some amount of leisure and surplus means for the
lesser enjoyments of life. And it must be remembered

that never in the whole course of human history has there been a century which has added so much to man's command over the forces of nature, and which has so enormously extended his power of creating and distributing all forms of wealth. Steam, gas, photography, and electricity, in all their endless applications, have given us almost unlimited power to obtain all necessaries, comforts, and luxuries that the world can supply us with. It has been calculated that the labour-saving machinery of all kinds now in use produces about a hundred times the result that could be produced if our workers had only the tools and appliances available in the last century. But even in the last century, not only was there produced a sufficiency of food, clothing, and houses for all workers, but an enormous surplus, which they had to give to the landlords and other wealthy persons for their consumption, while large numbers, then as now, were unprofitably employed in ministering to the luxury of the rich, or wastefully employed in destroying life and property in civil or foreign wars.

Taking first the anti-capitalistic or social legislation, we find that, though the horrible destruction of the health, the happiness, and the very lives of factory children has been largely reduced, there has grown up in our great cities a system of child-labour as cruel and destructive, if not quite so extensive. Infants of four

dwellings have been provided, and education has been
systematically urged on, with the final result that one-
fourth of all the deaths in the richest city in the world
occur in workhouses, hospitals, etc., and, in addition,
unknown thousands die in their miserable garrets and
cellars from various forms of slow or rapid starvation.
Can a state of society which leads to this result be
called civilization? Can a government which, after
a century of continuous reforms and gigantic labours
and struggles, is unable to organize society so that
every willing worker may earn a decent living, be called
a successful government? Is it beyond the wit of man
to save a large proportion of one of the most industrious
people in the world, inhabiting a rich and fertile country,
from grinding poverty or absolute starvation? Is it
impossible so to arrange matters that a sufficient portion
of the wealth they create may be retained by the
workers, even if the idle rich have a little less of profuse
and wasteful luxury?

Our legislators, our economists, our religious teachers,
almost with one voice tell the people that any better
organization of society than that which we now possess
is impossible. That we must go on as we have been
going on, patching here, altering there, now mitigating
the severity of a distressing symptom, now slightly
clipping the wings of the landlord, the capitalist, or

the sweater; but never going down to the root of the evil; never interfering with vested interests in ancestral wrong; never daring to do anything which shall diminish rent and interest and profit, and to the same extent increase the reward of labour; never seeking out the fundamental injustice which deprives men of their birthright in their native land and enables a small number of landlords to tax the rest of the community to the amount of hundreds of millions for permission to cultivate and live upon the soil in the country of their birth. Can we, then, wonder that both workers and thinkers are getting tired of all this hopeless incapacity in their rulers? That, possessing education which has made them acquainted with the works of great writers on these matters, from Sir Thomas More to Robert Owen, from Henry George to Edward Bellamy, from Karl Marx to Carlyle and Ruskin; and, possessing as they do ability and honesty and determination fully equal to that of the coterie of landlords and capitalists which has hitherto governed them, they are determined, as soon as may be, to govern themselves.

Now, I believe that the great work of this century, that which is the true preparation for the work to be done in the coming twentieth century, is not its well-meant and temporarily useful but petty and tentative

social legislation, but rather that gradual reform of the
political machine—to be completed, it is to be hoped,
within the next six years—which will enable the most
thoughtful and able and honest among the manual
workers to at once turn the balance of political power,
and, at no distant period, to become the real and permanent rulers of the country. The very idea of such a
government will excite a smile of derision or a groan of
horror among the classes who have hitherto plundered
and blundered at their will, and have thought they were
heaven-inspired rulers. But I feel sure that the workers
will do very much better ; and, forming as they do the
great majority of the people, it is only bare justice that,
after centuries of misgovernment by the idle and wealthy,
they should have their turn. The larger part of the
invention that has enriched the country has come from
the workers; much of scientific discovery has also come
from their ranks ; and it is certain that, given equality
of opportunity, they would fully equal, in every high
mental and moral characteristic, the bluest blood in the
nation. In the organization of their trades-unions and
co-operative societies, no less than in their choice of the
small body of their fellow-workers who represent them
in Parliament, they show that they are in no way inferior
in judgment and in organizing power to the commercial,
the literary, or the wealthy classes. The way in which,

during the past few years, they have forced their very
moderate claims upon the notice of the public, have
secured advocates in the press and in Parliament, and
have led both political economists and politicians to
accept measures which were, not long before, scouted
as utterly beyond the sphere of practical politics, shows
that they have already become a power in the state.
Looking forward, then, to a government by workers and
largely in the interest of workers, at a not distant date,
I propose to set forth a few principles and suggestions
as to the course of legislation calculated to abolish
pauperism, poverty, and enforced idleness, and thus lay
the foundation for a true civilization which will be
beneficial to all.

I. That the ownership of large estates in land by
private individuals is an injustice to the workers and
the source of much of their poverty and misery, is held
by all the great writers I have alluded to, and has been
fully demonstrated in numerous volumes.   It has led
directly to the depopulation of the rural districts, the
abnormal growth of great cities, the diminished cultivation of the soil and reduced food-supply, and is thus at
once a social evil and a national danger.   Some petty
attempts are now making to restore the people to the
land, but in a very imperfect manner.   The first and
highest use of our land is to provide healthy and happy

homes, where all who desire it may live in permanent
security and produce a considerable portion of the food
required by their families. Every other consideration
must give way to this one, and all restrictions on its
realization must be abolished. Hence, the first work of
the people's Parliament should be, to give to the Parish
and District Councils (which will by that time be in
full working order) unrestricted power to take all land
necessary for this purpose, so as to afford every citizen
the freest possible choice of a home in which he can
live absolutely secure (so long as he pays the very
moderate ground rent) and reap the full reward of his
labour. Every man, in his turn, should be able to
choose both where he will live and how much land he
desires to have, since each one is the best judge of how
much he can enjoy and make profitable. Our object is
that all working men should succeed in life, should be
able to live well and happily, and provide for an old
age of comfort and repose. Every such landholder is a
gain and a safety instead of a loss and a danger to the
community, and no outcry, either of existing landlords
or of tenants of large farms, must be allowed to stand
in their way. The well-being of the community is the
highest law, and no private interests must be allowed to
prevent its realization. When land can be thus obtained,
co-operative communities, on the plan so clearly laid

down by Mr. Herbert V. Mills in his work on " Poverty and the State," may also be established, and various forms of co-operative manufacture can be tried.

II. The next great guiding principle, and one that will enable us to carry out the resumption of the land without real injury to any individual, is, that we should recognize no rights to property in the unborn, or even in persons under legal age, except so far as to provide for their education and give them a suitable but moderate provision against want. This may be justified on two grounds. Firstly, the law allows to individuals the right to will away their property as they please, so that not even the eldest son has any vested interest, as against the power of the actual owner of the property to leave it to whom or for what purpose he likes. Now, what an individual is permitted to do for individual reasons which may be good or bad, the State may do if it considers it necessary for the good of the community. If an individual may justly disinherit other individuals who have not already a vested interest in property, however just may be their expectations of succeeding to it, *ex fortiori* the State may, partially, disinherit them for good and important reasons. In the second place, it is almost universally admitted by moralists and advanced thinkers, that to be the heir to a great estate from birth is generally injurious to the individual, and is necessarily unjust to the community. It enables the individual to live a life of idleness and pleasure, which often becomes one of luxury and vice ; while the community suffers from the bad example, and by the vicious standard of happiness which is set up by the spectacle of so much idleness and luxury. The working part of the community, on the other hand, suffers directly in having to provide the whole of the wealth thus injuriously wasted. Many people think that if such a rich man *pays* for everything he purchases and wastes, the workers do not suffer because they receive an equivalent for their labour ; but such persons overlook the fact that every pound spent by the idle is first provided *by* the workers. If the income thus spent is derived from land, it is *they* who really pay the rents to the landlord, inasmuch as if the landlord did not receive them they would go in reduction of taxation. If it comes from the funds or from railway shares, *they* equally provide it, in the taxes, in high railway fares, and increased price of goods due to exorbitant railway charges. Even if *all* taxes were raised by an income tax paid by rich men only, the workers would be the real payers, because there is no other possible source of annual income in the country but productive labour. If any one doubts this, let him consider what would happen were the people to resume the land as their right, and thenceforth apply the rents, locally, to establish the various factories and other machinery needful to supply all the wants of the community. Gradually all workers would be employed on the land, or in the various co-operative or municipal industries, and would themselves receive the full product of their labours. To facilitate their exchanges they might establish a token or paper currency, and they would then have little use for gold or silver. How, then, could idlers live, if these workers, in the Parliament of the country, simply declined to pay the interest on debts contracted before they were born? What good would be their much-vaunted "capital," consisting as it mostly does of mere legal power to take from the workers a portion of the product of their labours, which power would then have ceased; while their real capital—buildings, machinery, etc.—would bring them not one penny, since the workers would all possess their own, purchased by their own labour and the rents of their own land? Let but the workers resume possession of the soil, which was first obtained by private holders by force or fraud, or by the gift of successive kings who had no right to give it, and capitalists as a distinct class from workers must soon cease to exist.

III. Another principle of equal importance is to refuse to recognize the right of any bygone rulers to

tax future generations. Thus all grants of land by
kings or nobles, all "perpetual" pensions, and all war-
debts of the past, should be declared to be legally and
equitably invalid, and henceforth dealt with in such a
way as to relieve the workers of the burden of their
payment as speedily as is consistent with due consideration for those whose chief support is derived from such
sources. Just as we are now coming to recognize that
a "living wage" is due to all workers, so we should
recognize a maximum income determined by the standard of comfort of the various classes of fund-holders
and State or family pensioners. As a rule, these persons
might be left to enjoy whatever income they now
possess during their lives, and when they had relatives
dependent on them the income might be continued
to these, either for their lives or for a limited period
according to the circumstances of each case. There
would be no necessity, and I trust no inclination, to cause
the slightest real privation, or even inconvenience, to
those who are but the product of a vicious system ; but
on every principle of justice and equity it is impossible
to recognize the rights of deceased kings—most of them
the worst and most contemptible of men—to burthen
the workers for all time in order to keep large bodies
of their fellow-citizens in idleness and luxury.

By means of the principles now laid down, we may

proceed to see how to deal with the present possessors of great estates, and with millionaires, whose vast wealth confers no real benefit on themselves, while it necessarily robs the workers, since, as we have seen, it has all to be provided by the workers. It will, I think, be admitted that, if a man has an income, say, of ten thousand a year, that is sufficient to supply him with every possible necessary, comfort, and rational luxury, and that the possession of one or more additional ten thousands of income would not really add to his enjoyment. But all such excessive incomes necessarily produce evil results, in the large number of idle dependents they support, and in keeping up habits of gambling and excessive luxury. Further, in the case of landed estates the management of which is necessarily left to agents and bailiffs, it leads to injurious interference with agriculture and with the political and religious freedom of tenants, to oppression of labourers, to the depopulation of villages, and other well-known evils. It will therefore be for the public benefit to fix on a maximum income to be owned by any citizen; and, thereupon, to arrange a progressive income tax, beginning with a very small tax on a minimum income from land or realized property of, say, £500, the tax progressively rising, at first slowly, afterwards more rapidly, so as to absorb all above the fixed maximum.

When a landed estate was taken over for the use of
the community, the net income which had been derived
from it would be paid the late holder for his life, and
might be continued for the lives of such of his direct
heirs as were of age at the time of passing the Act, or
it might even be extended to all direct heirs living at
that time. In the case of a person owning many landed
estates in different counties, he might be given the
option of retaining any one or more of them up to
the maximum income, and that income would be
secured to him (and his direct heirs as above stated)
in case any of the land were taken for public use.
In the case of fundholders, all above the maximum
income would be extinguished, and thus reduce
taxation.

The process here sketched out—by which the continuous robbery of the people through the systems of
land and fundholding, may be at first greatly reduced,
and in the course of one or two generations completely
stopped, without, as I maintain, real injury to any living
person, and for the great benefit both of existing
workers and of the whole nation in the future—will, of
course, be denounced as confiscation and robbery. That
is the point of view of those who now benefit by the
acts of former robbers and confiscators. From another,
and I maintain a truer point of view, it may be de-

scribed as an act of just and merciful restitution. Let us, therefore, consider the case a little more closely.

Taking the inherited estates of the great landed proprietors of England, almost all can be traced back to some act of confiscation of former owners or to gifts from kings, often as the reward for what we now consider to be disgraceful services or great crimes. The whole of the property of the abbeys and monasteries, stolen by Henry VIII., and mostly given to the worst characters among the nobles of his court, was really a robbery of the people, who obtained relief and protection from the former owners. The successive steps by which the landlords got rid of the duties attached to landholding under the feudal system, and threw the main burden of defence and of the cost of government on non-landholders, was another direct robbery of the people. Then in later times, and down to the present century, we have that barefaced robbery by form of law, the enclosure of the commons, leading, perhaps more than anything else, to the misery and destruction of the rural population. Much of this enclosure was made by means of false pretences. The general Enclosure Acts declare that the purpose of enclosure is to facilitate "the productive employment of labour" in the improvement of the land. Yet hundreds of thousands of acres in all parts of the country, espe-

cially in Surrey, Hampshire, Dorsetshire, and other
southern counties, were simply taken from the people
and divided among the surrounding landlords, and then
only used for sport, not a single pound being spent in
cultivating them. Now, however, during the last twenty
years, much of this land is being sold for building at
high building prices, a purpose never contemplated
when the Enclosure Acts were obtained. During the
last two centuries more than seven millions of acres
have been thus taken from the poor by men who were
already rich, and the more land they already possessed
the larger share of the commons was allotted to them.
Even a Royal Commission, in 1869, declared that these
enclosures were often made "without any compensation to the smaller commoners, deprived agricultural
labourers of ancient rights over the waste, and disabled
the occupants of new cottages from acquiring new
rights."

Now, in this long series of acts of plunder of the
people's land, we have every circumstance tending to
aggravate the crime. It was robbery of the poor by
the rich. It was robbery of the weak and helpless by
the strong. And it had that worst feature which dis-
tinguishes robbery from mere confiscation—the plunder
was divided among the individual robbers. Yet, again,
it was a form of robbery specially forbidden by the

religion of the robbers, a religion for which they professed the deepest reverence, and of which they considered themselves the special defenders. They read
in what they call *the Word of God*, "Woe unto them
that join house to house, that lay field to field, till there
be no place, that they may be placed alone in the
midst of the earth ;" yet this is what they are constantly
striving for, not by purchase only, but by robbery.
Again they are told, "The land shall not be sold for
ever, for the land is Mine;" and at every fiftieth year
all land was to return to the family that had sold it,
so that no one could keep land beyond the year of
jubilee; and the reason was that no man or family
should remain permanently impoverished.

Both in law and morality the receiver of stolen
goods is as bad as the thief; and even if he has
purchased a stolen article unknowingly, an honourable
man will, when he discovers the fact, restore it to the
rightful owner. Now, our great hereditary landlords
know very well that they are the legal possessors of
much stolen property, and, moreover, property which
their religion forbids them to hold in great quantities.
Yet we have never heard of a single landlord making
restitution to the robbed nation of workers. On the
contrary, they take every opportunity of adding to their
vast possessions, not only by purchase, but by that

meanest form of robbery—the enclosing of every scrap of roadside grass they can lay their hands on, so that the wayfarer or the tourist may have nothing but dust or gravel to walk upon, and the last bit of food for the cottager's donkey or goose is taken away from him.

This all-embracing system of land robbery, for which nothing is too great and nothing too little, which has absorbed meadow and forest, moor and mountain; which has secured most of our rivers and lakes, and the fish which inhabit them ; which often claims the very seashore and rocky coast-line of our island home, making the peasant pay for his seaweed-manure and the fisherman for his bait of shellfish; which has desolated whole counties to replace men by sheep or cattle, and has destroyed fields and cottages to make a wilderness for deer; which has stolen the commons and filched the roadside wastes ; which has driven the labouring poor into the cities, and has thus been the primary and chief cause of the lifelong misery, disease, and early death of thousands who might have lived lives of honest toil and comparative comfort had they been permitted free access to land in their native villages ;—it is the advocates and beneficiaries of this inhuman system, the members of this " cruel organization," who, when a partial restitution of their unholy gains is proposed, are the loudest in their cries of " robbery ! " But all the robbery, all the spoliation, all the legal and illegal filching has been on their side, and they still hold the stolen property. They made laws to justify their actions, and we propose equally to make laws which will really justify ours, because, unlike their laws which always took from the poor to give to the rich, ours will take only from the superfluity of the rich, not to give to the poor individually, but to enable the poor to live by honest work, to restore to the whole people their birthright in their native soil, and to relieve all alike from a heavy burden of unnecessary taxation. This will be the true statesmanship of the future, and will be justified alike by equity, by ethics, and by religion.

And now, what has been the conduct and teaching of those priests and bishops who profess to be followers of Him who declared that a rich man shall hardly enter into the kingdom of heaven, and who gave this rule as being above all the Commandments, " If thou wilt be perfect, go and sell that thou hast, and give to the poor, and thou shalt have treasure in heaven." Have they ever preached to the squires and nobles restitution of some portion of the land so unjustly obtained by their ancestors ? Have they even insisted on the duty of those who hold the land to allow free use of it to all their fellow-citizens on fair terms ? Have they even set before these men the inevitable and now well-known

O

results of land-monopoly, and the deadly sin of using their power to oppress the poor and needy ? It is notorious that, with some few noble exceptions, they have done none of these things, but have ever taken the side of the landed against the landless, and too often, whether in the character of landlords or magistrates, have so acted as to lose the confidence and even gain the hatred of the poor. We look in vain among priests and bishops of the Established Church for any real comprehension of what this land question is to the poor ; but we find it in the following words of a dignitary of the older Church, that good man and true follower of Christ, the late Cardinal Manning :

" The land question means hunger, thirst, nakedness, notice to quit, labour spent in vain, the toil of years seized upon, the breaking up of houses ; the misery, sicknesses, deaths of parents, children, wives ; the despair and wildness which spring up in the hearts of the poor, where legal force, like a sharp harrow, goes over the most sensitive and vital rights of mankind. All this is contained in the land question." But our archbishops and bishops know nothing whatever of all this ! They are truly blind guides ; and, as pastors of a Church which should be pre-eminently the Church of the poor, how applicable are the words of Isaiah, " They are all dumb dogs, they cannot bark ; sleeping, lying down, loving to slumber. Yea, they are greedy dogs which can never have enough, and they are shepherds that cannot understand : they all look to their own way, every one for his gain " !

And now, in conclusion, I will give one or two extracts from a book written by a self-taught worker for workers, to show how workers feel on the questions we have here touched upon.

"At present the working people of this country live under conditions altogether monstrous. Their labour is much too heavy, their pleasures are too few ; and in their close streets and crowded houses, decency and health and cleanliness are well-nigh impossible. It is not only the wrong of this that I resent, it is the *waste*. Look through the slums, and see what child-hood, girlhood, womanhood, and manhood have there become. Think what a waste of beauty, of virtue, of strength, and of all the power and goodness that go to make a nation great, is being consummated there by ignorance and by injustice. For, depend upon it, every one of our brothers or sisters ruined or slain by poverty or vice, is a loss to the nation of so much bone and sinew, of so much courage and skill, of so much glory and delight. Cast your eyes, then, over the Registrar-General's returns, and imagine, if you can, how many gentle nurses, good mothers, sweet singers, brave soldiers, clever artists, inventors and thinkers, are swallowed up every year in that ocean of crime and sorrow which is known to the official mind as 'the high death-rate of the wage-earning classes.' Alas! the pity of it."

And again, from the same writer—

"A short time ago a certain writer, much esteemed for his graceful style of saying silly things, informed us that the poor remain poor because they show no efficient desire to be anything else. Is that true? Are only the idle poor? Come with me, and I will show you where men and women work from morning till night, from week to week, from year to year, at the full stretch of their powers, in dim and fetid dens, and yet are poor, ay, destitute—have for their wages a crust of bread and rags. I will show you where men work in dirt and heat, using the strength of brutes, for a dozen hours a day, and sleep at night in styes, until brain and muscle are exhausted, and fresh slaves are yoked to the golden car of commerce, and the broken drudges filter through the union or the prison, to a felon's or a pauper's grave! And I will show you how men and women thus work and suffer, and faint and die, generation after generation; and I will show you how the longer and harder these wretches toil, the worse their lot becomes; and I will show you the graves, and find witnesses to the histories of brave and noble and industrious poor men, whose lives were lives of toil *and* poverty, and whose deaths were tragedies. And all these things are due to *sin;* but it is to the sin of the smug hypocrites who grow rich upon the robbery and the ruin of their fellow-creatures."

These extracts are from a shilling book called " Merrie England," by Nunquam. In the form of a series of letters on Socialism to a working man, it contains more important facts, more acute reasoning, more conclusive argument, and more good writing than are to be found in any English work on the subject I am acquainted with. When such men—and there are many of them—are returned to Parliament, and are able to influence the government of the country, the dawn of a new era, bright with hope for the long-suffering workers, will be at hand.

ALFRED R. WALLACE.

Social Teaching of the Early Fathers.

THOSE of us who owe most to the Tractarian movement cannot but regret the fact that the High Church-
man of to-day is content merely to occupy ground
already won. He considers himself to be the lineal
descendant of the Puseyites just because he can mimic
their tones and wrap himself in their old chasubles. But
when it comes to extending their principles, with their
old zeal, their strenuous and bold piety, their crusading
spirit, it never seems to cross his mind that such new
applications are possible, or if possible desirable, to any
other matters than ecclesiological ones. Granted that all
the Tractarians' reform began at the altar ; granted that
they showed that the associative principle is of the very
essence of the Faith ; still it does not follow that they
wanted to stop those reforms at the west door or the
lych-gate ; still less that they wished to store the leaven
of the Faith in the vessels of abstract and general
statement, and never to use it. Their work was to set

in order the Church ; to draw attention to her misunderstood doctrines, her broken discipline, her neglected
decencies, and her belittled claims. They had no time
to extend the rule of the principles they fought for,
to the street and the shop, the market and the law-
court. These and many other applications remain for
us, who come after ; and would that we could brace
ourselves to this work with anything like their reverent
and manful spirit !

Yet an application of Catholic principle to political
and social questions has been more than hinted at by
the Tractarians themselves. Let us take one extract
from the leader, who to us, in these later days, seems the
pre-eminent genius of the whole movement : " Strictly
speaking, the Christian Church, as being a visible
society, is necessarily a political power and party. It
may be a party triumphant or a party under persecution ; but a party it must always be, prior in existence to the civil institutions with which it is surrounded,
and from its latent divinity formidable and influential,
even to the end of time. The grant of permanency was
made in the beginning, not to the mere doctrine of the
Gospel, but to the Association itself, built upon the
doctrine (St. Matt. xvi. 18) ; in prediction not only of
the indestructibility of Christianity, but of the medium
also through which it was to be manifested to the world.

Thus the ecclesiastical body is a divinely appointed means towards realizing the great Evangelical blessings. Christians depart from their duty, or become in an offensive sense political, not when they act as members of one community, but when they do so for temporal ends or in an illegal manner; not when they assume the attitude of a party, but when they split into many. If the primitive believers did not interfere with the acts of the civil government, it was merely because they had no rights enabling them legally to do so. But where they have rights the case is different (Acts xvi. 37-39); and the existence of a secular spirit is to be ascertained, not by their using these, but their using them for ends short of the ends for which they were given. Doubtless, in criticizing the mode of their exercising them in a particular case, differences of opinion may fairly exist; but the principle itself, the duty of using their civil rights in the service of religion, is clear; and since there is a popular misconception that Christians, and especially the clergy as such, have no concern in temporal affairs, it is expedient to take every opportunity of formally denying the position, and demanding a proof of it. In truth, the Church was framed for the express purpose of interfering, or (as irreligious men will say) meddling with the world. It is the plain duty of its members not only to associate internally, but also to

develop that internal union in an external warfare with
the spirit of evil, whether in kings' courts, or among the
mixed multitude ; and if they can do nothing else, at
least they can suffer for the truth, and remind men of it,
by inflicting upon them the task of persecution." *

A candid examination of the writings of the "primitive believers" must lead us to see that if they had
possessed rights enabling them to interfere with the acts
of the civil government, they would have used these on
behalf of the frankest Socialism, and that in exact
proportion to their own orthodoxy.†

Where the Catholic Faith is merely latent, there the
Socialism is also less explicit. When the writer is unsound in his orthodoxy, then he is almost sure to favour
some form of individualist law or possession. When the
writer is sound and saintly, then he is always entirely
and unhesitatingly in favour of the common holding of
goods, of equality of opportunity, of social freedom ; and
even when he is not quite sound, he is always fiercely
opposed to the covetousness which calls itself enterprise, smartness, natural incentive to exertion, thrift,
and the like.

---

* Newman's "History of the Arians," pt. ii. ch. iii. p. 264.

† Of course, by "Socialism" we must understand the principles set
forth by the "Fabian Essays," and not the mere railing accusations which
sometimes usurp the name.

The whole meaning of the New Testament word "righteousness" has been narrowed down to include only the personal virtues. Yet the word δικαιοσύνη, which is used eighty-six times in the New Testament, has no such limitation. It ought, in the present state of our language, to be rendered "justice;" and its opposite, ἀδικία, which is used twenty-five times, should be rendered "injustice." Without this clearly before us, we should never be able to understand the patristic use of Holy Scripture.

St. Clement of Rome* asks the question how we may be found among those who wait for God and receive the promises? and he answers not only that we must be mentally settled Godwards, but also that "we must bring about a state of things agreeable to His holy Will, casting out from us all injustice, anarchy, covetousness, competition, ugly customs and deceitful ways, slanders, detractions and hatred of God, class arrogance, pretence, pomposity, and cliquiness. Those who peddle in such matters are hateful to God—ay, and not only those, but they too who compromise with them." St. Clement† pits the sympathy of the Gospel against what some modern Churchmen dáre to praise as a thing natural and inevitable, the greed and grab of modern business. Then, again, St. Clement regarded

* 1 Cor. xxxv. 2, Leipsic edit.   † 2 Cor. iv.

the world to come, not as a mere continuation of this world, but as its mortal foe. Yet he did not push his revolutionary tenets so far as to neglect present facts. He found rich and poor, and bade the former supply the needs of the latter, and the latter thank God for giving him a helper. We may say that the apostolic Fathers no more elaborated Christian Socialism than they did Catholic theology. But they laid down social principles, and those clearly—St. Clement of Reform ; St. Ignatius of Social Union ; and St. Polycarp of that Unworldliness without which no great reforms have been or ever will be carried. Yet St. Polycarp pointed out that the greatest obstacle to the work of the Church was money-loving.* St. Ignatius insists upon the power of Christ's grace to break every bond,† and distinctly tells us that indifference to social wrongs and woes is a note of heterodoxy,‡ although he did not specify either the way the bonds were to be broken, or the medicines to be used against social woes. The Shepherd of Hermas is perhaps of a slightly later date than these, if for no other reason, because the social teaching has grown. The rich Christians are there shown to us as round white stones, unfit for building into the Church triumphant until they be squared, by the paring off of their riches.§

* Phil. iii. 3.   † Phila. v. 8.
‡ Smyrn. vi. 2.   § Vis. iii. 8.

Indiscriminate alms is insisted upon,* and the writer
even assumes that the natives of the city of God are
likely to lose their lives at the hands of the ruler of this
world, "as rebels against his law."

This charge is, of course, the one which alone
accounts for the persecutions the Church endured.
Other things might be pretexts, but the reason for persecution was that the Faith was suspected of contradicting the constitution, of breeding slave wars, and of
denying the sovereignty of Cæsar. Hence the test
applied to Christians—the sacrifice to Cæsar, the god
of things as they are. Hence too, perhaps, the symbols
of the Lamb and the Dove, which marked the spiritual
warfare against the Wolf and the Eagle.

We should not be likely under these circumstances
to find the Apologists insisting very explicitly upon
the social bearing of the Faith. Yet Aristides,† in his
long-concealed Apology, tells us that the Christians
allowed no class distinctions. Athenagoras, who casually
admits that Christians held slaves, yet found Plato and
his social schemes not to be practical enough. It is
not a little curious that both he, Tatian, Theophylus
of Antioch, and Hermias, the literary Apologists of the
second century, should all ridicule the kings of old

* Sim. i. 6. Compare Διδαχή i. 5 and Ap. Constit. vii. 1.
† c, xv.

philosophy as mere " sky pilots "—the very charge which secularists now bring, not without reason, against some of our clergy. St. Justin Martyr had already explained * that "what human law had been unable to accomplish, the Word came to do ; " and that meant, and was understood to mean, that Christ came to fulfil our social and political deficiencies, and therefore to act also upon the plane of politics and the social life. St. Justin boldly applies the second great commandment to equality of possession, even in a stronger way than our modern Socialists would quite relish : " If one really loves one's neighbour as one's self, one will both work and pray to get him all the good things one gets one's self."† Justin's pupil Tatian distinctly tells us ‡ that he fell in love with the Church, not only because of the low morality of the Greeks, but because of their political anomalies ; " but these are the principles which will free us from our host of rulers, and enable us to have what God has sent for us." The Epistle of Barnabas, which cannot be later than Tatian's time, and which the most educated early Church—the Alexandrine—received as genuine, gives the whole pith of Christian Socialism : § " Thou shalt have all things in common with thy neighbour, and not call them thy private property ; for if ye hold

* Apol. c. xi.   † Tryph. 95.
‡ § 29.   § cxix. 8.

the imperishable things in common, how much more the perishable ? " Is not this exactly like the words of the Rev. Stewart Headlam : " Those who come to the Holy Communion are bound to be holy Communists " ?

Such teaching is all the more striking, and stands out in bolder belief, when we remember that there was no State then, in our sense of the word. There were governors above and subjects below, but the people were not, and indeed are hardly even yet, so organized as to be able to hold common property. Socialists had to be content for a very long time with almsgiving, bounty, and little communes, like the monasteries, in their slow approach to the new Jerusalem of Justice.

Irenæus, St. Polycarp's disciple, continued the same tradition. In his synodical letter from Lyons, he writes, " In whatsoever direction a man can do good to his neighbours and does not do it, he shall be deemed an alien from the love of God." Clemens Alexandrinus was a great and learned writer, and, though no saint, yet necessary to us for the defence of the canon. He has always been beloved of scholars from St. Hilary down to John Selden ; and in him we find that enthusiasm for Plato, especially for his Republic, which grew with the Church, as she grew in intellectual stature. Plato is for him the Attic Moses. Plato prefigures the Republic of Christ, St. Chrysostom thought.

His teaching is "hardly ever alien from the Church," and he is "the noble philosopher, whose disciples can with very little change bow their necks to Christ," as St. Augustine puts it. His philosophy has not unreasonably been called "the meshing of the gospel net." Clement takes pains to show us that it is Plato's Communism he approves of; and, indeed, so zealous is the Christian author for Socialism, that he actually wrests Holy Scripture on behalf of it. "Pythagoras poetically sums up the Mosaic teaching on justice, when he says one must not turn the balance (ζυγόν) of the scales ; that is, out of respect to justice one must not overstep equality in distribution.

> 'Friend leans on friend, and State depends on State ;
>   Each comrade bears about a comrade's fate.
> Equality is man's most natural law ;
> But always strife and days of war abide,'
> When Have and Have-not live here side by side '—

as it is poetically put. It was for this that the Lord said, ' Take My yoke (ζυγόν) upon you, for it is easy and light ;' and to those who were competing about social precedence, He gave one simple word of command—' equality.' He bade them become as little children. Likewise the Apostle writes that in Christ no one is slave or free, Greek or Jew ; for the new creation in Christ is non-competitive, non-covetous, and a just equality."

The entire condemnation of usury is so strong and

so well known that we need not insist upon that, for the Church continued her warfare against it until the days of the prophet Jeremy Bentham—so successfully that Renan * accuses her of putting back civilization for a thousand years ; because she would not allow that a man may lawfully take what he has neither frankly begged nor fairly earned.

But it is more significant that Clemens utterly departs from Plato on the slavery question.† " We must treat slaves as we do ourselves ; for if we would but see it, He is equally the God of the slaves and the free." St. Chrysostom, too, says that of course, when the Holy Ghost fell upon the Church, the slaves were all manumitted. St. Augustine contends that slavery is as unnatural as sin, and says that no Christian may " own a man, as he would own a horse or money ; " and, indeed, it seems to have been a received opinion among primitive believers that, as Innocent I. put it,‡ " nature bore men free, fortune made men slaves," and a slave " has such treatment as no man would inflict upon himself ; " and therefore that the conditions clashed with Christian law—an argument which also admits of wider application.

Of course, Clemens Alexandrinus fell foul of Plato

* Marcus Aurelius, c. xxxii.　　　† Ped. iii. 12.
‡ " De Vilitate Conditionis Humanæ."

upon the community of wives question. His attitude was that of Tertullian, who sarcastically tells the Imperial pagans "our Socialism ends just where yours begins." Indeed, the Christian criticism upon the Republic during the first six centuries is singularly unlike that one now hears passed. It is from the standpoint not of our genteel academies, still less from that of our episcopal palaces, but rather from that of the Guild of St. Matthew. St. Chrysostom, for instance, contrasts Plato's Republic and Christ's; "*His* doctrine can only be understood by the learned, but labourers, sailors, and masons can see ours; his plans are all city ones, but ours do in deserts too; his way needs full-grown men, but ours does even for babes." Or, in loose modern phrase, Plato was an aristocrat, but Christ democratic.

The early Christian writer who most nearly denies the Platonic Communism is Lactantius. "Plato adopted the Socratic teaching that the force of justice resides in equality. He says, 'Since all have an equal status at birth, they should own no private property whatsoever; but to get this equality which rational justice demands, they should possess everything in common.' This is sufferable so long as the question is merely one of money; but even that, how impossible and how unjust it is, I could show with much matter. But let it pass, and let us suppose it to be practicable." He then falls

P

savagely upon Plato's proposed community of wives, and shows that it would result in mere anarchy.* But even Lactantius could write thus : "Democritus is praised for throwing up his lands and letting them lapse into public pasture. I should like him if he had given them to the public ; but nothing is wisely done, which if it were done all round would be useless and evil." And later on in his life he was wiser still, and gave us plenty of excellent Socialism in his book on "Justice."

Clement of Alexandria, once more, has strong views upon what we should now call women's rights,† holding that as both men and women already have one God, one schoolmaster, one Church, common virtues and common senses, a common grace and a common salvation, equality in the Love-feast and an equal education, so they must have but one moral code.

The thesis that the Christian Church was strongly Socialist in tone at this time, is borne out not only by the attacks of her enemies, but by the exaggerations of heretics.

We have already noticed the great fact of the persecutions, which sifted the *cæremonia illicita* from the *cæremonia licita*, and decided that our Faith was one of the worships which contradict the constitution. Let us now turn our attention to Clement's great pupil

* " De falsa Sapientiâ," lib. iii. † Ped. i. 4.

Social Teaching of the Fathers. 211

Origen, and his controversy with Celsus. The gravest charge made by the latter against the Church was "that the Christian and the Jewish religions both originated in revolution (στάσις)." *

The charge was cleverly made, for "Israel came out of Egypt" with something very like a great brick-makers' strike, and the Christian Society is assuredly one which aims at turning the world upside down. Origen's answer was first a challenge to his opponent to name any armed rising the Christians had caused ; and secondly, an appeal to Christ's law, which works no violence, nor does men to death ; but the defence evades the gist of the charge, and merely emphasizes the fact— possibly well known to Celsus—that the Church does not appeal to that clumsy weapon the sword.

As to the exaggeration of heretics, we may mention Epiphanes and Basilides, who both taught Communism very much in the acrid spirit of some of our anti-religious Socialists. Among other things, those heretics, like some modern writers, laughed to scorn the notion that one should not lust after one's neighbour's wife ; and when they were confuted, since this was the only tenet which was attacked, may we not say that the rest of their teaching, though not their tone, was approved by implication ?

* Origen (Migne), iii. 7, p. 451.

Origen, in his zeal for allegory, often dissolves the plain New Testament denunciations of the rich into warnings against the pride of intellect, and makes the blessings pronounced upon the poor fall upon the head of the Gentiles. Nevertheless, when he does take these literally, his fierceness of invective against those "unclean and twisty camels" the rich, knows no limits, and he bears emphatic testimony to the fact that the Word teaches equality. "As you can see in most of the orthodox Churches, especially in the large towns, the leaders of God's people take no precedence ; and they make no exception even for the most perfect disciples of Jesus." *

We are now passing on to the Arian heresy and the times of the Greek Doctors. This heresy, for all its subtilty, not only had a political and social bearing, but this side of it was to the civic authorities the chief side. The question as to whether the Divine Son was in any way inferior in essence to the Eternal Father, meant in effect : Is the Mystical Body of Christ, the Church, in any way inferior to that Natural Society, the State, which in its way expresses the natural order, and God the Father ? In other words, is the Empire to rule the Church or to get out of her way? This is why the emperors were Arians. This is why the Imperial party first pooh-

* iii. § 724.

poohed the Catholics, and then persecuted them with such inconceivable fury. The history of the fourth century is no less a history of social reformers fighting against reaction because the battle was fought out in the schools and on the lofty plane of accurate and technical theology. SS. Basil, Gregory Nazianzen, and Athanasius were none the less Socialist because they were fighting for the very citadel of fundamental theory and not for mere legal applications. Often they declare the same themselves. St. Basil, for instance, says bluntly that "the Word calls us to socialism, altruism, and realism " * (or correspondence with Nature), "for man is a social and an interdependent animal." So far from thinking poverty and slavery to be natural and inevitable, these Fathers regarded them as the diseases which were bred of sin, and which the Church has been founded to cure. Here is St. Gregory Nazianzen's view †—

" Do let us remember God's law, which is highest and first. He rains upon the just and upon sinners, and makes His sun to rise upon all alike. He has prepared the earth, field, springs, rivers, and woods for all the dwellers upon dry land ; the air for the winged things, and the water for those whose life is of that. He has given the necessaries of life to all jointly, without limit or stint ; not impossibly conditioned or legally hedged,

* In Psalm xiv. 6.   † xiv. 25, Oratio.

not prescribed by partitions ; but He has bestowed the
same in common and richly, and has left no want
unsupplied. He regards the natural equality of rank
by an equality of gift, and displays the riches of His
kindness. But men must needs get gold and silver
and all sorts of soft clothes, and useless shining stones,
and all such matters, which are the symbols of war
and rebellion and tyranny. With these they are
stupidly elated, and shut up their mercy against their
kindred in distress, and refuse to succour them even
with necessities out of their own superfluities. What
blockishness ! What stupidity ! Whatever we do,
pray let us reflect that poverty and riches, what we
call freedom and slavery, and similarly named things,
are later effects on the race of men. They are the
common diseases which have fallen upon our baseness,
and the symptoms of that. But in the beginning it
was not so. He who first formed man, made him free
and a master, bound only by the law of God's commandment, and rich in the luxury of Paradise. All this He
wished to bestow upon the rest of mankind, who should
spring from the first man's seed."

St. Athanasius also is far from thinking that the
Divine Word operates only in the sphere of the personal
and immaterial life, and provides some ready-made hereafter for those, who have despaired of God's republic

here. He goes out of his way to tell us that the work of atonement would be incomplete, and Christ would not have reeeived His due, unless all things were given Him, including the earth, including food and rest for the workers and burden bearers; and that if we did not have rest and food, the primal curse would not be removed.*

While SS. Athanasius, Gregory, and Basil were defending the Catholic theory, St. Chrysostom was speaking to the common people, and speaking clear and concrete things. Take his sixth sermon on the First Epistle to the Corinthians. He is examining into the checks which the Church has received, though the Word abides still with her, and concludes that these checks have come, not because we have no miracles, but because we have let go the Pentecostal Communism, "the angelic life," and fallen back on private property. " But if we lived as they did (with all things in common), we should soon convert the whole world, with no need of miracles at all." Indeed, St. Chrysostom is full of the plainest and most emphatic Socialism. Take his explanation of πλεονεξία, covetousness,† as the desire for more things than those to which our faculties can correspond — over-endowment we might call it ; whereas φιλαργυρία is that "thrift" which is now preached to the poor as a virtue, and practised by those of us

* Migne's Athan., i. p. 212.   † Hom. xxv. Acts

whose wills are sworn under such huge sums. St.
Chrysostom was always impressing upon people that the
Communion which the Apostles taught " was not only a
matter of prayer and doctrine, but extended into their
political and social relations." *

In his eleventh sermon on the Acts, St. Chrysostom
points out that private bounty tends to vainglory, but
the early Christians gave in their corporate capacity—
nationalizing everything, as we should say.   Waxing
warm over that beautiful text, " Great grace was upon
them all, neither was there any that lacked," he points
out that thus, and thus only, can we get great grace.
He thunders against social inequalities.   He points out
how all could be made rich by a total renunciation of
private property.   Amid the cheers and groans of his
hearers, he sketches the effects of the Apostolic Communism applied to his own city ; urges that if it were
possible when believers were so few, much more is it
possible now ; and he then descends into political
economy, and shows how much cheaper co-operative
methods are than separative and competitive ones.   To
St. Chrysostom the Christian warfare was no scramble
for the best in a hereafter.   It was a war of emancipation here.†   He had a keen sense of the horrors
of competition, and is as furious at it in labourers

* Hom. vii. Acts.   † Ephes. vi.

and hucksters as in society ladies and merchant princes.*

If the Greek writers excelled in ἐπίγνωσις, the Latins bear the bell for αἴσθησις. If the former are deeper, quicker, and more subtle, the latter put their principles more immediately to work. In them, too, it is true to say that they are Socialist in exact proportion to their orthodoxy.

Tertullian, in his Apology,† redeems a rather conservative and questionable passage, wherein he prays for "the delay of the end" by a splendid passage upon the fraternity, which Christians so believed in, that they extended it even to their pagan persecutors. "Why, we are even brothers in income, the very question which almost tears your fraternity to tatters. So we, who are one in mind and soul, make no balk at common property. Everything we have is our common and equal property, except wives. Our Socialism ends just where yours begins."

St. Cyprian ‡ insists that none of the gifts of God are given us to be our private property, or ought to be claimed to the exclusion of others. The land and its products ought to be as common to men as are the sun, clouds, winds, sleep, stars, and moon ; and he calls

---

* Hom. x. 1 Thess.   † Ap. 39.
‡ " De Opere et Eleemosynis."

upon landlords and crop-lords to use these, as God shows how, for the common benefit. That this is "bounty" and not "State Socialism" is, of course, only because, as we have said, the State, in our sense of the word, was not yet evolved.

St. Jerome again and again points out that salvation without active labour is impossible,* and ordered the Egyptian monasteries to let no one off his work and labour. Indeed, the monastic life altogether is itself a witness to the fact that throughout the ages the Church has believed that the higher life is inconsistent with private property.

St. Ambrose, too, held opinions which would certainly have brought him into no little trouble in the modern Church. This is how he regards the fowls of heaven : " They are a great example, truly, and one worthy of our faithful imitation ; for if God's providence never fails to supply the fowls of heaven, albeit they use no husbandry, and trouble nothing about the prospects of the harvest, the true cause of our want would seem to be avarice. It is for this reason that they have an abundance of suitable victuals, because they have not learnt to claim as their private and peculiar property the fruits of the earth, which have been given to them in common for their food. We have lost common pro-

* Cf. "Ep. ad Rusticum Mon."

perty by the claims of private property. Yet nothing can be one's own, when all is so transitory ; nor can there be an assured plenty, when the disposal of it is uncertain." This is how he meditates upon Naboth the Jezreelite : "How far will your mad lusts take you, ye rich people ? Till you dwell alone upon the earth ? Why do you at once turn Nature out-of-doors, and claim the possession of her for your own selves ? The land was made for all ; why do you rich men claim it as your private property ? Nature knows nothing of rich men : she bore us all poor." With this we can compare another passage : * "The philosophers thought that justice might be defined as keeping common or public things for public purposes, and private ones for individual uses. This is quite unnatural, for Nature lavished all things for all in common. So, likewise, God bade all things to be produced, that all should have common pasture, and the land should be a kind of property common to all men. Nature, then, produced common property ; robbery made private property." Proudhon himself could have hardly put it more bluntly ; and these are no isolated instances. Justice is as much associated by St. Ambrose with nationalized property as it is with Plato himself.

St. Augustine was not one whit behind his great

* " De Off. Minist." cap. xxviii.

teacher.* "That is a most harmful counsel which a man gives to himself—to seek his own, and not the things which are God's. But in His heritage because He is ours, when He deigns for our solace to manifest Himself, we with the saints shall suffer none of the social miseries which come from love of what is our own, the so-called private property. Indeed, that most glorious city of God, when she comes into her promised inheritance, where none is born and none can die, will not have citizens who privately enjoy their separate possessions, for God will be all in all. And whosoever in this our pilgrimage faithfully and earnestly has longed for His society, makes a practice of always preferring common things to private ones, seeking not his own, but the things which are Jesus Christ's." In a similar vein he interprets the psalm *Memento David.* If a man has a house or bed of his own, he will never find or be a "place for the Lord." "Private property is the cause of lawsuits, jars, duels, revolutions, party feuds, scandals, sins, injustice, and murders;" and "so let us keep from private property altogether, or, if that is impracticable, at least from the love of it."

St. Augustine also struck a note which the Church has never let die, and which is a death-knell to the pseudo-social reforms such as vegetarianism, teeto-

* Enarr. in Psalm cv. (Vulg.).

talism, and the like. " It was not for pork, but for pippins, that the first man met death ; and Esau lost his birthright, not for poultry, but for pottage. I know, too, that Noah was given for food, all kinds of flesh which can be eaten ; that Elijah was refreshed with flesh food ; and that John, endowed as he was with marvellous abstinence, was not defiled with the animals—to wit, locusts—which fell to his food. Yes, I know Esau was deceived with the lust of pottage ; and David severely rebuked himself for his desire for water ; and that our King was tempted, not with butcher's meat, but with bread." *

St. Leo, in one of his sermons, lays down the usual maxim that collective property is always to be preferred before private property, because the general watch and ward over is more likely to secure a right use of it.

There is one author with whom we may fittingly close this essay, St. Gregory the Great, the friend of the English. Both the necessity of his unhappy, disorderly time, and his own ruling spirit, tended to make him a friend to authority and a foe to innovation. His teaching upon social subjects is cautious, and he tries to balance his utterances. If he tells us that riches are very dangerous to the spiritual life, he almost immediately tells us that the faithful Abraham

* Cf. S. Bernard *in Apologetic.*

was rich.* If he tells us that the Gospel calls equally
to men of every class, he is careful to add that to each
type of character the call comes in a different manner.†
If he has to point out that men who have heard the
voice of God often defy the powers that be, he is
careful to show that they also burn with charity
towards those whom they rebuke. ‡

Yet St. Gregory, in his "Pastoralis Cura," a book
which " has always been a text-book for the formation
of members of the ecclesiastical hierarchy," § and
which more than any of his works bears the mark
of extreme care and compressed thought, distinctly
explains his theory of almsgiving, and explains it from
a strongly socialist standpoint. This is all the more
telling, because the boundless generosity of the saint,
and his severe attention to sympathetic almsgiving,
are the keynotes of his whole life. He was more
renowned for his almsdeeds even than for anything
else in his strenuous and valorous career ; and those
who came after him blamed him, if for anything, for a
charity which exceeded his very powers of giving.
His words to those who are called upon to teach the
Faith are these : ‖ "This is how we must preach to

---

* Magna Moralia, iv. 60, 61 ; x. 41–49.   † Ibid., vi. 21, 22.
‡ Ibid., vii. 53, 54.   § Father H. J. Coleridge, Preface to Dialogues.
‖ De Cura Pastorali, Tertia pars. c. xxi.

those who neither covet other men's goods nor yet bestow their own in alms. We must make them clearly understand that the land which yields them income is the common property of all men, and for this reason the fruits of it which are brought forth are for the common welfare. It is therefore absurd for people to think they do no harm when they claim God's common gift of food as their private property, or that they are not robbers, when they do not pass on what they have received to their neighbours. Absurd! because almost as many folk die daily as they have rations locked up for at home. Really, when we administer any necessities to the poor, we give them their own; we do not bestow our goods upon them. We do not fulfil the works of mercy; we discharge the debt of justice. Hence it was that Very Truth, when He told us to be careful to show mercy, said, 'See that ye do not your justice before men.' In harmony with this the psalmist too said, 'He hath dispersed, He hath given to the poor, His justice remaineth for ever.' For when he reviewed a lavish generosity to the poor, he chose to call it justice rather than mercy, because what is given us by a common God is only justly used when those who have received it use it in common. Such people must also be told to consider carefully the barren fig tree. The husbandman quarrelled with it, because it merely held the land. Indeed, a barren fig tree holds the land when the mind of the owners idly keeps what could benefit so many. A barren fig tree holds the land when a fool overcasts with the shadow of his inactivity a place which another could use with the sunshine of good work."

It is with social teaching of this sort that the English people received their Church—teaching which was no idle whim of a few loose thinkers, but the settled conviction of the highest and saintliest of the Church's own teachers. And when, after a long winter of protestant discontent and commercial individualism, such teaching is once more found among us, we might expect that our leading and most learned Churchmen would welcome it indeed. Such, unhappily, is not yet the case.

CHARLES L. MARSON.

Meliora.

THE feeble folk wane through the ages, and careless
   the Mighty Ones smite them ;
   Who is there that shall avenge the shedding of inno-
   cent blood?
Over the earth and the sea, the spoiler and slayer
   triumph,
   Till the low sobs grow to a shriek, and the tears to a
   flood.
Careless are they, the strong, secure of the fathomless
   Future ;
   As it has been, shall it be down to the pitiless end ?

In dark dens, by the hills, or the sea, long ages the
   bickering cave-men,
   Armed with their sharpened flints, rob and ravish
   and slay ;
The smoke of the Aztec victims steams up from the
   Mexican altars,

Q

And the quivering heart is torn by the priests from
the living breast;
The bearded Assyrian treads on the necks of the van-
quished foemen;
The shafts from the chariots pierce the huddled
wretches who fly.
On the tombs of the Nile's grave lords still marches the
doleful procession—
The captives go forth to swift death or the lifelong
doom of the slave.
Laurel-crowned, up the Capitol's steep the heavy-eyed
Cæsar advances;
Splendid the triumph rolls by, with the fettered
captives behind;
The famished lions leap forth on their prey in the
bloody arena,
And for ages no pitying thrill touches those merciless
hearts.
Thro' all time under African skies, the tyrant or slaver
oppresses.
The red man slays and is slain on the limitless plains
of the West.
Thro' the weary suffering Past, far and wide, on land
and o'er ocean,
The feeble are trampled down, and only the mighty
are blest.

Comes there no end of these things ? shall men murder
 and ravage for ever ?
Shall not a mightier hand give to the desolate
 Peace ?

And thou, my Britain, unconquered, untrod by the foot
 of the foeman,
Hast thou deep Peace indeed in thy borders, or
 imminent strife ?
Thou who slayest the savage with bolts from thy mur-
 derous death-dealing engines,
And lettest thy children starve in the midst of the
 plenty around,
Tho' to-day thou seemest at rest, shalt thou scorn the
 lesson of ages,
Singing thoughtless pæans of Peace in a time wherein
 no Peace is ?
When the graves of the slain lie thick, Lorraine, on thy
 vine-covered hillsides,
And the New World groans and throbs with the stress
 of a fratricide strife ;
When Europe, half ruined, reels 'neath the load of her
 armèd battalions,
And the peoples, affrighted, shrink back from the
 thought of the terrors to be ;

When fiends plot together in secret, driven mad by un-
reasoning hatred,
Flinging death and destruction unmoved, tho' only
the innocent bleed,
And the groans of the strong men rise, who fain would
labour, but may not,
While their pale-faced children starve or rot in their
fever-fraught dens ;—
What heart has a man to tell of an Infinite Mercy and
Pity,
Whose ears grow deaf with the noise of the woes and
the sorrows around ?

Shall the common lot take thee too, O dear land, the
doom of the feeble,
When the strength that was thine is spent, and the
foemen beleaguer thee sore ?
Nay ; spare thou the reckless savage, who flings his rude
manhood against thee,
Whom thy pitiless engines mow down as a mower the
grass of the field.
But keep thou thy Power unassailed, and be just and
fear not the future ;
With equal and merciful laws make thou thy wide
Empire, rejoice !

Be to thy children a mother, be they as brother to
    brother,
Acting the precept divine which was taught by their
    Teacher and Lord.
Let thy strong sons raise up thy weak, through a Christ-
    like strength of compassion,
Bearing each other's burdens, and lightening each
    other's woes.
Let not the State any more turn with careless aspect
    averted
From the sight of the people's pain, unheeding their
    pitiful cry.
Scorn thou the pedants who prate of dead laws stern
    and unbending,
Based only on selfish instincts, and spurning the
    general good.
Knowing one limit alone to the Commonwealth's pro-
    vince of mercy ;
That no action of all shall mar the life-giving effort
    of each.
Let thy Empire of self-governed men prove how weak
    is the arm of the despot,
How mighty the sum of the strength of myriads
    obeying the law.
Save thou the weak from themselves when strong temp-
    tations assail them,

The Curses of Greed and of Sloth, the Demons of
    Lust and of Drink.
By patient toil without price, raise thou in the hearts of
    the lowly,
The white bloom of knowledge, to swell to wisdom's
    ineffable fruit.

Destroy not the humble home, when the strength of the
    worker has vanished,
    And the young have gone from the nest, and the
        cottage is silent and still.
Let the State, with wise providence, aid the faithful
    servants of labour
    To an honest wage for their toil, and relief from the
        sorrows of age.
Raise the myriads of poor and cast-down from the
    sloughs where to-day they languish,
    Teach them the civic sense ; their duty to man and
        to God.
Join thou and thy children your strength, till the nations
    learn the unreason,
    The folly, the mischief, the crime of the murderous
        evils of war ;
Let a mightier Union of Peace dispel the jealous sus-
    picions,

Meliora.

The anger, the senseless rage, which divide and
distract men to-day,
Till the clear Voice of Justice is heard, August, Inviolate,
Awful,
Where now are the myriad cries of causeless passion
and hate.

Then let the Judge ascend to his Throne, and the strong
and the weak be judged.

LEWIS MORRIS.

A Lay Sermon to Preachers.

I⊤ is not without a sly feeling of good-humoured revenge that a layman, who in his early days suffered much at the hands of preachers, finds himself at length in possession of the pulpit with his former tyrants for victims.

There is something so sweetly seductive to Englishmen in preaching and being preached at; it suits our national character and climate so well, that I do not doubt when the present unintelligent and unintelligible gabble of our two hundred sects is at length silenced, or at least neutralized, by the bawling of mutual contradiction, the desire of being preached at will still be the fiercest prompting in the average Englishman's breast, and he will demand from other teachers that spiritual profit which he now supposes himself to derive from the various expounders of the various systems of current theology. In those perhaps not far distant future days he will possibly ask the lights of science or the drama to edify him on Sunday evenings and to see to it that his valuable Day of Rest is not wasted in mere idleness or relaxation, but is turned to account and made the means of his moral and spiritual improvement. For I take it that spiritual *"profit"* is what our nation chiefly demands from its spiritual teachers. That same keenness and business persistence which scourge Englishmen to the pursuit of money-making for six days, till the end is entirely lost in the means and the pursuit of money becomes an end in itself, also scourge them on Sundays, and make them as greedy and "pushing" for the good things of the next world as on week-days they are greedy and pushing for the good things of this.

Nothing gives me greater food for thought than to watch the various English congregations streaming in and out of churches and chapels on Sundays. Indeed, so instructive and suggestive do I find it to watch church and chapel goers from the outside, that it is only by the rarest chance that I go inside. I do, indeed, number amongst my most valued friends priests, clergymen, and ministers of all creeds, sects, and denominations, but I find them so generally obliging and tolerant that they make no more ado about my unbelief than my doctor does when I express doubt as to the efficacy of his drugs. He merely replies good-naturedly that he has no very great faith in them

himself, but that they work all sorts of marvels on those
who do believe in them. And, besides, the drama has
lately been so cordially recognized by the Church as a
fraternal institution, that I hope there is no presumption
in my dealing with theological abuses and absurdities
in a spirit of kind inquiry and brotherly interest—in
short, as one of the craft. Only, as I say, I find so
much is to be learnt, so much spiritual instruction is to
be gained outside churches and chapels, that I have no
time to spare for the minor controversial matters which
occupy the preachers and congregations within.

But I will first let off my intended victims and
descend from the pulpit. You are free, reverend friends.
I have myself suffered too much from preaching to
wish to subject any fellow-creature of mine to such
useless torture. I have no wish to preach to anybody
upon any subject under the sun. Nothing amuses me
more than to find myself described as having theories
about education, about the drama, about this, that, and
the other. God be praised I haven't a theory to bless
myself with, and as for pretending to elevate my fellow-
creatures, or to be any better than the rest of them,
I hope I shall never do anything so mean and disagree-
able.

So, reverend gentlemen, I will not preach to you.
All I will ask you to do is just to chat these matters

over with me, and perhaps you don't mind if your congregations stand by and listen.

Well, first of all, reverend and lay friends, suppose some Sunday morning you each lay aside that rather greedy and selfish wish you have to profit your own soul by repeating that you are a miserable sinner; suppose you stay outside and watch church and chapel goers in London or some great English city. In short, dear good people, try for once to see yourselves from the outside on Sunday. Shall we go through London one Sunday?

Very well—what do we see? Here are thousands of churches and chapels, wherein are being taught nearly two hundred different sets of doctrines. Do try and realize what that means. Either one hundred and ninety-nine of them are teaching what is false : or one hundred and ninety-nine of them are teaching what is non-essential and useless : or, in varying proportions, they are teaching, on the one hand, what is false, and, on the other, what is useless and non-essential. There is no escaping from one of these three conclusions.

Now, my dear Mr. Brown, do, please, for a moment leave off trying so earnestly to save that soul of yours next Sunday, and try to see in how ridiculous a light your own particular persuasion appears if judged by this test. You will say, my dear Mr. Brown, that you

are *sure* your own sect is right and all the other one
hundred and ninety-nine wrong. With all respect for
your judgment, my dear Mr. Brown, I cannot think, if
you will lay aside your own notions for a moment,
you will really affirm that you are any more likely
to be right than Mr. Smith, who holds notions so very
contrary to yours. He is quite as good a business
man as you, and I, who have no notions to enforce, and
am not very anxious to save my soul, must really beg
you to acknowledge that our friend Smith is *quite* as
likely to be right as you. But if Smith is as likely to
be right as you, how, my dear sir, can you, who are
such a good business man in other matters, continue
to keep up a separate organization from Smith, and
support a different expensive agency, and send mis-
sionaries into all parts of the world to teach notions,
which by your own acknowledgment may be non-
essential and useless, or possibly even false ?

And by the way, my dear Mr. Brown and my dear
Mr. Smith, how is it that this stupendous supernatural
scheme of yours is so often housed in such shabby
architecture ? Granted your own notions on justification, sanctification, or the eastward position, or what
not, are correct ; and granted that I shall be damned
for not being able to comprehend them ; granted this,
my dear Brown and Smith, I don't think you have

any right to make our English streets ugly, even if you are quite sure you are saving your soul and doing a good turn to your co-believer Robinson the builder, in the process.

I do beseech you all, without for a moment preaching to you—I do beseech you to dwell for one moment on the absurdity, the waste of time, the waste of money, the waste of resources, the waste of brain power, the waste of opportunities of gaining knowledge, the waste of opportunities of healthy enjoyment implied in the present organization of religion in England. Two hundred sects all mutually contradicting each other on notions that none of them can clearly explain! Now, my dear Mr. Brown, do watch all these people coming out from other churches and chapels, all of them sup-posing that in some way or the other they have bene-fited their souls by affirming curious metaphysical doctrines they do not understand, and that they have in some indefinite, unimaginable way helped on the movement of the universe and the march of events in this planet in certain complex matters where the efficacy of their prayers cannot be put to proof.

Of course I know, my dear Mr. Brown, you recoil from the alternative that one hundred and ninety-nine of these sects can be engaged in expounding and propagating useless and non-essential doctrines. But granted this, or granted the other alternative—that one sect only is right and all the others wrong—either way, see what your belief implies. Every member of each of these two hundred sects, every believer in any one of them, must of necessity also accept (though he will not own it to himself) this monstrous and necessary deduction from his belief. Every believer of the accepted doctrinal Theology must also believe that the Author of this universe, whose remote stars flash light that started on its voyage to our eyes hundreds of thousands, and perhaps millions, of years ago ;—that the Author of this universe, at certain periods a few thousand years ago, so far departed from His apparently eternal method of governing the universe as to vouchsafe a miraculous dispensation to this planet, and to authenticate it in Person ;—that this extraordinary supernatural message which gave Him so much suffering and weariness to deliver was so loosely conveyed and so badly understood by those to whom it was confided, that from the very beginning there have been all sorts of quarrels and quibbles about it ; that after taking the trouble to deliver it in Person, He did not take enough trouble to see that it was plainly and unmistakably written down and attested in such a way as to prevent you, my dear Mr. Brown, and you, my dear Mr. Smith, and dozens of other equally intelligent and earnest Browns and Smiths, from all holding different and mutually contradictory notions as to what is or is not necessary to believe for the salvation of your souls. Now, my dear Mr. Brown, I do not care a fig to which of these two hundred sects you belong ; I do not care a fig about historical criticism upon the authenticity of sacred documents ; I say that if there is only one honest, intelligent doubter on the face of this planet, one man who, with the strength of the reason ·given to him, as you will say, by that same Power, calls in question the authority, or the reasonableness, or the righteousness of this supernatural scheme of yours, the whole of it is condemned. See how you degrade your Maker by supposing Him to have hung the eternal happiness or misery of you His children upon the comprehension of a curious, illogical, metaphysical scheme, of which scheme there have been during the ages all sorts of conflicting interpretations or misinterpretations ; of which scheme there are to-day in England two hundred conflicting interpretations or misinterpretations ; and concerning which scheme, what parts are necessary and essential, what parts are unnecessary and non-essential, and what parts are false and mischievous, scarcely two honest searchers can be found to agree.

But, my dear Mr. Brown, you will say that you

are all agreed about essentials. Then do pray tell
me what are essentials. Will the next Church Congress
or the next Congregational Union affirm what are
essentials?—for instance, is Hell an essential? I am
not preaching to you, reverend fathers, God forbid! I
am only asking you to make up your minds what my
friends Brown and Smith are to believe. For my
own part I have been in perfect peace for many years
about all these things. What are essentials? What
belief is necessary? Plainly and simply, is there a
Hell to which my friends Brown and Smith will go if
they don't believe in it? Yes or No? And is it eternal?
Yes or No? And is it physical or spiritual torture?
Yes or No? Will the next Church Congress answer
these questions? Surely this is not asking too much?
Surely if there is a revelation it must be definite and
unmistakable, at least on such vital points as these?
And what about other dogmas no less in dispute?
Don't think me irreverent, reverend fathers in God.
While you are squabbling about miracles, and the
Atonement, and this, that, and the other, England is
getting at bottom less and less religious. You have
so bound up incredible dogmas with the simplest
dictates of honesty and morality that the rough
common sense of the people, plainly seeing your
dogmas to be so much moonshine, is making short

work with them, and in the summary process is making short work too with morality and honesty, thinking *them* to be moonshine also.

I believe—I stand accountant for the words to That which gave me the power of thinking and writing them —I believe that if the time and money and thought now given in England to the propagation of wholly incredible doctrines, which are no sooner uttered in one pulpit than they are repudiated in another—if this time and money and thought were given to the understanding and scattering abroad of the simplest laws of national economy, of physiology, of health and beauty, in another generation our England would be greater and mightier than she has ever been. I believe a knowledge of the necessity of fresh air, of the value of beauty, of the certain disease and national corruption and deathfulness hidden in our present commercial system, to be worth far more than all the books on theology ever written. I believe faith in constant ventilation and constant outdoor exercise to be a greater religious necessity than faith in any doctrine of any sect in England to-day.

At the last Church Congress at which I assisted, a reverend gentleman was wildly applauded because he condemned certain young ladies for playing lawn-tennis on Sundays. When I remembered the great physical

R

development of our upper-class English girls in this generation, I thought how much better a preparation these girls were making for their duties of motherhood by playing lawn-tennis than by repeating barren Church formulas. I remembered that spiritual and mental demoralization are always caused by physical demoralization, and I thought how wise these girls were, and how *religious* to spend their Sundays in lawn-tennis and keep themselves healthy, thereby saving their descendants from the necessity of bothering clergymen with their hysterical distresses in days to come. How is it that clergymen and ministers are always the last to understand the religious necessities of the age?

But I forget—I'm getting preachy. Think these things over, my dear Mr. Brown and my dear Mr. Smith. Meantime, you gentlemen in black, suppose, as there seems to be great disagreement amongst you as to what is religion and what is not, and what is sound doctrine and what is not—suppose we take it that religion consists in just what Jesus Christ is reported to have said it consists, especially as we are all agreed about so much, " Thou shalt love the Lord thy God with all thy heart," which, by your leave, good gentlemen, I will interpret as standing reverently in face of the mystery of the Universe, and loving our Mother Earth with so deep a love that we dare not make her ugly and profane : "and thy neighbour as thyself," which I will interpret, good gentlemen, as meaning, amongst other things, not grinding his face if he is poor, not cheating him by promoting rotten companies, not hurting his body by selling him quack bodily medicines, or his spirit by selling him quack spiritual medicines.

"Oh, but this is too simple!" I hear my friends Brown and Smith saying. Alas! it is because religion is so simple that it is so much misunderstood!

HENRY ARTHUR JONES.

The Ancient Faith in Providence.

THE Market or the Temple, that is the question.

The Auctioneer or the Redeemer, that is the issue.

I or Another, that is the cry.

There are two gospels—which will you preach?—the one of the Mallet, which estimates man at the market price ; the other of the Cross, which proclaims that man was bought with the precious blood of the Martyr, and that he is not for sale.

Between the Exchange and the Temple there is a deep gulf fixed. Between the Auctioneer and the Redeemer there is an abyss yawning. Between the two gospels of the Mallet and the Cross, of Cain and Abel, there is a gaping chasm.

It is impossible to place a beam across the fissure, and pass the sons of men over into the Temple ; baptize them ; title them " heirs of God," " inheritors of heaven," " dearly beloved brethren," " immortal souls," dismiss them for six days into the Market, to be brought and sold as cattle, to be ticketed "labour," to be knocked down at the hammer. Impossible save in pantomime and panorama.

There are the two ideas, and an abyss is between them as deep as that 'twixt the burning veined limbs of Dives and the cool streams of heaven—man is a brother and in the Temple ; man is another and in the Market.

The one idea has no religion. It may have—it has—priests, churches, sacraments, salvations ; but in truth it is more atheistic than any Voltaire. The other is the very idea and the very blood and the very soul of Jesus.

" Oh, what extreme ideas ! "

How snugly the Lilliput Christians imagine that they have built the Church in the valley of Compromise between these two ideas! How musically ring the bells in the ears of the labourer, as he washes his large, melancholy, weather-beaten face, and puts on his sabbath clothes ! Behold him at last in his pew ! Behold Hodge, peasant, pauper, "labour," transformed into " the dearly beloved brother " !

Only eighteen hours ago, at five o'clock p.m., Saturday—it is now twenty minutes past eleven, Sunday morning—O immortal man, thou wert estimated at half a guinea and thy small beer. Three months ago—well, it was in December, and it is now the middle of March—

thou, O child of God, wert too dear at any price. Thou,
O brother, worth a soul's ransom, didst not last winter
fetch a worm's ransom. Not a brother would bid for
this brother sixpence a day. The heir of heaven failed
to command a quotation. (*The organ strikes up.*)

How beautiful might the music of the sanctuary be!
The ploughman looks thoughtful. Is he wondering
how it is that He who hath made such melodies for the
human ear hath set such miseries for the labourer's
flesh? Does he query why it is ordained to quiver
with hunger? Is there no sacred music of rest for the
toiler's limbs? No divine music of food for the
peasant's stomach? Ah, the devout ploughman excuses
God and accuses man. He is a real religious fellow is
Hodge. There is not one of this sanctimonious congregation who would touch with the tips of his fingers
in gloves the keys of this grand organ here in the
smock frock—their brother. No; they can play to
God on instruments of brass and wind made by man,
but not on this instrument of life and mind made by
the great Organ-builder Himself. Yet, if ye strike not
these human keys, my sacred music-masters, woe unto
your temples—they are already sepulchres!

The book is opened, and the Rev. Timothy Glebelands, M.A., reads, " Are not two sparrows sold for a
farthing? and one of them shall not fall on the ground

without your Father. But the very hairs of your heads are all numbered. Fear ye not therefore, ye are of more value than many sparrows " (Matt. x. 29–31).

Is the ploughman so stupid that he cannot think, my lord in the pew? He is thinking, I assure your lordship. He is slowly, but surely, untying the knot why his mate, Jack Coulter, is at this moment in gaol. It was hard times with Coulter when he picked up that pheasant. He and his family were starving. Were they not of more value than the pheasant? My lord in the pew and my parson in the pulpit were the judges on the bench, and they gave him three months for his crime of overestimating the value of five human beings. Jesus said that they are worth much more than the bird ; the judges said that they are worth much less.

This priest who was reading the Scriptures, and is now expatiating upon the precious value of the immortal soul, is the same who (under the *alias* of J.P.) three days ago pronounced Jack Coulter's soul and body together to be not worth half a crown.

I will not allow you to interrupt me. You preachers do not allow us pewmen to interrupt you. I know there is something more than the mere bird—"the sacred rights of property." Yes, the sacred rights of property which Jack Coulter possesses in his life and the

life of his family. Still you interrupt me, " There
was no necessity for them to starve—there is the Poor
Law and the workhouse." Silence, sirs! silence! you
preach Jesus and accept His valuation of a human
being. The Poor Law valuation is another affair. It
arrives at another figure. It is just what I want you to
tell us when you are in the pulpit next time—and your
words are heard in Heaven as well as in church—I
want you to tell us how you explain two such valuations
of one man, the Poor Law valuation and Jesus Christ's
valuation.

Shall we slip out of the steeplehouse into the
conventicle over the way? There are some simple
folk amongst the Dissenters who believe that if religion
is once freed from "State patronage and control" even
the ring-marks on her ankles would soon disappear.
Tom Flail, whose white hairs the child can number—
how much more the Heavenly Father!—has not found
that the air of the Baptist Chapel is altogether perfumed
with liberty. There is the stench of patrons and con-
trollers even in the conventicle. What matters it to
Flail whether the State or the Church governs religion,
if the mill to which she is yoked grinds him betwixt
the same hard stones of oppression and starvation?
What matters it to the labourers whether the Church
is a State institution managed by State ministers, or

a *laissez faire* kirk managed by free ministers, if in either case *they* are not free?

No, this little Baptist Chapel was not freed from "patronage and control." Flail's master is in the cloth pew, and though the preacher hath the roar of the lion, and looketh to have the back of a Cromwell Ironside in the pulpit, yet hath he his masters also in the cloth pews, which problem you would see demonstrated and chalk up Q.E.D. on the door, on looking into the minister's vestry after the sermon is over, and behold you the Reverend Pastor under "the patronage and control" of Deacon Gold (stockbroker and gambler) and Deacon Brass (thimble-rigger and flesh-grinder).

O sad spectacle in the vestry, the voice and the spine of the minister of God have become the voice and spine of the flunkey of men. No doubt, however, the good pastor prayeth in secret for backbone. Would to God it was whispered, he prayeth to eternally preach in secret!

And yet how keenly one feels for the fine preaching organisms here and there in the Free Churches—fine-bred animals, whose sides oft spurt with blood from the spears of the vulgar money savages and insolent heresy hunters who corner the Temple as they corner the Market! Shall these preachers come out and enter the Establishment? Sometimes they feel tempted, I dare say. Yet they must reflect that the curates, who form the vast majority of the State clergy, are no better off than themselves. Not any form of Church constitution at present in existence seems to secure the ideal both for teacher and congregation, either in the State Church or the Free Church.

But the Reverend Charles Unction—for that is the name of the minister of the Baptist Chapel—is not yet in the vestry, but in the middle of his sermon, and a pious "sister" hands us his text, which is, "Consider the ravens: for they neither sow nor reap; which neither have storehouse nor barn; and God feedeth them : how much more are ye better than the fowls ? "

How much more is Tom Flail better than the fowls ? The white-haired old tasker sits in the chapel, and is no doubt reflecting, "After fifty years of sowing and reaping and stowing of corn, I have not a fowl-house to roost in, nor a fowl's picking at the barn doors. I am much worse off than the fowls, and "—shall he think it ? is it blasphemy for him to think it?—"Jesus is no longer to me the Truth ; He is a betrayer like Judas Iscariot, and a parable-spinner like Unction, and a gambler in providence like Gold, and a taker-in like Brass, and a false brother's keeper like Straw. God is not a Father ; He feedeth the fowls, perhaps, but He has left me to fill my belly with air."

O ye Christians, who scoff at infidels, and turn men out of the House of Providence, and ticket to eternal perdition those who believe not on Jesus and you—see for the price of a few sacks of corn, how nearly you (not the devil) tempt Tom Flail to deny his Lord and perish his soul !

Here is the story of Tom Flail, real Christian. The great crisis had come against which he had trembled and hoped and prayed for years. His body (being seventy-three winters old) could no longer be maintained at a profit, and as the relations of Straw to Flail outside the conventicle were £ s. d. relations, and as £ s. d. standeth not for "Lord save Demos," but "Lord save Dives," Flail's name (after being on the dirty pages for forty-two years) was on Saturday (yesterday) struck out finally and for ever from Straw's book of life. In too real a measure it was to Flail God's Book of Life, though only Straw's wages diary. It seems strange, by the way, that whilst God keeps, with His own hand, the ledger of providence for the ravens, He lets such a cheat as Straw (the farmer could hardly help himself, poor man !) square his accounts with His labourers. Who knows, if God hath inspired men to write the Scriptures, it may be that He hath sent also chartered men to tot up Straw's figures, and to show that after one half-century's toil (for Flail began

to work in the fields at the age of seven) a larger
balance than one half-sovereign on Flail's side.

Verily, the Church wants not preachers, but God-
chartered accountants—divine wranglers, who can go
into the Lord's figures, and do such a sum as this—

Given, "The earth is the Lord's, and the fulness
thereof," what is the equitable share of fulness and
emptiness due separately and individually to Flail
(labourer), Straw (farmer), Acres (landlord), and Gold
(usurer)?

If you Christians will only read your Bibles as well
as the infidels do, you will find an old wrangler there
who dismisses the last two as equitable empties, with
no claim to eat a snail.

Now, Straw and Flail were baptized in the same
water, have partaken of the same Lord's Supper, are
members of the same household of faith. Inside "the
Church" Flail is declaredly and undoubtedly in name
Straw's "brother;" outside, he was (for forty years
ended yesterday) Straw's "hand," and now is (shame!)
Straw's CASTAWAY. What relation are they to one
another? What relation is Straw to himself?

However puritanical at times she seems, Religion
is the child of the drama. It does not follow, however,
that God is not her father. And here, in her dramatic
environment, we have a half-explanation of the curious

and immoral inconsistencies of the Christian. This "one man in his time plays many parts." He is elaborately theatrical in his representation of God and himself. His Deity, for example, appears on the grand stage in three persons ; so does his man. And sometimes Satan, in the theological play, does not get "behind" God, as Jesus ordered him, but takes a leading part. This man appears in three personalities —body, soul, and spirit ; his enemies in the piece are three also—the world, the flesh, and the devil. There are his three ages of man—original Adam, travailing Adam, new-born Adam. There are, at least, three acts—election, belief, baptism. There are two compartments—the World and the Church. And one great partition divides his fabric—the spiritual from the material. As for geographical scenery and historical situations, these are many ; but in broad impressiveness these three are his main continents and crises— earth, heaven, hell.

The Indian philosopher, we may add, with a still further eastward and oldward position than the Christian, has also his three Da's. His Vedantic plays have likewise their several acts. His Vedanta, like our New Testament, is a scriptural rejection of his Old Testament—his Samhitas and Brahmanas. It is impossible here to go into the Indian faith, with its atman (or self), its parama-atman (or highest self). These two selfs run astoundingly parallel with St. Paul's two egos (so pathetically described by him in Romans vii.).

I don't think in St. Paul there was any moral danger, even though he says, "Now if I do that I would not, it is no more I that do it, but Sin that dwelleth in me." But there is a great moral danger with such a doctrine rattling inside a man like Brass. Now, I wish to ask Christians to make surer of their identity in the future. Paul was a tent-maker, and worked with his own hands; he did not employ a thousand hands, like Brass, thimble manufacturer, to do his work and get his living for him. The apostle carried his Christian identity into the world as well as into the Churches. In the Tent he was the same simple hero as he was in the Church. (When will some bishop resolve to be a shoemaker, and lay once more the hard and thorny palms of toil upon the heads of the " successors of the apostles " ?)

I say, with all this " one man's many parts " and many compartments, with all these back doors and side doors and front doors, and with all this "one man's " *dramatis personæ*, how can you expect him to know what relation he is to himself, or what relation another man is to him ? It is true that a good man

The Ancient Faith in Providence. 255

must be like Paul, a tent-maker, and, like Truth, a
tent-dweller. He must always be on the move towards
his brother and his Father. There is something healthy,
cheek-glowing, broadening, plain-seen and plain-seeing
in migrations and campings-out under the great skies
and over the wide prairies. But these bandbox
migrations, these soul and body flitations, these church
and world doors, these acrobatic somersaults, confuse
a man's conscience and lose a man's entity, where he
is only too glad to lose it. I believe in conversion—
in more than one conversion. I rejoice that Simon
and Saul should be so transformed that it is even well
that, like the actors, they should take the new names
of Peter and Paul. But I see a danger in these aliases
and doubles, in these compartments sacred and secular
—that men may play at hide-and-seek with themselves
and their duties.

Look at Deacon Gold, saint and stockbroker.
Yesterday he had the visage of Satan and the pulse
of—well, not of a saint, for yesterday he was in the
Exchange, staking the million mites of the poor. As
he sits there now in his pew, he looks as refreshingly
cool as if he had just come up out of the baptistery.
Indeed, he has in his own mind no connection whatever
with Gold, of Capel Court. He has tossed that trans-
gressor and all his transactions (especially his losses)

upon Jesus (he takes good care to retain the old
rascal's gains), and he is listening to Unction as
though in those heavenly ears of his there never had
sounded the yells of bulls and bears (verily, there never
hath sounded therein the flying blood-spats of his
murdered Africans, or the eternal pat, pat, pat of the
sweat of his Country's brow)! Now he is listening;
but harken thou to-night to his voice in the conventicle prayer-meeting. How soft and wet it is, as
if his lips were dripping with the very milk and honey
of the promised land! You would, if there, indeed
exclaim, "Of a truth, this saint deals in eternal
futures!" and even though an angel from heaven
whispers the soft impeachment, "This pious fraud is
a boomer of cotton futures and war and famines, and
his wet lips will crack to-morrow with gambling hell-
fire," you would not believe that angel.

It is well for a man to be " on 'Change." Without
growth and change there is no life and no use in him;
but Gold's change was skipping between Hell and
Church. To say that he did not know what "conversion"
is would be wrong, for it takes place with his coin every
day at the bank.

In short, Gold the saint is only paint—wet paint.
Sirs, be so good as to put up a notice outside your
steeplehouses and conventicles: "Beware of the Paint."

This is the second time I have spoilt my Sunday clothes, rubbing against your saints. Better far—carve these letters in eternal stone over each entrance, and put an angel on guard at each door, with a flaming sword : " No Golds admitted here save on the business of true repentance, and on solemn oath that they never will speculate in futures and God's sweat any more."

Now, as to these fearful fluctuations in human values, some authoritative information can be got from Gold. He is professor of the science of fluctuations. He specs in famines, and locusts, and blights, and dearths, and wars. He bets on plagues and whirlwinds. To look at his long list of current prices, it is plain that the earth is not the Lord's, but Gold's. I thought that the Almighty was the Universal Provider. I am wrong ; it is Whiteley ; and Gold is his broker. I was simple enough to imagine that, as God found all the capital at the creation for most of His joint-stock companies, at least some shares would still stand in His name. He has apparently sold out. If Gold was God's broker at the time of this big sale, he must have made a good thing of it. I presume this is how we came to have landlords—they are the rich men who bought up God's shares, and took the Lord's title. It puzzles me (I am not learned, like the Duke ——)where theygot the money from. It is hardly likely that the Great Inventor would

S

part with His patent rights in the universe, with all its wonderful contrivances of sun and moon, winds and rains, seed-times and seasons, growth and food, for a mere song. And, so far as I can read up Rent's ancestors, it was only a doggerel verse or two they could offer for the universe. I have always had the reverent fancy that God must love music and poetry. Perhaps Rent's ancestors were Alpine herdsmen, who exchanged copy-right for freehold, and bartered their *ranz des vaches* to the Almighty for cattle ranches. Yet I can hardly believe that the Great Artist would sell His exquisite landscapes for a mere song. Then there comes in a trifling ethical question. Suppose the ass were to say to her Maker, "I will sell you *my* music if we can come to terms;" would it not be possible that the Maker might reply, "You ass, how could you bray or pray unless I gave you the trumpet?"

"Enoch walked with God: and he was not; for God took him." Rent bargained with God (it seems); it has yet to be written, "*He* was not, for God took him." I am not an infidel; I am not going to blaspheme against the sacredness of contract. I am not an anarchist; I am not going to dynamite private property. Yet I must observe that there is a religion more ancient, more simple, more solid—yea, more majestic than any, and that is the religion of Providence. And, sirs, if

God has no property in the earth; if He be without means ; if He has sold out ; if Rent, Gold, Brass, Straw, and Company have acquired His universe and His rights ;—what is the use of His religion ? Is it not more politic to fall down and worship Rent, Gold, Brass, and Company than the Almighty (so called)? Verily, it seemeth to me that the poor better pray to the promoter than the Creator, under these sorry circumstances.

Who is surprised that, with this bad environment, the Church is a social failure, and that Glebelands and Unction—the " State " and "Free " parsons respectively —are not the priests of the Most High, but of the Main Chance? Whenever you find in history the Chimney corner disestablished, and the Exchange corner endowed, you will be sure to know where to find the priests—round the corner. But as to God and the true religion—they are not to be found this side of the creation, for Rent and Company have purchased (as we have seen) the whole tract 'twixt here and there, and even a large sweep beyond. No wonder that Tom Flail becomes a stone-broker, munching flints, if there be no God, or (what is the same thing) if Lord Rent is the man in possession.

Until the Church can return to her simple and ancient and beautiful business of Many-making (the business which Jesus followed), and can convert the

Christians to the faith that their calling is not Money-making; until the Church can restore Providence and the Father to the human body and child; until she has the courage to take a scourge in her hand and lash out the land-sellers and sweat-dealers from the temple of nature;—there must remain, and remain, the present miserable state of affairs.

Let the Church restore once again to her temples and her bosom the truths of Nature and Providence; let her put in her creed St. Paul's dogma of divine crescendoism—that doctrine which acknowledges that "God gave the increase;" and that this increase is common property; and she shall behold again the Shekinah upon her altars and the people within her congregations.

"What then is Apollos? And what is Paul? Ministers through whom ye believed; and each as the Lord gave to him. I planted, Apollos watered; but God gave the increase. . . . Now he that planteth and he that watereth are one: but each shall receive his own reward according to his own labour. For we are God's fellow-workers, God's tilled land, God's building."

Here you have the doctrine of "the unearned increment" laid down with much larger grip than the touch of the two Mills. It is true that in another connection John Stuart Mill wrote, "No man made the land ; " but, if my memory serve me rightly, he never wrote, "No man made himself." Paul says, " The Lord gave to him " what he is. How can a man who cannot claim private property in himself, claim private property in the earth, or others, or the products even of his labour? If his hand is not his own, how can that which his hand makes be his own ? In truth, a man makes nothing alone. And the apostle takes us this step when he writes, " He that planteth and he that watereth are one."

In other words, the world is a stage, and so intricate and multiple are the parts, so interlaced and interlooped is the web of the great drama of society and nature ; so much of it is an inheritance from the past ; so much the spinning of insects and weaving of plants ; so much the work of cattle and birds, and winds and floods ; so much do we owe to the innumerable fingers of the ages ; —that though each one plays even many parts, it is utterly impossible for that one to shout (unless he is mad), "Get away, all ye ages and ye men and ye vermin ; I can play the parts without you." And hence we find in history that the great Cæsar has to give up the stage to a worm, and that the dread Herod's thunder has to be stopped for the " muling and puking " of an infant.

It is claimed that one man shall only count one.

This is a great bill of rights against the millionaire who counts himself a million. But can one man be reckoned as one ? Shakespeare says—

> "Learning is but an adjunct to ourself ;
> It adds a precious seeing to the eye."

These "adjuncts to ourself"—to its eyes, to its ears, to its hands, to its feet, to its world, belong as much to another as to me, and I am really unable to define my "one." And as science goes on making telescopes and telephones, and society goes on making "adjuncts to ourself," while the "one" grows larger every year, yet it is becoming less "one" at every age—that is, it is more and more a common property of the All. Science seems at times to lead as with a torch of lightning, leaving us in greater darkness than ever. Yet behold her—what rapid tracks she is taking towards heaven ! She is making inevitable the final breaking up of the individual, and the turning of the world into one common. The phenomena of the millionaire and the *imperataire* are simply the last chaotic upheaval of *laissez faire.* These gigantic "trusts" must force on trust in the people. And these "rings"—pray don't fix them to the snout of the swine—we will use them presently at the marriage of All and One.

Come with me into St. Paul's temple, ye labourers. Come in your work-clothes and with your watering-pots. There, don't wipe the drops from your brow. The baptism here is the baptism of sweat. (Look how like is Paul to Gladstone! The same face and eyes. The same doubt of women, and faith in man and God. One's a wood-chopper, the other a tent-maker—that's all the difference 'twixt them. Equally scholars and gentlemen, conservatives and liberals, equally word-drawers, and always both coatless democrats—"hard at it.") This is the apostle's text: "Ye are God's pals and mates, for He works in the same universe as you, and we are all on the same job." And then he makes a word-tent of matchless imagery (what a cooling shelter for the labourers on a hot day!): "For we are God's fellow-workers, God's tilled land, God's building."

Unction's sermon is over, so is Glebeland's, and Paul hath finished; no, *he* is an eternal preacher. And here is Flail also finished, and—well, when I met him some weeks after my visit to the Baptist Chapel, I found him broken-hearted and broken-winded, and with the great tears rolling down his face. Unction had abandoned him, and so had Saint Gold and Saint Brass. Had God done likewise? Now, my answer to this question shall not be that of these brace of saints and of their pastor. Here is the answer: The Church has abandoned Providence. (I think Providence has abandoned it.)

It has abrogated its function of fellow-workers with God. It has given up the old social occupation of its primitive days. It has turned its temples into spiritual distilleries, with tall chimneys for steeples. It has forsaken nature and God's increment, and the planting and watering business—so healthy, so quiet, so good for mind and body—for supernatural and superfine and very smoky manufacturing.

This is how it has all come about. The strong seized hold of the land. The artful seized hold of the Hand. Then the two took possession of the Church. When the landlords came in, we find bodies chucked out of the Church, and souls put in their place. When the handlords and the Manchester School came in, with *laissez faire* for master, we notice the introduction of mansions in heaven, and glory and hallelujah factories. The Church is bound to go into the other world for its stock-in-trade if you turn it out of this. When Rent, Gold, Brass, and Company seized the property of Providence, it is plain that the Church could no longer keep on with its old social business. It is true the State Church has still some glebelands, and a few slums, and one or two public-houses left to it, but these scarcely pay the salaries of its archbishops and bishops.

Instead of a State Church, it is possible we may have again a Church-State, but these are idle questions. THE

PEOPLE ARE GOD'S CHURCH. It was with the multitude
Jesus left His gospel. It is they who will become the
voice of God in the future. Aristotle said that the
multitude had many eyes and many ears and many feet,
and that they were more philosophers than the few.
Jesus agreed with Aristotle. All His gospel was
preached to the people—they know it by heart—and
now the people will re-preach it to themselves. Jesus
was impressively a Socialist. He lived in the midst of
a labour crisis. Thousands of workmen had been dis-
charged from the building of the Temple, and hundreds
of His hearers must have been "the unemployed." The
two thieves that were crucified with Him were probably
no thieves at all, but half-starved workless artisans, who
had taken from some rich man what he had robbed from
them. All the parables of the young village Carpenter
are perfumed with nature, and lilies, and cornfields,
and sheepfolds, and labourers.

All the words of His mouth sound of rural work and
wages and hours. He had dangling at His waist the
key of the social problem. He unlocked the door and
showed the rich out of Heaven and State and Church.
Peremptorily He locked and bolted the door of the
Kingdom of God against them. Only two rich men
were even distantly His disciples—we do not find
that they were let into His inner society—the one

said he gave half his goods to the poor, and restored much of the remainder to the wronged ; and the other was a secret disciple, and only appeared on the scene by night to bury the Lord's body. Jesus deposited with the people a terrible gospel to be preached to the rich, and, as the Church has abdicated its social functions, the people have put the State in its place, and to-day from the pulpits of the people the gospel of Jesus is being preached (and with power) to the multitude by the multitude.

If two men are on an island, unless they be Cain and Abel, they can get along with very little religion. But when there are thirty millions of people on an island, it is necessary to have a great deal of really good religion.

And Providence, therefore, hath two Hands—with the one He institutes the law of increase in the plant, and with the other He establishes the law of increase in the heart, so that the will of men towards each other shall co-operate with Him in His will towards them.

Here are a few figures which show that the first Hand does its work well (and rest assured that in the evolution of society the second Hand will also do its work well). Prince Krapotkin, in the *Forum* of 1890, writes :—

"Mr. Hallett, by a simple selection of grains, will

obtain in a few years a wheat which bears 10,840 grains on each stem grown from a single seed ; so that from seven to eight hundred of his stems of wheat (which could be grown upon a score of square yards) would give the yearly supply of bread for a full-grown person."

This would make out that one acre could furnish an annual budget of bread for two hundred and forty-two persons ! Lord Lauderdale computed that one acre would feed four persons. Those who doubt that the dear soil of old England cannot hold her own against the world should read this. It is from a letter (dated February 20, 1894) written by Sir J. Henry Gilbert, who, and Sir John Bennet Lawes, Bart., have done more for English agriculture than any other two men :—

" The average yield of wheat per acre in the United Kingdom is about twenty-eight bushels. We can get more than this by special manures, but such practice could not be followed on the large scale. The yield above mentioned is higher than the average in any other country in the world. Indeed, our unmanured plot, kept free from weeds, has for fifty years in succession given an average of thirteen bushels per acre, which is more than the average of the United States, and is, in fact, the average of the whole of the wheat lands of the world ! "

According to the Rothamstead Tables, we find that the "special manures" give in some years an increase of ten bushels, making thirty-eight bushels to the acre. If, therefore, you had the two million acres of wheat land in the United Kingdom put under "the small scale"—which really means "the large scale"—we should add to our wheat-yield twenty million bushels, and certainly one labourer per acre. Our total "agricultural and fishing class" only numbers in England and Wales 1,284,919! We should, with "special manures," add at least two millions to these on our present bread lands. But with special labourers, and without special manures, we could, on a moderate and careful policy, put back five million people on good soil in England within five years, and five millions more in the next five. If we cannot place the man, let us put the child, on the land. *He* will grow.

England to her own rescue! Scotland to her own rescue! Ireland to her own rescue! And gallant little Wales to hers! After all, God inspires the Nation, if not the Church. Thy land is crushed with stones and lords; crown it with bread and men! It is the promised land! Arise, thou, and be the Promised People!

JOHN HEATHER.

Principles and Practice.

Is Christianity used up, or does there yet remain any effective good in the principles of Jesus of Nazareth? Are those ideas of Jesus applicable to the affairs of modern society and practical life? and if not, why? If God is the Father of all, and caring for all equally, how is it that so many of His children are in a condition such as should shame an ordinary savage?

When talking of these things, we often hear it remarked that "One half of the world does not know how the other half lives." There may be, and no doubt is, lack of knowledge of the sufferings of the "other half," but ignorance on this subject cannot be accepted as an excuse for the "one half," or relieve them from their responsibility in the slightest degree. In this as in other matters, what we do not know will not be the standard by which we shall be judged, but what we ought to know, and, by the application of common sense, could know.

We will give due weight to the fact that this is a

busy age, and admit that even a Christian cannot be expected to know and do everything. Nevertheless, there are some things which that portion of the community calling themselves Christians cannot neglect with impunity and at the same time retain their Christian standing ; for example, the investigation and consideration of those circumstances and conditions which hang like a black pall over Society, and which are too often looked upon as a fabric of nature that must not be touched, much less removed ; or even as irremovable.

Man is declared by Scripture to have been created "a little lower than the angels." We find, however, that the majority of men live a devilish rather than an angelic existence ; all lofty aspirations are crushed, all noble faculties abortive—their heartstrings strained and broken. In numberless cases, homeless, breadless, workless, diseased, and degraded to a level lower than the beast of the field—their little children are crying for bread in the land of plenty ; their daughters making their very virtue a marketable commodity on the streets in order to provide for themselves and others the necessaries of life.

While few, if any, can be found who will deny that a social sore exists on the body politic of a character and extent which can scarcely be estimated, and while expressions of sympathy are often heard—how little is being done by the Christian world to rectify those foundation wrongs upon which the social problem stands!

It is not an answer to say that ever since Society has been, these things have always existed to a greater or lesser degree. It is not sufficient to argue that these things are not so bad as they once were. What we as Christians have to ask ourselves is, Is it right that these conditions should exist at all? Is it in accordance with the will of God that they should continue? Will any one dare to assert that the " All-Father " has called into being a larger number of His creatures than His provisions in nature can provide for or for whom the earth can find sufficient space? To admit, or even to think, such things would be surely to commit "the unpardonable sin," and to put in the place of the All-wise Father, a monster of iniquity whom every true man should loathe instead of love.

We who profess the name of Christ cannot allow that either the Divine love or the Divine plan is, or can be, a failure in any degree.

If this last proposition is sound, why, then, are things socially in the wretched condition they are? Who is to blame? and what action ought Christians to take to deal with the situation ?

The view, however, which Christians will take of their responsibilities depends upon the value they are prepared to place upon Christ's utterances. Before these can be rightly gauged, there must be a decision as to His personality. Permit me, therefore, to ask you, What think ye of the Nazarene?

Was He the Christ of God or an impostor?

Both He could not be, even in degree.

If we apply this principle to Christ, and give Him the authority which He claimed for Himself, then we are bound to accept what He says, without attempting to read into His words our own opinions or preconceived ideas.

"When ye pray say, Our Father. . . . Thy kingdom come, Thy will be done on earth as in heaven."

This is a very simple and plain direction, and one concerning which there does not appear to be much room for misunderstanding; and yet, plain and simple as it is, Christians have failed utterly to grasp it.

The faith they have in Divine declarations is perfect enough, when dealing with the "joys laid up for the saints" in the "sweet by-and-by"; but faith they appear to have none, when the claims of humanity in general as regards temporal things are pressed upon their attention. Yet, if the words of Christ mean anything, they make it clear beyond dispute that He was concerned with things temporal as much as with things eternal. Every parable He told—every word-picture He painted — showed His practical human sympathies.

Christianity, however, in practice, whatever may be its theories, refuses to admit that in the Divine plan there is any concern for things temporal. The latter-day Christ remains crucified on Calvary—a distant historic or angelic figure. His self-styled followers to-day do not pretend their Christ has anything but a spiritual connection with poverty-stricken, struggling humanity; in fact, should any urge that the principles of the Son of man are for practical application here and now, the religious convictions of these dear souls are greatly shocked, and they sanctimoniously declare that what is proposed would "drag religion in the gutter."

If the Divine plan, however, is two-sided—body and soul—the Christians have become one-sided. That which God joined together, they seek to put asunder, the soul from the body. The separation of religion from so called "worldly" affairs has consequently tended to make those connected with religious movements intensely impracticable. Religion and business, religion and politics, religion and pleasure, we are taught must be antagonistic. The affairs of the world are handed over to the devil. It is no uncommon thing, therefore,

T

to find that those, who on the sabbath are intensely religious, are during the other six days of the week intensely " worldly."

The teachings of the Christ of the gospels are considered to be too far-reaching to be taken literally, and are only accepted as a mere ideal concerning which it is the duty and privilege of Christians to sing sentimental songs—an ideal to be worshipped afar off, but never possible of attainment in this life.

" He that would be My disciple," said Jesus, " let him take up his cross daily and follow Me," at once dis-proving the notion that religion was concerned only with the inner life and a world which is to come.

If we are His disciples, we must take Him as a whole, or throw Him overboard as a whole.

I know it is argued by many good people that the Scriptures cannot be taken literally, that there must be compromise in all things. Whatever may be said for compromise in other directions, so far as the principles of Christianity, as laid down by Christ, are concerned, to compromise is to give place to evil.

Christ by His pronouncements proved Himself to be the regenerator of conditions, as well as of men. Christians, however, instead of giving to His utterances their all-round application, cramp them into narrow bigoted doctrinal channels, which at once destroy their practical utility in temporal affairs, and make them only an emotional sentimentalism.

Christ was not a mere word-spinner, neither was He a manufacturer of riddles. In spite of all the mystery that organized religion has endeavoured to weave about Christ's words, "On earth as in heaven" meant both the possibility and practicability of an organization of earthly affairs in which truth, love, and happiness would prevail. Surely a condition of things as reasonable as it is desirable.

Christ's foes are indeed of His own household. They seek to strike off the shackles of mythology, simply that they may replace them by the shackles of theology. Ofttimes a distinction without a real difference. A new heaven they profess to believe in, but it is the heaven of dogma.

It is part of the creed of some that heaven and earth are, and must be, in deadly combat. That the ideals of time and eternity are, and must be, antagonistic. Some even tell us that it is part of the Divine plan that the powers of evil shall rule and govern things temporal— that the starving of the multitudes and the sufferings of the poor are but evidences of their sin, and directly ordained to give to the "elect" an opportunity for a display of their generosity. Hence we have the damnable doctrine that suffering and affliction are in accordance with the Divine will, and that contentment with injustice on earth will act as a passport to the favoured circle in the world which is to come. It is a fact worth noticing, however, that they who preach this doctrine take every care to suffer themselves as little as possible.

Judged from the standard which Christ Himself set up, the present-day Christianity could not be in a worse condition or farther away from the realization of those ideals which its Founder intended. Why is this? Is it because the principles of Jesus are impracticable, or is it because Christians are impracticable? The latter. And I will tell you where you can find the reason for these ideals remaining in the clouds.

It is to be found in the fact that Dives reigns, to please whom the family of God has been rent and riven into classes, with all the accompanying evils of a divided brotherhood of man. On the one side the rich ; on the other side the poor. Between the two— the middle classes. Yes, Dives reigns, and to this fact can be traced the failure of the truth and the failure up to the present of Christ.

Dives has cursed and corrupted the Church, as he has cursed and corrupted the world. The golden calf is set up as of old. That Dives reigns is demonstrated in the gorgeous equipages and powdered flunkies, who wait while land grabbers, capitalistic sweaters, brewers, and slum rack-renters mumble their prayers in "dim religious light" with less sincerity, and certainly with less expectation, than is felt by the "heathen Chinee" who prostrates himself before his "joss."

Dives, the rejected of God, is the accepted of the Churches. Hence the Churches have no power, either with God or the people.

In spite of the truths contained in the "needle's eye" parable, Dives goes on accumulating riches, adding increment upon increment, increasing the gains of the luxurious classes, while at the same time the toiling masses are sweated, starved, and slain.

Dives reigns in pulpit and pew, creed and choir. They all play to his habits, tastes, and wishes.

Christ's response to the rich young man, who sought counsel of old, was, "Go sell that which thou hast." The young man turned away "sorrowful, for he had great possessions." Wealth was his curse ; it has cursed men since ; it curses men still. Experience proves to us that millionaires should be considered monsters ; since one individual cannot accumulate great wealth without directly or indirectly denying to other members of the human family those necessaries and comforts of life which that wealth could procure.

If the distribution, and not accumulation, of wealth was in old time the first condition of discipleship, it must be so still. But whoever hears of any leaving the church sorrowful in these days because they are rich? It is their wealth which makes men desirable acquisitions to religious institutions. Wealth ensures its possessor the best seat in the church, and even the church itself is his " gift."

Dives simply, because of his riches, becomes the patron of the "house of God," and the paymaster and employer of His "servants." Is it any wonder, therefore, that the latter fail to make war upon those conditions which enable their patrons to fatten and flourish?

Dives dominates the church as truly as he governs the world. The sanctuary is often nothing more than the receiving house for stolen property. For that is what the costly altars represent when erected by men whose wealth has been wrung from the very life's blood of the poor. What are many of the "endowments" but the results of plunder? Organized religion may, in truth, be said to have committed a double sin—the taking of Dives' bribes while neglecting Dives' victims.

To be true to Christ's principles the Church should be the tender nurse of *all* the people, without regard to class or distinction. The Church should be the first to demand from those in authority practice as well as precept, and stand in the breach as the champion of the weak against the strong. Does the Church rise to these responsibilities?

We read that it is righteousness that "exalteth a nation;" but how shall the nation learn righteousness, if by example the Church fails to demand from those within her own borders a practical compliance with the fundamental principles of righteousness?

Wealth is *the* power in the Christian Church, and, as a result, Dives has usurped the place of the Divine Founder.

The representatives of organized religion make much of their charities; but it is justice, not charity, the people need. Charity demoralizes. It is the dole that curses and saps true manhood.

Rich men and the grinders of the faces of the poor salve their consciences by restoring a portion of their illgotten gain to its owners. They build cathedrals with beer-barrels, and mash-tub millionaires are welcomed as they endow the sanctuary.

The reign of Dives in the Church is to be seen in the existence of that curse of man—competition. Do not so-called Christians compete with each other as they fawn and flatter Dives to secure his patronage and legacies? Within the Church is not competition fostered? Are not churches built, restored, beautified at "the lowest tender," thus nourishing a form of

competition which has its firstfruits in dishonesty and
sweated labour ?

Within the borders of the Church we find extremes
of the most pronounced form—bishops with palaces
and retinues; archbishops with £300 per week salary;
bishops at £100 per week; deans £50 to £60 per
week; canons from £10 to £20 per week. By the side
of these unnecessarily high salaries place the wretched
conditions of the drudges of the Church—the curates !

Of a truth we need not go to the Gentile capitalist,
or the Israelitish taskmaster, to find worse sweating
dens than those in the Church of England of to-
day.

There can be no room for Jesus or the practical
application of His teachings while Dives rules and
reigns within the Churches. Christ and His teachings
must be forsaken in the tenacious clinging to old
abuses.

The reign of Dives has destroyed even common
consistency. There are, amongst orthodox Churchmen, those who would not hesitate to drive a Non-
conforming teacher from a Board School as a heretic
and a sinner. Yet they joyfully join hands with any
propertied politician, though a Unitarian or a Jew, in
their anxiety to retain their hold upon the parish
charities. They will fight for creed to the last gasp,

but they will compromise when it is only the principles of righteousness and justice which are concerned.

The reign of Dives in the Church is demonstrated by the greed and demand for fees, which meet us at every turn. A man can neither be religiously born, wed, nor buried without a fee. A stone to mark the spot of his last resting-place cannot be erected without a fee. The most sacred feelings are played upon, so that the dust of our loved ones cannot be laid away in what is termed "consecrated ground" without a fee. Over £8000 a year are paid by cemetery companies in London to the representatives of the Established Church in nine parishes alone as toll for the dead. There is more of Shylock than Jesus in proceedings of this kind.

The reign of Dives is again clearly to be found in the traffic of souls which shamelessly goes on. "Spiritual" charges and church preferments are sold at public auctions as so much merchandise. Could anything be farther from the teachings of Him whose chief aim was to bring heaven to earth?

Is it too much to say that in these practices lie the causes which have destroyed the power of Christian doctrines, and provide a sufficient answer to those who ask "why the Church, as an institution, has lost touch with both the human and Divine"?

She has sold herself to Dives, and, as a consequence, partakes of his damnation.

These facts have in a measure forced themselves to the attention of those in authority, and latterly they have been setting their caps at the masses, coquetting with Radicalism in general, and "labour leaders" in particular, the object being to attract the masses once more. But all these efforts will fail unless Dives be dethroned.

Do not suppose that by the Church the Establishment alone is alluded to. This institution is by no means the solitary instance of the damnation by wealth. The democratic denominations are in the same damnation. It is true they have not the rotting influence of a State endowment to sap their foundations ; but here, as elsewhere, Dives is the man in possession, holding mortgage on the heritage of the children of the King. Is it unjust to say that in many instances money, and not piety, is the standard by which men are valued even in Nonconformist bodies ? The publican and distiller, for example, may enjoy the luxury of the best pew, while the poor and pious widow of a ruined drunkard must needs take a back seat because she cannot pay.

Such is the existing condition of things within the Churches, a condition which should cover us with shame and fill us with a spirit of true repentance.

In spite of the social problem existing in the most unmistakable form at their very doors, so-called Christians do not realize it. There are thousands of churches and chapels from whose pulpits the affairs of everyday life, and the wrongs suffered by the poor, are never mentioned from year's end to year's end. Can the occupants of such claim to be doing God's will? Surely it is the duty of the pastors and teachers to concentrate the intellectual and spiritual forces of their flocks towards the solving of the social problem! They should be directed as to the part they ought to take in the emancipation of their fellows from material burdens as clearly as their duty is pointed out and action counselled for the spiritual emancipation of man.

Many excuse themselves from interference with temporal matters because they hold that such efforts belong to the political arena, and say that "religion has nothing to do with politics." That religion should have no connection with "party" politics I admit. That the principles of Christ are opposed to political action on the lines of justice and reform I deny.

I know also the argument is frequently used that the spiritual emancipation of man is of greater importance than any material question.

Is it a matter of no moment that a hundred thousand homeless souls roam the land condemned to beg, steal,

or starve, the majority of whom have been thrust into
that plight by circumstances over which they had and
have no control ?

Is this the will of God ?

Are the claims of the pauper class too insignificant
a matter for the Christians to pick up ? They are a
class as large as the population of London. Is this
social blot a matter of no importance to us as Christians,
or do we say it is the will of God ?

What of the ninety per cent. of the actual producers
of wealth, whom Mr. Frederic Harrison so graphically
describes—who " have no home that they can call their
own beyond the end of the week ; have no bit of soil,
or so much as a room that belongs to them ; have
nothing of value of any kind except as much old furni-
ture as will go in a cart ; have the precarious chance of
weekly wages which barely suffice to keep them in
health ; are housed for the most part in places that no
man thinks fit for his horse ; are separated by so narrow
a margin from destitution, that a month of bad trade,
sickness, or unexpected loss brings them face to face
with hunger and pauperism. . . . This is the normal
state of the average workman in town or country "?

Will Christians go on praying with the lip for the
coming of His kingdom, but never raise a hand to
assist in the bringing of that kingdom ?

Is it a matter of no importance to Christians that three children die in some parts of London and our great towns to one in other parts, because of the vile and insanitary conditions which surround them in the hovels and slums to which poverty condemns them?

Not a day passes without our newspapers containing accounts of death from starvation of the most shocking character. Is this the will of God? or are these things possible simply because Christians neglect their duty?

It is true that now and again there is a spasmodic burst and a conference. We have had one lately at the Mansion House, where Dives, anxious to *appear* to be moving in the right direction, held solemn inquest on Lazarus, assisted by a jury of capitalists, guinea-pigs, and dividend-mongers, with a cleric or two staged in for effect. This capitalistic mountain, after passing through the throes of its stupendous labours, has brought forth a mouse, in the shape of the usual report, which, under the influence of the Charity Organization Society, has the impudence to suggest that the miseries of the poor are the result of their criminality and vicious-ness. Yet hardly a word of protest is heard from any of our pulpits against this cold-blooded document.

Turn, again, to the Conference of the "Jerusalem Chamber" on the "Living Wage." How hopefully

beat the hearts of many as that day of meeting drew
near ; but how those hopes were shattered ! Dignitaries
of the Established Church and Nonconformity—alike in
the enjoyment of a luxurious wage—joined hands with
Dives and shouted in chorus that a living wage was
" indefinable."

To have arrived at the conclusion their Master
would have advocated would have offended Dives.
They preferred, therefore, to belie the principles of
Jesus.

If Christians want the kingdom of heaven to come
to earth, they must insist upon the right of each to
live by their labour, as well as to enjoy all the fruits
of that labour. They must destroy once and for all
the iniquity of one class living in luxury on the toil
of another class. Some will say that drastic action of
this kind amounts to " confiscation." My reply is, that
if any have robbed, they must restore. The restoration
of stolen property, be it land, or the resources of nature,
or anything else, is but common honesty. Those who
exist on the manipulation of capital and " vested interests " are aware that heavenly conditions mean their
destruction, and Dives, therefore, is only too willing to
subsidize handsomely Church institutions for the pulpit
to cry peace, when there is no peace. Therefore it is
that Dives packs the Legislature to resist reforms,

making the political representatives of the people mere pieces of a party machine, the object of which is to crush, instead of elevate, the people ; and thus it is that amidst starvation and suicide, smug Christianity covers his face with his hands and thanks God for "inexorable economic law."

But what shall we do ? Attack those who make sin, as well as damn the sinner. Let the prophets of God in these days be as uncompromising as they were of old. Thunder out the truth that the earth is the Lord's, and *not* the landlords'. Trumpet that the earth, and all that is in it, is the gift of the Creator to all men, and that they who rob men of, or hinder them in any way from enjoying, the full use and benefit of the Divine gift, are enemies of humanity of the worse kind.

Send forth the fiery cross against unholy competition. Sweep out from all religious communities the makers and sellers of strong drink, as those upon whom a share of the drunkard's damnation will fall in time as well as eternity.

The duty that lies first to the hands of followers of Christ is the overthrow of Dives within the borders of the Church. We "cannot serve God and mammon."

The next step is the dethronement of Dives in the Legislature, so that party politics will be known no

more, and principle in place of policy be the guiding
force. Then the dethronement of Dives in the commercial world.

These are the foundations upon which the heavenly
kingdom will rest; and when these are laid, as men
and women of religion could and should lay them, we
shall neither have to wait or pray for the kingdom of
heaven to come—*it will be with us.*

FRANK SMITH.

Preachers and Churches.

I MAKE no apology for writing this chapter upon preachers and Churches. In our day every institution is open to criticism, and rightly and necessarily so ; and although—if this should meet the eyes of preachers— many of them will doubtless consider it presumption on my part to attempt even to deal with such a sub- ject, let it be so. We live in England, and not in Russia—plutocratic England, it is true, but with de- mocracy getting a good grip. And if by writing this I simply lay myself open to criticism, it may still be the case that I shall have served some small purpose by helping to make clear what it is we object to in orthodox preachers, with their orthodox doctrines and congregations. It cannot be that I am wholly correct, it may be I am very wrong ; but feeling strongly upon the subject, and often indulging on Labour platforms in sentiments identical with those I have here given expression to, I now venture (upon invitation) to place

U

before another audience the views I hold, as well as those I condemn.

At the outset, I desire to say that I am fully alive to the fact that there are clergymen, ministers, Sunday-school and Bible-class teachers, who cannot be covered by the general terms of censure I have made use of in what follows. I am happy in possessing the close friendship of not a few who, I am quite sure, are not merely as devoted as any men and women on earth to the cause of truth and righteousness, but strive continuously to make right-doing prevail in every sphere of life. But it is just these who, more than others, feel and know what a terrible responsibility rests upon preachers and teachers as a whole ; and who also know, to their sorrow, how shamefully deficient the Churches are in supplying the much-needed correction and stimulus and light.

The Churches set up a claim to be the moral and spiritual guides of humanity, to whom all men should look for guidance as to their conduct in this life, and qualifications for life hereafter. The question I propose to examine is : Do they fulfil these functions ?

In a complex society like ours, where the average person, on reaching girlhood or boyhood, must perforce begin work of some kind to obtain a maintenance, a very large share of one's time, thought, and energy must of necessity, under present conditions, be devoted to the mere work of obtaining a living. Indeed, it is the paramount question, by the side of which all others fall into comparative insignificance. Consequently, if guidance is needed anywhere, it is in connection with the means whereby a livelihood is to be obtained. The virtues—including honesty, sobriety, and obedience to superiors—are all emphasized in the Sunday schools, Bible-classes, and churches ; exactly how to apply them being, of course, too great a task. A general condemnation of " sin," and urgent advice to " flee from the wrath to come," and find salvation by reliance upon the sacrifice in the crucifixion of Jesus, sums up the teaching of the average school, church, and chapel. Where does this land a man ? Judging by a lengthened experience, I unhesitatingly declare that I find that the average church or chapel goer, who is influenced primarily by what he obtains from its functions, becomes a narrow, saving, squeezing creature, taking little or no part in the vigorous life of the community, but very commonly becoming, by his isolated action, a source of weakness in any real democratic movement. If he takes part in municipal or political life, he usually does so on the flimsiest party lines. He generally attributes the cause of the poverty of the poor to their utter degradation, caused by their dissolute habits, brought about by their unchecked evil tendencies, the human heart being desperately wicked and deceitful above all things. Very rarely is he connected with a trade union. As a rule, he is most loyal to the injunction, "Servants, obey your masters," and will side with his kindred "brethren" to blackleg against his fellows.

The tricks of trade he necessarily becomes familiar with; and, like a business man, he not only indulges in them, but becomes an expert thereat. He will attend a prayer-meeting and bless God for the good things of life, and pray for the salvation of the poor sinners in the slums, and will take, as evidences of God's blessing in return, the possession of a few more shares that will pay ten per cent.; and if fifteen per cent.—why, the more cause for thankfulness, of course! Let none tell me I am concocting a case; such men can be counted by thousands. And why? Because that upon which they have been fed is devoid of real vitalizing force. Instead of giving moral discernment to enable a man to understand how, where, and when moral or, if you will, religious principles should be applied, the preachers land him in a complete fog. Beholding those who are held in high esteem in the Churches, that they include the bankers and stock-jobbers, and the company promoters and capitalists and landlords, he follows them rather than the simple carpenter's Son. Between such select and exalted personages and mere labour agitators, trade unionists, socialists, etc., there is, as surely there ought to be, he concludes, a great gulf.

The Church is in a helpless backwash, having lost the true courage, mental and moral vigour, power of discernment, and hence capacity, to apply what humanity now demands. The parsons, clergymen, and ministers are, for the most part, a feeble folk, who, daring not to lead, are therefore bound to follow.

Other men labour, and in the course of years the Church slowly is dragged along; for the pioneers of righteousness we must look elsewhere than to so-called Christians. The man who is truly religious wants no driving to do his duty. He does not try to make all manner of excuses for the exploiters of the industrious community, and pile up the trifling misdeeds of an unfairly handicapped proletariat. A truly religious body of men, whose religion enabled them to understand between right-doing and wrong-doing, and furnished them with the requisite courage to face all foes, would never be content with the sunny complacency of the average parson in the midst of the life-destroying conditions of our industrial centres.

Shame, say I, and a thousand times shame, upon so

feeble a religion as that which can tolerate the awful
social life which exists in London at this very time.
There are not less than four hundred thousand persons
in London alone in a state of semi- or actual starvation.
There are among these at least a hundred thousand
adult males out of work ; tens of thousands of women,
having no one to rely upon to support them, but in
multitudes of instances being responsible for children
(or aged or crippled relatives) in addition to themselves,
who, over and over again in the course of a year, are
deprived of the means of obtaining a livelihood ; tens
of thousands of children setting off to the Board schools
every morning with less than a tenth part of that which
is necessary for physical sustenance. Scores of miles
of streets, with wretched dens in the background, furnish
enormous rents—to whom ?   To the men of the world ?
No ; to the rich members of your congregations, the great
subscribers of your salaries, O preachers ! who turn up
at your church or chapel service and follow you in praying, " Thy kingdom come ; Thy will be done, as in heaven,
so upon the earth." Can they, do you think, believe
that there is anything in heaven corresponding to the
wretched slum-dwellers of Whitechapel or Spitalfields ?
Are there any in heaven corresponding to these Christian
rent-takers, who wax fat at the expense of the down-
trodden ?   What are you ministers and plutocratic

members of the rich churches and chapels doing to make earth like heaven? Why, it would need an entire change in the basis of society, and the means whereby incomes are obtained. Are these religious plutocrats and preachers trying to change the basis of society, so that better conditions shall prevail? Assuredly not. On the contrary, they are determined opponents of those who do try to make such changes.

The fact is, preachers and congregation are bound hard and fast in a system that is grossly materialistic, utterly soulless in good, and without a single noble aspiration. The Hobbs & Co. Liberator phenomenon indicates how completely swamped is the average Nonconformist soul. Not only did it make haste to get rich, but by the most damnable means that the most cunning Jews and Gentiles combined could devise. Morality! Religion! Where is the religion or the morality in taking ten per cent. usury? Yet who among the orthodox in faith and practice objects to ten or more per cent.? Honesty! Righteousness! Who that believes in the doctrines of Jesus can uphold industrialism whose very basis from top to toe is ten per cent.? " The man that will not work, neither shall he eat," is an apostolic injunction; but how many ministers or members of our swell churches and chapels believe it? "Yes, but even Hobbs and Wright worked," some will say.

Ah, so they did; as did also Mr. Charles Peace of
burglar notoriety—the latter with less scoundrelism
than the former.

The average preacher or church-goer does distinctly
believe, not only that it is right to eat without working,
but to get fed, clothed, housed, insured, and buried into
the bargain. Who among them condemns as a religious
duty the taking of interest and rent? And if these are
defended, and I can get sufficient interest or rent to
keep me and mine without working, what religious
principle comes in after that to say I must work? Or,
am I to work like the Yankee millionaire—on six days
a week endeavouring to amass the biggest fortune on
record, entirely irrespective of how many will be ruined;
and on Sunday attending church, receiving the blessing of the minister, and helping to carry the collecting-
plate to show how godly I am? If ever Deity was
insulted, it is by these devourers of widows' houses, who
receive direct sanction and approval from orthodox
exponents of orthodox religion. Let none rise to say,
"Oh, but we would never endorse the enormities of
the Liberator Company." If not, where, then, would
you stop? The whole shoal of interest-takers and
stockbroking gamblers are specimens of the same
type in embryo. Not so successful as the millionaire,
perhaps—why? Because they lacked opportunity.

Never had the brains to scheme like the others, and the courage to come down a resounding crash at the end. Why? Because they hadn't had time to go far enough. The difference isn't in kind ; it is only in degree. As in the time of Nahum, so now, to describe London we must indeed say, " Woe to the bloody city ! it is full of lies and robbery."

I do not state or imply that all this is done hypocritically; what I do say is "that the truth is not in them." Christians need to be " born again." Orthodox religion is acquiescing in an irreligious condition of Society. Christianity is made part and parcel of the national commercialism, and wholly subservient to the individualistic acquisitiveness of the age. The Fatherhood of God and Brotherhood of Man have come to be mere threadbare phrases when used by an ordinary religionist. Church or chapel is regularly attended, not indeed to obtain guidance out of the industrial and social wilderness, but to maintain tradition and keep up appearances. Some Christians positively believe, doubtless, that religion consists in church-going, hymn-singing, and muttering over the words found in the Prayer-book, or offered up by the minister ; failing to realize that these are but the means to an end. If they are used as the end itself, then indeed does moral darkness assert itself.

It does appear to be the case that with industrial England, as with pastoral Israel in the time of Amos, the outward ritual is made the chief concern. At that time the Mosaic ritual was jealously attended to, but the message was: "I hate, I despise your feast-days, and I will not smell in your solemn assemblies. Though ye offer Me burnt offerings, I will not accept them : neither will I regard the peace offerings of your fat beasts. Take thou away from Me the noise of thy songs ; for I will not hear the melody of thy viols. But let justice run down as waters, and righteousness as a mighty stream" (Amos v. 21–24). This is a sweeping condemnation of fashionable church - going whilst the state of society is unsound. See v. 11 of the same chapter : "Forasmuch therefore as your tread-ing is upon the poor, and ye take from him burdens of wheat : ye have built houses," etc.

Now, it was not the custom even in brutal Israel for one man to literally knock another down in order to take his wheat from him. There were more refined methods of exploitation then as now—though, doubtless, modern civilization even in Christian England could give the old Jews many points, and beat them at legalized robbery ; for it is this legal robbery that is here condemned as much as any other kind.

But nothing puts the case more clearly than the

condemnation by Jesus of the orthodox professors of religion of his time (see St. Matt. xxiii. 13, 14)—

" But woe unto you, scribes and Pharisces, hypocrites ! for ye shut up the kingdom of heaven against men : for ye neither go in yourselves, neither suffer ye them that are entering to go in. Woe unto you, scribes and Pharisees, hypocrites ! for ye devour widows' houses, and for a pretence make long prayer : therefore ye shall receive the greater damnation."

No language could be stronger, and yet this was directed against the respectably religious of that day. These Pharisees have their exact counterpart to-day in England.

I know the risk I run by any attempt to deal with the subject of future salvation. But with a keen remembrance of the influence orthodoxy exercised over me,—of the years of unrest, of the flimsiness and mimicry with its pretences of solemnity and make - believe solidity,—I feel bound to deal with the subject. I know many young men who have striven hard to find " salvation ; " and with blind guides to lead them, many years were spent in finding what ought to have been reached in a few months. The talk about the one thing needful under orthodoxy (it will be noted that I continually guard myself by referring to "orthodoxy") means nothing more than fixing attention upon Jesus as the

Saviour, He having been sacrificed to reconcile mankind to the Father. I make no comment upon this doctrinal point. What I want to expose is the demoralizing effect produced by the individual being taught that salvation for him consists in reflecting upon and believing in his acceptance with God, because of Christ's sacrifice, irrespective of the life he leads. " No one says this," some will cry. Yes ; but, indeed, it is said and taught in nineteen churches out of twenty, and the effect is to cause the individual to think of himself or herself, and to value, out of all proper proportion, his or her own personal salvation. Selfishness begins this, and with selfishness it usually ends. Whilst one can admire the energy put forth and the trouble taken in the voluntary street-corner preachers and singers, one can only pity those who speak, as well as those who may in any way be influenced by what is said. A million times over is the same story told—personal salvation by faith in Christ. It seems to me it would be a truly religious act if all such received a severe castigation for wasting so much time trying to assuage the sorrows primarily brought about by a vicious industrial system, instead of boldly tackling that industrial system itself.

Salvation surely consists in living in accordance with Divine harmony,—in loving order and living it,—in hating disorder here on earth, and striving might and main to remove it so that earth may be more like heaven. Oh, the unworthiness of followers of Jesus being primarily concerned about their poor little souls! He that seeks to save his soul on these lines will lose it; but he that will lose his own life by working for the salvation of the community,—all such must be saved. Up! off your knees, young men! Let us have more effort directed to the removal of evil! Don't go continually begging of God to do that which you ought to do! This world is wrong, and wants righting, and you and I are responsible for doing our share towards righting it. What horrible villainy have you been guilty of, that half your time needs be taken up in praying for forgiveness? The man that loves righteousness will seek to live righteously, and all such are already saved. His duty is to be at work removing the cause of wrongdoing.

A little less time spent at orthodox mission meetings, and more time spent in helping on effective industrial organization, to ensure right-doing in the business of life, is sadly needed just now. This orthodox mission work is exactly what our exploiting plutocrats rejoice in. It is so gracious of them to give an occasional ten pounds to keep a mission going, that they may with reasonable safety exploit an additional twenty from

their employées, and still receive the praise and blessings of the faithful.

"Go to now, ye rich men, weep and howl for your
miseries that shall come upon you. Your riches are
corrupted and your garments are moth-eaten. Your
gold and silver is cankered ; and the rust of them shall
be a witness against you, and shall eat your flesh as it
were fire. Ye have heaped treasure together for the
last days. Behold the hire of the labourers who have
reaped down your fields, which is of you kept back by
fraud, crieth : and the cries of them which have reaped
are entered into the ears of the Lord of sabaoth " (St.
James v. 1–4).

What have our landed aristocrats and capitalistic
plutocrats who go to church and chapel regularly to
say to St. James? Dare they claim to be better than
those whom James condemned? If so, in what way?
And if not, are they not condemned by the book in
which they make a pretence of reading? Not that I
am affirming that every rich man is necessarily a
candidate for hell. What I do contend is that, be we
rich or poor, if our mental and moral standard is such
that we continue to support the present hellish system,
—which the ordinary capitalist upholds, and is sanctioned in upholding by the average Church,—then we
are violating every genuinely religious principle.

I am not condemning religion, but the lack of it. Religion to me consists of those ethical principles that serve as a guide in all matters of conduct—social, political, and industrial alike; and the essence of the whole thing is this: the choice between a life whose actuating motive shall be self, either in acquiring wealth, renown, prestige, or power, and a life which shall have primary regard for the well-being of the community as a whole. To do this is to engage in making it possible for "His kingdom to obtain on earth as in heaven." If I am asked, "Do I think that all that is necessary is a perfected industrial machinery on socialistic lines?" I say emphatically, "No! I don't think that is all."

I do distinctly believe in the necessity for Socialism out and out, and that it is my duty to work for its realization. But I know also that something more than good machinery is necessary, if really good results are to be obtained. I desire to see every person fired with a holy enthusiasm to put a stop to wrong-doing. Before this is possible, individuals must submit themselves to much and severe discipline. The baser sides of our nature must be beaten down, that the higher and nobler side may develop. Regard for the brethren (brethren meaning all) must be the mainspring of our action; the development of the highest possible qualities in ourselves is undoubtedly a religious duty, but for this chief reason—that we may be of the greater service.

"He that would be greatest among you, let him be servant of all."

This to me is the ideal test and standard. As Jesus was the servant of mankind, so I, as a follower of Jesus, must learn to be of use. The irreligious man is not only the deliberate maker of mischief, but equally so the indolent and useless man. Swedenborg has well said—

"All religion has relation to life, and the life of religion is to do good." Further : "Heaven consists of those of all nations who love God supremely, and their neighbours as themselves. Hell is the assembly of the selfish,—of all who love themselves supremely and gratify their lusts at any cost to others."

The astounding anomaly of our time is the complete separation of religious principles from everyday industrial life. Spiritual pastors teach the young to regard God as the common Father ; and when the young become of age to reflect upon the shameful inequalities created and maintained by our social system, they are discouraged by their elders from trying to alter it, and are treated as agitators and destroyers of the peace.

Honesty demands a frank statement that the so-called religions of our time are afraid to apply the principles of Jesus. They make a pretence of championing His cause; but in reality the Socialist agitator and the Trade Union organizer is doing far more than the preachers and the Christians, the Missionary Societies and the Bible Societies to make Christ's gospel prevail. The Churches are afraid of Socialism. Why? Because the wealthy in their congregations are anti-socialists. If any say this is not so, then it will not be difficult to give an effectual reply by quoting instances where the minister has seen the light and dared to proclaim the truth, and where the men who "have great possessions" (relatively) have very soon taken their departure. I have heard of complaints from one or two such ministers that they not only lost the employer class by their boldness, but that they did not succeed in securing the adhesion of any counteracting proportion among the workers. There is less to be surprised at in this than some seem to think. The Churches having gone astray worse than lost sheep, are not likely very easily to win back democracy. Whether they will ever do it or not is an open question.

The clergyman is undoubtedly at a serious discount as an adviser. "Serve him right," say I. Nor will he ever redeem his position except by honest effort on behalf of democracy. Not that democracy will suffer materially if this is not done. The greatest trouble is

X

past. Democracy is learning how to provide for itself, and never was the democracy so truly religious as now. And it is gradually getting more so. This religious evolution will increase as the bad environment is altered on one side, and the ethical gospel is lifted up and followed truthfully on the other.

I know that many preachers contend that industrial and economic matters are nothing to them ; theirs is a religious work, and men must be left to themselves to find out how to apply religious truths. " If they were to take sides, it would mean the break up of the Church," and so on. To endorse a religion apart from principles that are to guide our everyday behaviour is monstrous. If one's religion does not compel one to take sides in favour of a righteous basis of society, the sooner it ceases to encumber the earth the better for all concerned. A minister who can't find time to make up his mind as to the direction in which he should travel on industrial and economic matters, will probably not find time to be of any practical use to the world, nor yet to the denomination to which he may belong. I am fully aware of the fact that by declaring in favour of Socialism, many who might have been disposed to consider the possibility of some mild action favourable to democracy, now stand off. To such let me say: I have purposely avowed myself a Socialist here, so that those who read this may know what I expect from those on whose behalf I can speak. We do not want, and will not have a person's patronage, or goody-goody advice. If there is to be a *rapprochement* it can only be by the parson getting off his high horse, stopping his goodyism and meeting men and women frankly as such. If he doesn't, he'll get left high and dry for a certainty.

I am not here demanding that every parson who is to be of use, shall be an out-and-out Socialist right off. I am telling him that we workmen who happen to be Socialists are adding largely to our numbers every month, that the whole trend of modern effort in our Trade Unions, Co-operative Societies, Town and County Councils, and Parliament is distinctly socialistic, and if parsons and ministers want to stop it, they had better refurbish their weapons. I can easily understand that some genuine men among the clergy will be dis-quieted by wondering whether the Socialists are coming round their way for a general sharing-out arrangement, and so they are slow to make a move. Such is the enlightenment that exists in these quarters! Let me hasten to reassure all such that if they are to subscribe to the following very mild statement of John Ruskin, they need not be seriously alarmed :—

"So far am I from invalidating the security of

property, that the whole gist of my contention will be found to aim at an extension in its range, and whereas it has long been known and declared that the poor have no right to the property of the rich, I wish it also to be known and declared that the rich have no right to the property of the poor" (" *Unto this Last* ").

That surely should be a self-evident proposition to the mind of a moralist, but it goes rather a long way, as it would mean nothing less than a righteous distribution of wealth. It is to be hoped that no preacher will ask what business is this to him. Surely " Thou shalt not steal " is emphatic enough, and when we add Carlyle's trifle to it, " Thou shalt not be stolen from," it gains a little in clearness. The Church will doubtless concern itself in a few generations to come about such an elementary subject as the enforcement of honesty. We workmen contend that honesty of distribution should become a fact. Forty-nine-fiftieths of present-day poverty, and the bulk of the crime and villainy that now disgrace our country, would disappear, if the Society thieves were to disappear.

But timid Christians and their preachers are likely to reply that, " to bring about such a change is impossible ; human nature won't admit of it." If not, what becomes of the Lord's Prayer: " Thy kingdom come . . . as in heaven so upon the earth " ? If this is a pious fraud, please be frank enough to say so. Some of us, when we say the Lord's Prayer, do indeed mean it, amongst whom I am glad to be one. I am not willing to be included with those cowards who say it is impossible of realization. Whatever is right we are bound to work for, even if its fruit is in the dim and distant future. We believe that the Lord's Prayer is not only realizable, but we are of those disciples who will make it so. This done, the question of a "living wage" will be settled.

As yet in this Christian land we haven't been able to establish a living wage, even when it means nothing more than a sufficiency of material necessities to maintain life. Many in connection with the Churches have recently said that a living wage is impossible, *i.e.* that it is impossible in this "religious" country to see that each of God's children, our own brothers and sisters, shall be as well fed as a horse. Let Carlyle again be heard—

"There is not a horse in England, able and willing to work, but has due food and lodging, and goes about sleek-coated, satisfied in heart. And you say, 'It is impossible.' Brothers, I answer, if for you it be impossible, what is to become of you? It is impossible for us to believe it to be impossible. The human brain, looking at these sleek English horses, refuses to believe in such impossibility for Englishmen. Do you depart quickly ; clear the ways soon, lest worse befall. We for our share do purpose, with full view of the enormous difficulty, with total disbelief in the impossibility, to endeavour while life is in us, and to die endeavouring, we and our sons, till we attain it, or have all died and ended ! " ("Past and Present ").

This is the correct spirit in which the modern crusade against our social villainies is to be conducted. It is especially the work of the Church to set the pace. It ought, but we don't expect it will, and yet, I feel sure that those young men and women who are certain to be touched by the devotion and fervour of our modern crusaders, will not require much converting to our side. They are too noble to remain in the ranks of the inactive and selfish. They too will come forth to join in the noble work of social reconstruction. We have a glorious and an inspiriting work in hand,—nothing less than the purifying of the industrial and social life of our country and the making of true individuality. For, let it be clearly understood, we labour men are thoroughly in favour of the highest possible develop-ment of each individual. We seek no dead level of uniformity and never did. Our ideal is: "From each according to his capacity, to each according to his needs." We can't reach that right off, but when we have done so, we shall not be "far from the king-dom."

To engage in this work, is to be occupied in the noblest work the earth affords; to do it well, we want not only men and women of good intention—the Churches have these now—we shall want men and women of sound sense who will understand the science of industrial economics, as well as of the highest standard of ethics. To mean well is one thing, to be able to do well is a better thing, and we cannot do well except by accident, unless we know something of the laws that underlie and control the forces with which we shall have to deal. By way of indicating what we hope to reach, it may prevent fear and trembling if I say it is neither more nor less than that set forth by John Stuart Mill, in his "Autobiography," where he says—

"The Social Problem of the future we considered to be, how to unite the greatest individual liberty of action, with a common ownership in the raw material of the globe, and an equal participation for all in the benefits of combined labour."

Nothing very awful in that surely, and yet there is sufficient to revolutionize modern society! What does a really religious man care how far it goes? To him the one important question is: "Is it right?" Does duty demand that he shall endorse it and work for its realization? To me all other duties sink into comparative insignificance. I will yield to none if I know it in facing the straight path, and honestly endeavouring to walk in it. I dare not take my eyes off this big problem.

Much has already been done in removing barriers. The work of the Trade Unionists for the last sixty years has borne good fruit. In the early years of the present century, capital had complete sway. Unrestricted industrial competition was the accepted gospel universally applied in Great Britain. In Parliament the landed aristocracy had complete power. In industrial life, the then infantile but now powerful plutocracy had undisputed control. The law was against combination, consequently there were few Trade Unions. Neither was there anything in the nature of Factory Acts. And what was the result? Our industrial history of that period is the blackest page in England's life. Not only men, but women and children had to work fifteen to sixteen hours a day. Children too, of six, even five years of age, were called to the mills at five o'clock in the morning ; if they were a minute late, an overseer with a slave-driver's lash stood there to thrash them and the girls and women like dogs. Some power of revolt existed, and this country owes more than it thinks to the revolutionary course of the early Trade

Unionists. We still have England's industrial prestige maintained by child labour at ten and eleven years of age.

In thousands of instances the standard of life is such that when a man is in full work, so little does he earn that the wife and mother must not only get up herself at five o'clock in the morning, but must also wake her children, and take the infant out into the raw wintry air to leave it with some nurse, while she, the mother, must go to the mill, reaching there at six, to take her stand by the men, work all day, and return home at night to commence house duties, and this because the family would starve if she did not. Oh, Church people! if ever a crusade were needed it is here in England now. The honour of our country is left with us to guard. For humanity's sake, let us see to it that we wipe out these accursed blood-red stains. There is much to be proud of in Britain's history, but whilst such conditions remain, we cannot wait to comment upon the work done in face of so much waiting to be done. Who shall do it? Every man and every woman is expected to contribute a share. The social salvation of the entire community is the religious duty in which you preachers and people are called upon to engage.

Oh! rich women of the Churches, have you no social and political duty? You, who spend so much on your own persons, have you no care for the body of society? Yea, I tremble for your future, women of the middle classes, who have a great power; will you not use that power to wipe out these stains on our national and Christian character? If you take up a determined stand in connection with the Churches, they will be compelled to become active. The work will be done with or without you, but quicker with you than without you.

> Women! who shall one day bear
> Sons to breathe New England air,
> If you hear without a blush
> Deeds to make the roused blood rush
> Like red lava through your veins,
> For your sisters now in chains,
> Answer! are ye fit to be
> Mothers of the brave and free?

TOM MANN.

Christianity and Social Advance.

THE Christian Church has surely occupied herself dis-
proportionately with endeavouring to map out dogmas in
a realm of high and sublimated truth, which admits of
little accurate definition, where intuition, vision, symbol,
are rather at home and appropriate than exact propositions for the understanding. Hence interminable, barren
disputes, quarrels, and persecutions, and a comparatively
meagre record in undertakings of practical, secular
advantage to mankind. I say "comparatively," yet
we must admit that many temporal benefits of the
highest value have come to men through Christianity.
Can it be doubted that the proclamation of Christ, as
the Elder Brother of men, and as One who revealed,
through His Incarnation, the very mind and heart of
the Highest ; as One who abased Himself from heaven
to earth, from a condition of equality with God to that
of a poor mortal man belonging to the working, not
even to the privileged class ; who is venerated as having

borne our sins and carried our sorrows, lived a life of
lowly ministration to human need, and, lastly, submitted
to an ignominious death for our sakes ;—can it be
doubted, I say, that such a proclamation must have
had an incalculable effect in restraining the natural
selfishness of men, and inspiring them to the redress
of injustice and mutual service? As a matter of fact,
we do find it so. The Christian community at the
beginning had all things in common, neither said any
man that " aught that belonged to him was his own."
Now, this was evidently the more immediate result and
outcome of Christ's personal influence, and His personal
teaching, as well as that of His apostles. For it is pretty
evident from 2 Cor. viii. 13-15, that if communism
actually prevailed only in Jerusalem, it was the desire
of St. Paul that it should also be the rule in the early
Christian societies which had been formed elsewhere.
Christianity succeeded, says Professor Sidgwick, "in
dominating the social chaos to which the barbarian
invasions reduced the Western Empire;" it played an
" important part in producing out of this chaos the new
civilized order to which we belong."

One is unquestionably impressed, in reading the early
Fathers, with the very democratic tone of their utterances
concerning the relations which ought to exist between
employers and employed and the possession of private

property. " The communism attempted," says Professor Sidgwick, " in the Apostolic Age was cherished in the traditions of the early and mediæval Church as the ideal form of Christian society." " Private property and slavery were both regarded as encroachments on the original rights of all members of the human family, since men were naturally free and the fruits of the earth naturally common; both would disappear in the future when Christ's kingdom came to be realized." He adds, that the Church maintained the Jewish prohibition of usury, with certain reserves and accommodations, down to quite modern times.*

In the Middle Ages the Church certainly stood often between the poor and the grinding tyranny of kings and nobles, though she also invoked the secular arm to punish and prevent doubt or disbelief of her own dogmas and the progress of free thought. She has produced a St. Catherine, a St. Teresa, a St. Francis, and a Curé D'Ars ; while in her later reformed history we find an Oberlin, a Mrs. Fry, a Sister Dora, Wilberforce, Henry Martyn, Livingstone, and Gordon. When we are rightly denouncing corrupt and interested hierarchies, worldly, luxurious, and bigoted priesthoods, for their narrow intolerance, fierce cruelty, immorality, ambition, greed, and blind obscurantism, for their opposition to social

* " Hist. Ethics."

and political, as to intellectual progress, let us in justice
remember that to the leaven of Christian ideas also we
owe many of those great reforms which the more retro-
grade, self-seeking, and short-sighted Churchmen banned
and sought to arrest. In whose name, if not in that of
Christ, did Wyclif, Savonarola, John Huss, Luther,
Erasmus, and the Puritans inaugurate and carry out
their great forward, religious, popular movements ? They
fought with an open Bible in their hand against aristo-
cracies of privilege, whether religious or secular ; they
fought the battle of the common people, of the enslaved
multitude ; though it must be granted that the peasant
wars waged by Wat Tyler and Munzer were not approved
by Wyclif or Luther.

Yet these popular movements were indirectly, and in
great measure, the result of their preaching, or of the
spirit and temper aroused by them and that revolutionary
iconoclasm, with which the moral and intellectual atmosphere of the time was highly charged. The fanatical
and immaturely educated pushed their principles to
extreme consequences. Yet W. Morris has rehabilitated
John Ball for us.

But Savonarola became himself the champion of
popular liberty in the pulpit. "Feeling," says Mr.
Symonds,* "that in the people alone lay any hope of re-

* " Renaissance, Age of the Despots."

generation for Italy, he made it the work of his whole life to give the strength and sanction of religion to republican freedom. This work he sealed with martyrdom." "The spirit of the creed which he bequeathed to his partisans in Florence was political no less than pious." "What prophet of Israel, from Samuel to Isaiah, was not the maker and destroyer of kings and constitutions?" For many years the name of Savonarola remained the watch-word of Florentine freedom. But, on the other hand, that illustrious prince and monster, the head of the Christian Church, Alexander Borgia, was his mortal enemy, and a Bishop of the Christian Church was the man who conducted his execution and stripped his friar's frock from him.

Yet all great Christian reformers have endeavoured to bring back their religion to its primitive simplicity and purity, to its popular, human, democratic ideal.

The second of our great revolutions in favour of constitutional liberty, that of 1688, was made, like the first, to a great extent by religious men in the name of Christ. The trial and acquittal of the Anglican bishops for resisting the king's authority was the culminating point of the crisis under James II.

It was in defence of religious liberty, too, that the good ship *Mayflower* carried the Pilgrim Fathers to the shores of America, where they helped to found those colonies that grew up from so small a seed into the greatest of modern democracies.

Of the Liberal movement in Scotland again (1577), Green, in his " History of England," says, " Amidst the turmoil of the Reformation a new force had come to the front. This was the Scotch People, which had arisen into being under the guise of the Scotch Kirk." With splendid boldness the preacher Melville told James, "There is Christ Jesus the King, and His kingdom the kirk, whose subject James VI. is, and of whose kingdom not a king, nor a lord, but a member."

The French Huguenots, persecuted and exiled by their own king on account of their religious convictions, carried to other countries, to the shores of England and to the mountains of Switzerland, the sterling excellence and strength of their moral qualities, as well as their characteristic industrial skill. These were found again in Spitalfields and at Geneva, while, by intermarriage, the exiles invigorated the current of free blood, stiffened the backbone of liberty in those peoples among whom they settled ; though in eliminating these Protestants from their own race, the shortsighted bigot was depleting French veins of very life.

The Swiss patriots on the Grütli, by the shores of their dark water, in the presence of eternal mountains, as they vowed to achieve the independence of their

native land, raised their hands, rough with holy toil to
the winter stars, making solemn appeal to that God,
before whom king, governor, and serf are equal.

But it must be granted that, while the vindicators
of a righteous cause have sought help from Him whom
the founders of their faith proclaimed righteous, the
officials of the Churches that call themselves by His
name have too often been found ranged on the side of
injustice. Self-interest has too often pointed in that
direction—ambitions, pomps and vanities of this world.
If it be so that in our own day sweaters, or land-
grabbers, or money-makers at any price, now and
again elect their deacons and ministers, or present their
clergy to good livings, even as a board of slum-owners
elects the sanitary inspector, what can you look for?
Modern papal Rome again, before it became part of the
Italian kingdom, was probably as badly governed as
any city in Europe. While of the rival popes at
Avignon and Rome, and their proceedings, the less
said the better—or of the welcome they extended to
the revelations of men like Galileo, Bruno, or Savonarola,
organs of the Divine-Human Spirit in process of
evolution. But all this only shows that official
Christendom needs perpetually to return for purification
to the pure fountain head of her Faith, and that her
broad river, as it flows through the ages, should welcome

Y

tributary streams from every region—alike from modern philosophy, ancient wisdom, and Indian lore, for in all these God speaks to man,—as of old that same river gathered volume from Greece, Alexandria, and Rome.

The great war of liberation in the Netherlands, under William the Silent, was waged for the vindication at once of civil and religious liberty, as well as for the delivering of a nationality from a detested foreign yoke. It was, however, in the main, a religious war. But here again Christ is found arrayed against Christ. That good and conscientious king, Philip of Spain, with his satellite Alva, thought it right to burn, torture, and massacre, in the sacred name of that ancient two-headed idol, Tyranny-Superstition. But the "infidel" may be found now and again fighting on Christ's side, and the "orthodox" fighting against Him, for He has no party save that of justice and mercy, then or now, and all the world over. Whatever he call himself, the leader, ecclesiastical or secular, who fights against these Divine attributes is an Antichrist, an adversary, a Satan. For the kingdom of Christ is not of this world; it is the moral order of humanity.

I maintain, therefore, that there are now, as there have always been, two antagonistic tendencies in the Christian Church, the Conservative-reactionary, and the Liberal-progressive. When Christianity became the State religion under Constantine, there began to creep in the worldly spirit of self-aggrandizement; the corrupting influence of power and prosperity began to prevail. Much of the failure to sympathize with popular causes may, in every age of the Church's history, including our own, whether in England or on the Continent, be attributed to this same paralyzing and malignant blight. In England the clergy have, as a rule, belonged to the higher and privileged class ; many of them are wealthy ; peculiar worldly honours and distinctions are accorded to their bishops, and other dignitaries, over and above large emoluments. In Ireland, on the other hand, where the Roman Catholic clergy spring from the proletariat, they are one with the people in their aspirations ; they are leaders and powerful auxiliaries of the people.

. It is sometimes contended that the Church should refrain from taking any part whatsoever in politics ; so far as temporalities are concerned should confine herself to relieving the wants of individuals and the adminis-tration of charities. But, as a matter of fact, she has not done so. She has interfered very much when her own authority and emoluments were threatened, as under Henry VIII., and perpetually in favour of the rights of private property, even when that property has consisted of human beings. Thus the clergy in the

Southern States of America thundered from every
pulpit in defence of slavery, when that institution was
imperilled ; while her members to-day are generally
found to be in sympathy with the English squire on the
magisterial bench when he passes his severe sentence
upon the poor man who steals a crust of bread for his
starving family, or a stick from the park to keep them
warm ; upon the poacher who appropriates one of the
sacred birds ; upon the little ragged child who picks a
flower from the hall garden, even if it be only in
innocent ignorance, as her offering of affection to a sick
mother. The propertied clergy have often and often
endeavoured to steal common lands from the people,
and to enclose them for their own benefit.

But, then, it is not fair to charge all this upon the
religion of Christ. In any human institution, which
becomes established and powerful, the baser and more
evil elements in human nature are bound to come to
the front. I think it would be equally unfair to
designate such a temper as " the pagan " spirit ; Epic-
tetus would repudiate it as indignantly as Jesus ; but it
may certainly be designated as the satanic, worldly, and
anti-Christian spirit, against which precisely the religion
professed by these men protests, although such are the
self-sophistications we practise upon ourselves, that
Christians have been too ready to do what Christ

would have disapproved and repudiated, in the very name of their Founder.

But, on the other hand, when we come to later times, modern philanthropy may be said to date from the religious Evangelical revival under Wesley and Whitefield. The lethargy and luxury into which the Anglican clergy had sunk in the early part of the eighteenth century, produced no measure for the benefit of the people. But following upon the Methodist, and concurrent Evangelical revival in the Church of England, we find the beginnings of popular education, the building of hospitals, the endowment of charities, endeavours to abolish the slave-trade, together with efforts to reform our prisons and criminal system.

I am not for a moment maintaining that the sources of human progress are only to be found within the pale of Christianity. The polity of our Teutonic ancestors was essentially democratic. The Pagan nations have their own characteristic lessons for us. The love of abstract truth, the intelligent delight in beauty, and in art, the genius for jurisprudence, may have to be sought elsewhere; but the ethical and religious impulse so essential to the direction and regulation of life, and, above all, the "enthusiasm of humanity" do flow in fullest volume from Christ.

The revival of learning that was accomplished at

the end of the (so-called) Dark Ages counted for much in the emancipation of the human soul from darkness and error. But surely the impulse to universalize, and impart to the people in general this intellectual illumination was due to the specially Christian idea of human dignity and human brotherhood. Eventually, at any rate, it would come to be regarded impossible (as of old in the Pagan States founded upon slavery) to reserve culture for a few elect spirits, in order that they might tyrannize by virtue of it over the weaker and ignorant majority; at least, so far as that spirit did prevail in the mediæval republics and monarchies, it was a survival of the Pagan spirit, and in conflict with that of Christ. Though, indeed, we must admit that the privileged hierarchy had tried to keep whatever learning they possessed very much to themselves, their pretension to supernatural authority and miraculous power tempting them to arrogance and spiritual tyranny.

There is, I admit, a great apparent difficulty in the reflection that serfdom, and even slavery, continued to be the rule for so many centuries after the proclamation of Christianity. But may not this be accounted for by the fact that such institutions were part and parcel of the tribal systems, of the national customs, among those who were converted to Christianity, whether Roman or barbarian, and that the organization of the new society according to Christian principles, could only proceed very gradually in transforming institutions so rooted in racial character by long habit and custom? Human nature is a tough and stubborn thing to mould,—even when the Spirit of God is the moulder, not over-malleable, no very ductile clay for the potter's hand. The primeval matter, or "*hyle*," on which the Creator was, by some thinkers, conceived to work, was tractable to the reception of His image in comparison. And, even if it be right, as I believe, to regard the human soul as itself the Divine Spirit fallen into conditions of limitation in time and space, the same difficulties remain to hinder the regenerative process from within—the resistance being, indeed, essential to the process.

Thus I found, when travelling in Corsica, that the "enlightened" conscience of Corsica still insists on the traditionary blood-feud from generation to generation as strictly just and honourable ; while the arbitrament by private duel in cases of mere trivial difference between man and man is still sanctioned by the continental code of honour. But Herbert Spencer, for one, has abundantly shown that institutions which appear quite immoral to those who live under changed conditions, may not only seem right, but be really advantageous and indispensable under less developed and

earlier stages of civil polity. Social evolution is the
law, and, like physical evolution, it is necessarily slow ;
yet the principles of universal freedom were implicated
in the truths proclaimed by Christ, just as the typical
glory of a full-blown flower lies folded in the germ.
They require, however, for their full consummation the
maturing influences that correspond to sunshine, rain,
and a more genial season.

Secularists may urge that when we come on to the
French Revolution, the ideas of liberty, equality, and
fraternity, which inspired it, did not derive their origin
from that religion which so many intelligent minds had
ceased to believe, but rather from the teachings of
philosophy and science, giving birth to the conviction
that man as man has rights, and to a purely natural
benevolent passion for human happiness. Undoubtedly
these counted for much. Intellect and character were
ripening. There was a desperate and furious revolt
against monstrous injustice, against the selfishness of
privilege, secular and spiritual, against the corrupt
Christianity of interested classes. Yet may it not be
contended that the work of Rousseau, which counts for
so much in that volcanic outburst of the revolutionary
era, derived much of its inspiration from a desire to
rediscover the simplicity, sense of human brotherhood
equality before God, and universal benevolence of primi-

tive Christianity, overlaid, forgotten and confused amid
the corruptions and perversions of a selfish hierarchy, and
its monarchical or aristocratic allies ?   Surely we may
infer as much from the doctrine of Rousseau's " Vicaire
Savoyard." Renounce luxury, return to the simplicity
of primitive manners. Help your fellow-creatures, learn
that we are equals and brothers. Remove unjust restrictions and barriers ; that is the gist of the doctrine.
" The noble savage," so unhistorical, was but an accidental feature of this philosophy. Though on the
Continent, no doubt, the reaction against gross superstition and tyranny, priestly or feudal, was more violent,
sudden, and sweeping than it was in England, where
changes came little by little.

Certainly the revolt of fettered thought against arro-
gant, but blind uninformed authority, and the emancipated use of understanding, unchastened by reverent
feeling, affection, and conscience, has led many thinkers
far in the anti-religious, in some cases even in the anti-
ethical direction. The new scientific study of physical
nature has absorbed attention so exclusively as to
become positively disqualifying for the study and comprehension of philosophical or spiritual truth, the organs
that function in these sciences becoming atrophied
through disuse, and the mind acquiring an exclusive
crook toward an entirely different order of investiga-

tions. Thus the Encylopædists, and more recent
English, as well as German scientists, became material-
ists through their exclusive devotion to physical research. This Darwin virtually confesses to have become
more or less true of himself. But the benevolent and
humane bias given to successive generations by Christian education remained in the kindly and virtuous
natures of many such men, and they have often taken
up the popular cause with genuine earnestness. They
feel that the education which has lately been given to
the masses makes their demand for further corresponding privileges imperative on all. For through their
political enfranchisement they have become the real
governing power.

But save for such considerations, what are the social
and political lessons to be learned from modern scientific doctrine? Theories of natural selection, and the
survival of the fittest, suggest—that the weakest must
go to the wall—devil take the hindmost—*Vae Victis*—
eliminate feeble and diseased individuals for the benefit
of the race. Indeed, unless I have misunderstood him,
a conviction that this is the wisest course for statesmen
to pursue has been avowed by Professor Huxley and
others who think with him ; while Herbert Spencer is
an uncompromising individualist, and foe to State
regulation. So that though the older school of Radical-

ism, the Manchester School, bound up with the elder political economy, may claim the high-priests of science as allies, the newer Socialism, the co-operative, as distinguished from the competitive ideal of human society, can hardly expect to enlist them as very ardent supporters.

I admit, of course, that many modern anti-religious or agnostic thinkers have lately put themselves in the van of the new political economy; the less hope of redress elsewhere, the more need they feel of just conditions here; yet I must maintain that those to whom we are entitled to look for most effective assistance are the followers of Jesus Christ. For how can it be questioned that the social ideal, which has lately emerged into so much prominence and favour, is entirely in accordance with the principles by Him proclaimed? It was not only, as I have said, the rule of life that commended itself to the early Christian, as also to those who bound themselves by vows of poverty in the Middle Ages, but it was an ideal which inspired the protesting Lollard, the German mediæval Protestant, and those eminent founders of Modern Christian Socialism, Maurice and Kingsley. It commends itself now to the great creative poet of Russia, Tolstoi; to the English poet-critic and political economist, Ruskin; to the true poet and disciple of Walt Whitman, Edward Carpenter, as also to the clerical members of those influential Anglican bodies, the Christian Social Union, and the Guild of St. Matthew, which number among their adherents men like Bishop Westcott, the Bishop of Rochester, Charles Gore (late of Pusey House, Oxford), and Canon Scott Holland, of St. Paul's Cathedral ; to these, as also to Stopford Brooke, Dr. Clifford, and other prominent Nonconformists. Nor should the often admirable and impressive secular work of "General" Booth and his "Salvation Army" be forgotten.

But if, as I believe, religious worship, and the quest after truth or beauty flow from one common fountain, and find, although meandering, the same great sea, one would expect the same maxims of human conduct as were enunciated by Jesus, and incarnated in His life, to be ultimately discoverable by metaphysical, as well as physical philosophy, and to be capable of systematic application to the circumstances of daily life. Therefore that men who do not believe in the dogmas of Christianity—men, for instance, like the poet William Morris—should arrive independently, by their own different methods, at conclusions similar to those truths, which the Divine vision of Christ enabled Him authoritatively to teach on the subject of the ideal commonwealth centuries ago, is only what might be expected. Only you cannot be sure that at any given period there

will be perfect coincidence in the religious and secular
teachings upon a given subject, because, until the ripe
season arrives, secular thought cannot attain to certain
conclusions, thought being an organic growth, with progressive stages of evolution and development, while, on
the other hand, the religious magnetic needle is liable
to be deflected by subtle influences from interested
prejudice, and confusing intellectual theory. But in
recent years German philosophy, notably that of
Fichte and Hegel, and physical discovery, notably in
the regions of history and biology, have established
the solidarity and organic unity of the human race,
which reflects intelligible illumination upon the Christian
doctrine of Divine immanence, and God's incarnation in
humanity.

Personally I cannot pledge myself to any ready-
made or complete system of socialistic teaching as
indubitably true, and, even in the case of those maxims
which I recognize as well-founded, to their immediate,
or unconditional adaptability for realization in our code
of law. But still I hold this new democratic agitation
to be on the right tack, its current setting towards the
best and safest political haven. Surely that man or
woman is no Christian at all, except in name, in so far
as he or she remains indifferent to the awful abyss that

yawns between rich and poor; to the insufficiency of
the share in our immense wealth which falls to the lot
of those who produce it; the unjust, inhuman, and
horrible condition of the toilers in monstrous cities,
herded together like swine, with no leisure or opportunity for living a human life, perpetually starved,
stinted, stunted, maddened by carking care and anxiety
for the health, well-being, and very life of themselves
and of those nearest to them; the image of God well-
nigh crushed out of them by the cruel machinery that
makes us clean, comfortable, and virtuous, with a virtue
and happiness that have their root in a misery, and
moral degradation a millionfold more terrible than
those of the slave in Greece, Rome, or modern
America!

I do say that he or she who will acquiesce in an
earthly paradise for himself or herself, which is founded
upon this hell of innocent fellow-creatures, whatever
else he may be, cannot be a Christian. A Christian, on
the contrary, will move heaven and earth to alter it,
whatever risk and loss may be entailed upon him and
his. Orthodox and precise may be his definitions of
the human and divine natures, chaste and continent he
may be in his sexual relations, puritanical or ascetic
in his attitude toward certain forms of amusement,
though (somewhat arbitrarily) much less so towards

luxury and good living. But he can hardly be a follower of Him who appeared as the poor working Carpenter, a friend of publicans and sinners, denounced the rich man and proud religious Pharisee, uttered the terrible saying that a rich man can hardly enter into the kingdom of heaven, bade the virtuous and amiable youth whom he loved sell all he had and give to the poor.

The teaching of Christ is simply saturated with contempt poured upon the great and powerful, the ambitious master seeking great things for himself; its note throughout is exaltation of the weak, humble, poor, and despised, as more capable of the true inward spiritual riches; for it was the common people who heard Christ gladly; while the greater part of His life was devoted to making the outward condition of needy men more tolerable and happy, healing their sickness, ministering to their necessities, exhorting the wealthy and powerful to do justice and show mercy, although at the same time enforcing patient submission to the in- evitable as God's will, with an unseen purpose for good at the heart of it. "Ye cannot serve God and Mammon." " Lay not up for yourselves treasures upon earth."

It is true that He did not urge men to violent revolution. The hatred and cruelty implied in violence was foreign to His Spirit, nor were the times ripe for anything of the kind ; moreover, as Wyclif said, "God must sometimes serve the devil ;" yet Christ was in revolt against the orthodox religious rulers of his race, who crucified Him, and He knew that the actual result of His teaching would be to bring "not peace, but a sword." The slave was not emancipated without war ; the oppressive man will resist interference with those unjust but time-honoured privileges before which, if only they be effectually guarded, the slaves and cowards of the world cringe, nay bow in devil worship, that they may so propitiate and conciliate the powers of evil. But violence, tending as it does to reaction, can only be justified as a last resort. Rather would Jesus permeate men with His own Spirit, and then will new institutions grow quietly in place of the old, which will fall like the leaves of yester-year.

What St. Paul says to the elders of Ephesus in Acts xx. 33–35, is absolutely to the same effect as the words of Jesus—that we ought to labour with our own hands in order to support the weak, which is certainly the principle of modern Socialism. And there are many similar passages in the epistles, notably 1 Tim. vi. 17–19. But if anything in the Bible can be stronger still, it is the Epistle of St. James.

Charitable, helpful, and kindly indeed, many of our present clergy and ministers are, very fathers of their

Christianity and Social Advance. 337

flock, helpful to them in many ways. But I would urge
that they ought to go further, for I have already
traversed the plea that they ought not to interfere in
politics. The spiritual guides ought certainly to urge
upon the rich and powerful the duty of showing justice,
mercy, and kindness toward those dependent on them ;
while it becomes increasingly evident that the fundamental relations existing between these classes of the
community are wrong and indefensible, because incom-
patible with the claims of justice toward the producers
as a body, although the injustice be capable of redress
in a particular instance by a good master. And if that
should turn out to be so, it is clearly as much the duty
of a spiritual guide to proclaim the fact as it was the
duty of John the Baptist, according to his lights, to
withstand Herod in the matter of Herodias. In fact
the same cause will assume a new guise in matters of
detail at different periods, and in different circumstances.

The emphasis now laid by modern research upon
the organic unity of the race suggests that it is only
possible in a very imperfect fashion to save your own
soul, or the individual souls of other people from
future penalties in another world, and from bad habits
in this, unless you pay due attention also to the present
welfare of the race or nation as a whole, to the conditions

z

under which the majority, or a great multitude, are in this world obliged to live, think, and feel. Such is now known to be the influence of atmosphere and environment that you can hardly count upon remaining yourself, with your family and belongings, permanently healthy in body and soul—which (note it well) are now known to be only phases, or integral correlative elements of the same one entity, spirit, or person,—if you leave the moral and physical slums around you severely alone. Hence the growing sense that charity and justice should aim rather at a radical and general, however judicious and timely, alteration of established institutions, than at the relief of isolated individual wants, although of course these, in the meanwhile, cannot be left unregarded.

You may depreciate the "dark ages" and feudal times! At least in those days there was an acknowledged human and humanizing fellowship between the classes, though the members of one class might not be able to step over into the other. But while the one gave service, the other gave protection, food, and shelter; the lord and his dependent ate at the same table—at least, that was the theory; though the absolute rights claimed by the lord led to many instances of individual cruelty. But now there is no human relation at all existing, or even pretended, between employer and employed. A master—and far worse a company—regards " the hands " as mere impersonal machines for producing so much of material, exchangeable commodity; and the only question with them is, how cheaply will "the hands " do it? how little may we pay them? how nearly like the ownerless Pariah curs of some Eastern city will they be content to live? How much will just keep body and soul together, that they may work for us? How long, for how many hours out of the twenty-four will they consent to abrogate their rich and multiform humanity on our soulless, unbeautiful, and monstrous treadmill? For how many hours will the pale-faced, unfed, sick English girl do it, while the dingy room swims before her hollow eyes, while the mean walls go round, and even in the brief fevered sleep snatched by her burning head upon the poor pillow, she still stitches, and sews in a dream? In what asphyxiating and venomous sty will "the hands " be content to wallow? But no matter ; out of our ill-gotten gains we will endow churches, and give considerable sums, that cost us no self-denial, in charity. If "the hands " do not like it, there are thousands of hungry dogs waiting to snatch their morsel, and to take their places. In this way one may rob, starve others, and grow rich quite legally, quite respectably.

Out of the immense national wealth "the hands "

are indispensable for creating, what is their portion ?
"What porridge had John Keats ? " Such is this
vaunted modern demon-system of competition, such
these innumerable, warring human atoms, unlinked by
love or justice, untrammelled by mutual kindness, perfectly realizing before our eyes the imaginary "Levia-
than " of Thomas Hobbes, the lowest hell of selfishness
and anarchy.

Meanwhile the bishops, by their recent votes in the
House of Lords, are giving us an object-lesson in the
kind of attitude toward public questions peculiar to
dignified ecclesiasticism in high places. Meanwhile.
counties are depopulated that landlords may shoot
game ; families are evicted from humble ancestral
homes ; barbarian plutocrats, hereditary legislators,
claim a monopoly of forest, lake, and mountain, which
they are often too stupid and uncultured, or too satiated
by long and habitual possession, to appreciate or
understand.

Yet, from the spiritual rights of man proclaimed by
Christ, the secular rights of man proclaimed by Tom
Paine are an inevitable corollary—the secular rights of
every individual. It is, of course, easy for us who enjoy,
to sneer at and undervalue them. The inference, or
corollary, stands out as rigidly logical to-day, starts
forth as a deduction demonstrable and clear under

these changed conditions of the world, as a conclusion that the veracities and facts of the case compel us to draw, nay, to act upon without delay. For a man cannot enter into possession of or exercise any spiritual rights, if you utterly circumscribe and restrict him in the possession or exercise of rights, physical and secular. And these were little threatened when Christ spoke. Indeed, man had hardly awakened to the sense of them ; populations were less dense and hungry. But now human rights are threatened ; man is deprived of them ; yet education has made him desire them. "Stone walls do not a prison make, nor iron bars a cage," says the poet. Certainly this may be true of the hero or the saint ; " Minds innocent and quiet take that for a hermitage," he adds ; but such obstacles are apt to prevent the average, uninheriting, unmoralized, untrained man from even beginning to approximate to heroism or saintliness. The evil heritage and the evil environment smother and stint his virtue. There is not enough of it to be braced by adversity. When men prove unjust and unkind, God is apt to seem so too. You blow out the puny flame with the same breath that kindles the stronger, though smouldering fire into a blaze. A plant will not flower without congenial soil, manure, air, and water, much as you may look down upon these common things from your serene religious heights.

If you expect a man to sing, why you must first allow him to breathe. If he is to dance, you must give him room to turn round. A consumptive person is not strengthened, but killed, by going naked in a snowstorm, or by poor diet, though a Spartan athlete may profit by his black broth, or by roughing it all round. During the Wars of the Roses there was no literature to speak of; men were fighting for bare life. And so they are fighting now. What time or opportunity have they, and what heart, for the cultivation of virtue, let alone reason, or a taste for the beautiful? The Christian martyr was called upon to suffer for a great cause—the consciousness of that supported him through the flames; but for what great cause are these martyrs consciously suffering? Unconsciously? Yes, they are; but that is another matter altogether. They are victims sacrificed to prove that society is built on a rotten foundation. And our "pillars of the State" are letting the edifice collapse. Upon other foundations, with other piers must it be raised anew.

But then it may be asked, If the secularist and unbeliever take these matters up, why be so anxious that the Christian should do so likewise? And I answer : first, because we do not want our popular progress to fall into the hands of Anarchists of the type of Ravachol and Vaillant, a recent pamphlet, issued by that party,

as Karl Blind informs us, having for title "Up with
Bestiality!" And secondly, while we rejoice that
Secularists should advocate the popular cause — and
they do not always advocate it by any means—we
think that the Christian has in his keeping certain
important truths which cannot, without danger and
injury to the Commonwealth, be dispensed with. I
cannot, for my part, sympathize with those who regard
the Christian message as valuable, only in so far as it is
purely and directly ethical. (A clever book * recently
written by a young poet, Mr. Le Gallienne, takes this
view.) For though I believe much evil has resulted
from over-insistence on minute shades of dogma, yet as
scientific knowledge is valuable in the application of
scientific principles to practical purpose, so do I believe
also that certain important ideas are capable of being
reflected from spiritual intuition, or faith into the
understanding itself, and that man, consisting as he
does of both intellect and emotion—elements which
can by no means be isolated in his constitution—
requires some guiding light in his understanding, so
that conscience and emotion may be nourished, informed,
and regulated by reason.

Christ, unlike Buddha, proclaimed three great
intellectual truths, which are also moral, full of satis-

* " The Religion of a Literary Man."

faction for the noblest and deepest feeling. These
appear to be, first, the Fatherhood of God; second,
the divine sonship of man; third, the immortality
of the individual soul. He, unlike Spinoza, and the
Indian philosophy, taught that God, the Source and
Substance of our being, is both conscious Intelligence,
and moral, emotional Intelligence also; that Man, in
his deepest and truest individuality, is Image, or Word
of God, organically one with Him; that the highest
spiritual, human nature truly mirrors and expresses the
divine, however imperfectly, after its measure, even in
this mortal life; and that every individual soul in its
own distinctive personality is immortal, eternal, while
also organic, solidary, universal in essence; therefore
of quite infinite importance. Wiser than other great
teachers, Jesus does not exaggerate the duty of Altruism
into the Brahmanical idea of absorption into one dis-
tinctionless blank Unit, by philosophy named "Being,"
though indeed a mere abstract idea of philosophy, without counterpart in Reality, which is concrete, living
Spirit.

He bids us "love our neighbour as ourselves," thus
admitting that we owe a duty to ourselves, to our own
free and full development; that we cannot jump off our
own shadows. Which spiritual and moral proclamation
corresponds with the philosophical truth that there

cannot be unity without variety, that the two notions are correlative and necessary to one another; moreover that the conscious, self-identifying individual is indeed substantial, not merely modal or accidental. For without self-identification in conscious memory, without comparison by such self-identifying consciousness, both differentiating and identifying the data of sensation and perception, there can be no knowledge or experience of anything whatsoever, there can be no classified, known order of phenomena, contemporaneous and successive,—no world of Nature therefore, which is the name we give to the invariable relations or laws that are found to obtain among phenomena, and constitute our experience of what we call the material world. Even the faintest distinguishable sensation implies a one distinguishing personality behind it. Conscious individuality, therefore, is the permanent substance, underlying and supporting alike our own internal world of thought and feeling, and the so-called external world of phenomena, which we name material ; soul and body. But death of the body, being itself only one of these phenomena, or appearances, can hardly be conceived to affect the conscious substance, or subject of experience, in whose consciousness alone death can be regarded as an actual fact at all.*

* The Kantian and post-Kantian German Idealism, otherwise so help-

Now in such beliefs must undoubtedly be involved much ethical impulse, much moral strength and sustainment, through apparent failure or slow and laborious, progress. He who holds them has faith in one Divine purpose that runs through the ages, in a continuity of development for the human mind and character, under Divine guidance, whatever obstacles may be encountered; he believes that even these make for education and growth, for the bracing of moral muscle and sinew, through that long and tough wrestle with difficulty imposed. He is sure that this stage of existence, whatever disappointment, suffering, and ill-success may attend it, is only a stage in the infinite life and progress of every man or woman. Pessimism and discouragement, therefore, may invade the effort of another, not his. Cynical contempt for the petty, malign and despicable ephemeron of an hour, be it man or woman, may paralyze now and again generous desire for human welfare, but not his. Another may feel how little, after all, can be accomplished, how paltry our poor ability to contend with unknown and incalculable hostile powers.

ful, fails to inculcate the truth, that the universal Ego implies particular Egos, and that the latter are as essential and permanent as the former. But particular individuals are not fully developed until they have acquired a full realization of their solidarity with the race, of their universality, which is quite compatible with the perfect fruition of their own peculiar distinctive natures, as it was in Christ ethically, in Shakespeare intellectually.

The stern and awful sphinx, Nature, impassive and cold, regards man with blank, unspeculative eyes, till the wings of the animal-angel droop and wither, till the sword of the warrior breaks in his hand, the sword-arm falls numb and nerveless, as in the pessimistic poet's superb vision.   Then darkens again primæval night, and the everlasting ice enshrouds our weary, wandering, unpiloted planet, now the tomb of men and of all life. Shall we pine overmuch, wear heart and eyes and brains out to build the city of God—here?

Therefore do I prefer that Christians, who have a firmer hope, a surer and more ennobling word of prophecy, should lead our little army, whose faces though yet darkling, are turned toward the dawn, even though they be associated in command with those truly noble men who march forward, who wave the soldier on to victory, with despair in the inmost heart of them, or looking haggard forth from stern-set eyes.   Nay, but hear some of the spiritual guides, " Pray, gentlemen, take our place, for our sacred rights of private property must be secured at all risks.   Go forward, if you will ; in the name of Christ we turn again to nose out pestilent heresies, and to pursue the cultus of our golden calf."   But if these will not show us the way, then the people, marching forward, will trample upon them and upon their creed, which some of us will be sorry to see.

For the fact remains that, in order to the efficiency of
any institutions, and more especially of institutions
collective in character, mutual good-will, public spirit,
righteousness and honesty are essential. Without these
there will be failure, as without ripeness for a fundamental change there will follow reaction. But the
worship of a concrete personal Ideal, believed once
to have historically existed on earth, so proving the
nobler life to be possible, even here, and to be living
now in the unseen, gifted with a threefold power to
help, obtained for Him by this mortal triumph, this, I
believe, is capable of supplying the strongest motive
force, and the most reliable influence in securing the
result, we the friends of freedom, desire. Patient endur-
ance in face of disappointment and slow progress, per-
severance in hope and effort, mutual forbearance,
generous intelligent sympathy, confidence that One is
working in and for us, who cannot fail to conquer,
although His mills grind so slowly, this temper is
needed, and is most likely to be fostered by the religion
of Christ, purified from encumbering superstition, as
from antiquated and exploded dogma.

The proposition that politics and religion should be
kept apart seems mischievous and untrue, not more
true and profitable than the corresponding one that
politics and morality should be kept apart. Given a

religion which insists upon morality, or the performance of our duty to our neighbour as a religious duty, as the best way of serving God, or at least the one indispensable way of serving Him, then to affirm that religion and politics ought to be kept apart, is to affirm that in this sphere of the State's relation toward the citizens that compose it, and their relations toward the State, as well as in the relations of races and nations toward one another, such considerations as duty, justice, and honesty, are irrelevant. No more absurd and pernicious notion than this could be put into words.

The pagan states of antiquity may set us a good example as regards their inculcation of each individual's duty toward the state of which he is a member; and we are now returning to their conception of the individual as member of a human society, of an organic body politic. The Christian religion has hitherto treated the individual soul too much as if it were absolutely apart from its fellows and alone, teaching each to seek primarily his own everlasting salvation, or deliverance from wrath to come, and from bad habits here, by means of certain beliefs, or good works, partly consisting in religious observances, partly in acts of charity, and partly in abstinence from a few authoritatively specified pleasures, chiefly sexual. Little stress has, as a rule,

been laid upon the ordinary duties of man to his
fellow-men as a citizen of one state, or as a member
of the comity of nations. Still less on the international obligations of one people toward another.

And yet it is a familiar fact of every-day experience
that the gross injustice and cruelty, or fraudulent conduct of which a person in his private capacity could
not possibly allow himself to be guilty, he will yet be
guilty of with small scruple in his corporate or public
capacity, as member of some public body, say as director
or shareholder in a joint stock company. For one
who, by his own private speculative transactions, will
ruin without scruple thousands of innocent and helpless
families in pursuit of private gain (and alas! such
Neros and Borgias of our modern capitalist system
are all too common now), there are hundreds who will
do the same thing by shifting all moral responsibility
off their own shoulders, as members of a corporation
or company. And, again, a modern capitalist will avail
himself of any abstract maxims of a bloodless, inhuman
(though happily now nearly discredited), political
economy that may be current in justifying his hard
and unscrupulous dealings with those dependent on
him for employment, with no sort of reference to the
obligations which his Christianity might be supposed
to impose on him toward all men in general regarded

as brothers, and toward certain men and women in particular, as very closely connected with him in his capacity of master or employer, making use of their labour; although to him surely must consequently be committed the regulation and best disposal of their labour as a trust from God. To God he must nevertheless be answerable for his unjust, inhuman, and unmerciful exploitation of these human lives, which men and women and children are constrained, on pain of death, to place at his disposal in our competitive and overcrowded society, according to the conditions of its actual constitution.

And yet his religion, which prevents him from "stealing" a shilling, in the accepted criminal interpretation of that term, dost not prevent him from stealing the lives and health, the souls, hearts, and minds of innumerable sweated, trade-poisoned, and swine-styed fellow-creatures, who create his wealth; although the human rights and prerogatives which he denies them with a light heart and without a qualm, are claimed for them expressly by the very first principles of his religious creed. Howbeit this man may be a shining light, an eminent example of all the virtues as a family man, or as a member of his particular religious sect.

Now, does not the inconsistency arise from this arbitrary relegation of religious duty to the domestic, private, and other-worldly sphere, from the implicit and explicit denial of its authority in the province of public, or semi-public transactions? As a public man, as a wheel, or cog, or pinion, in the great machine, as the director and organizer of a large industry or business, which is indeed an integral element in our great national commercial system, a very artery of our complex national life, or one of its countless ramifications—in this capacity he must follow the usual course, the average current morality—into this province his religion cannot enter. Christian principles applied literally here would be too Utopian, too ridiculously unpractical. Business is business after all. And since this Christian does not in words draw the logical inference with respect to the Founder of his religion, which one would have supposed to be inevitable, why, his church or chapel is not obliged to call him a blasphemer, being indeed very far from desirous to do so, since it probably agrees with him.

But if one answers that all this is inevitable under the existing constitution of society, then I urge in my turn that assuredly a good Christian as such must desire to "interfere in politics," and get the existing constitution of society fundamentally altered, gradually and peacefully, if you will; organically; but as soon as possible. The Church has over and over again induced the State to enforce her own pretensions, as well as those of property or privilege by fire and sword ; let her now interfere to urge the claims of the people at large upon her sister, the State. The common people, who are suffocated and trodden upon in our English Black Hole of Calcutta, cannot well afford to wait for the better arrangements, which comfortable ecclesiastics assure them will be provided in some other world, to which, if they behave themselves, they may hope to emigrate after death. "While the grass grows," the proverb is somewhat musty. But the recent Jerusalem conference of clergy, which met to confer on the "living wage" of miners, was disappointing in the scanty attendance of eminent Church officials, and somewhat abortive in result.

We may remark, in conclusion, upon the notorious cynicism, cruelty, and profligacy, which have distinguished the proclamation and prosecution of international European wars, and especially the dealings of Christian peoples with those darker races, whom they are pleased to stigmatize as barbarian or inferior, though, indeed, we have ourselves not a little to learn from these. I believe that this may partly be explained by our refusal to apply the principles of our Christianity to the determination of public and political questions, save at least in the most haphazard and unsystematic manner. Whence it comes that passion and self-interest, inscribing certain isolated texts upon their banners, often applicable only to quite different periods and circumstances, have claimed the religion of Christ as a powerful advocate of evil causes, and with profane rites, have chanted "Te Deum" over Satan's victory.

Old Testament moral maxims adapted to an earlier and less developed condition of human nature have been regarded as equally sacred and binding with those higher revelations which have been made at a later time, and have been actually preferred as rules of action, in proportion as they proved more congenial to characters and dispositions, that are indeed a survival from primitive stages of moral growth. But, unfortunately, such survivals are the rule, while morally advanced natures are the exception; and yet the Old Testament, especially the prophets, are full of noble morality bearing upon the relations between rich and poor. I feel that I cannot conclude this essay in greater and more emphatic words than those of our Lord Himself: "Inasmuch as ye have done it unto one of the least of these My brethren, ye have done it unto Me."

RODEN NOEL.

The Social Creed of a Christian Democrat.

1. We believe in one God, the Father and Educator of Humanity.

2. We believe in Jesus Christ, His only Son, our Lord, the Redeemer and Emancipator of men's souls and bodies.

3. We believe that Jesus Christ, in proclaiming a Fatherly Will as the origin of all Life, and the root of Humanity, revealed to man the Divine Order under which he is living.

4. We believe that the Christian Church, in the idea of its Founder, had for its object the reorganization and restitution of Society, no less than the salvation and deliverance of the Individual.

5. We believe, therefore, that there is an Order of Society which is the best ; that towards this Order the world is gradually moving according to a definite Divine plan.

6. We believe that in the life and teaching of Jesus

Christ and His apostles, as recorded in the pages of the New Testament, the eternal principles of that Divine plan—the laws of the kingdom of heaven— were revealed.

7. But we believe also in the Holy Spirit of God as the living and acting motor of civilization, the inspirer and the purifier of the thoughts of men's hearts, "the light which lighteneth every man who cometh into the world."

8. We believe, therefore, that an educational revelation is ceaselessly descending from God to man, and that in each age of the world new portions of eternal truth are thus revealed.

9. We believe, therefore, in conscience, the revelation of life to the individual, and in tradition, the revelation of life to humanity, as the means given to us by God to comprehend His design, and that when the voice of conscience and of tradition are harmonized in an affirmation, that affirmation is the truth, or a portion of the truth.

10. We believe, therefore, that the revelation of the providential scheme is to be found in the witness of the facts of daily life, and is unceasingly continuous.

11. We believe that to limit that revelation to a given portion of time, to one sole people, to a single individual, to a single book, is essential Atheism.

12. We believe, therefore, that there is no finality in Divine Revelation, that the Will of God, the Word of God, is not yet all revealed, that—

> Slowly the Bible of the race is writ,
> And not in paper leaves or leaves of stone.
> Each age, each kindred, adds a word to it—
> Texts of despair or hope, or joy, or moan.

13. We believe in the Bible of God's continuous revelation, whose chapters are History, Politics, and Science, as well as in that other revelation of spiritual truth which we rightly reverence as the very Word of God.

14. We believe, therefore, in the duty of man to study the providential laws by which humanity has gradually been impelled along the path of social order and progress, and to co-operate with those laws in order that in human society this double manifestation of progress may be seen—all men approximating to a common level, but a level which is continually rising.

15. We believe, therefore, that in the " Notes " of the Christian kingdom—" righteousness, peace, joy "—we have the Christian translation of the old battle-cry of revolution—" liberty, fraternity, equality "—in which nothing of the old truth is lost, but all is interpreted, purified, transfigured.

16. We believe in Liberty—freedom—not to do what one likes, but freedom to do what one ought, and that, therefore, respect for individual rights must never blind us to the higher reverence we owe to social duty.

17. We believe in Fraternity—that we are all "one man in Christ Jesus," but that no man can say sincerely, "Our brothers who are on earth," who has not previously learned to say, "Our Father which art in heaven."

18. We believe in Equality—equality, that is to say, not of condition, but equality of consideration, and we express it in the maxim that everybody is to count for one and nobody for more than one.

19. We believe that in all the disputes and conflicts —industrial, social, political—which rend the body politic of this Christian State to-day, the prime necessity is frank Justice between class and class.

20. We believe that the first principle of Christian Justice is this—that the loss of one cannot, on the whole, be the gain of another in the unity of the one life.

21. We believe that to identify the increase of national wealth with the increase of individual wealth, is a gross social mistake; that, on the other hand, national wealth ought always to be treated with con-

stant reference to national life, and that therefore, in all questions of dispute between Capital and Labour, in the last resort it must be remembered that it is not a question about wealth, but about men.

22. We believe that the competition of Trade has been assimilated to the competition of War, and stands condemned by the assimilation.

23. We believe that in Christ's kingdom the law of life is service, not competition, and that no money therefore is legitimately earned which is not an exchange value for actual services rendered—services which minister to life and help on the common good ; and that consequently no wealth is honest wealth which is accumulated by taking advantage of the weakness or the ignorance of our neighbours, and rendering them no equivalent in reciprocal service.

24. We believe that although Christian Economics may quite justifiably show that Interest on invested capital is legitimate, when the advantage to the borrower is evidently as great or greater than it is to the lender, yet that the sin of Usury is not extinct so long as money remains the master, and not the servant of labour and industrial power ; and thus constantly falls under the temptation of making profits at the expense of wage.

25. We believe, therefore, that every Christian man

or woman who lends money and receives Interest upon it—who takes part, that is to say, in a commercial concern, and receives a proportion of profits in the shape of dividend, is bound not only to ask whether the business is *safe* to pay; but whether the business *deserves* to pay.

26. We believe, therefore, in the principle of the " living wage," by which we mean such a wage as will allow the worker not only to maintain his own working powers in the highest state of efficiency, but also to enable himself and family to live a decent, a joyous, and a reasonable life, according to " the standard of comfort " of his class.

27. We believe, therefore, in St. Paul's doctrine of wages, that " the labourer who worketh must be first partaker of the fruits ;" in other words, that the living wage must be the bed-rock of price, the first charge on the product of work, and that, therefore, some way must be found in a Christian system of trade for prices to follow wages, not wages to follow prices.

28. We believe that high civilization is not the destined lot of the few, while the destined lot of the many is to support the few by unremitting, joyless toil ; that it is no use any longer quoting or misquoting Scripture to prove that God wills the mass of mankind to be always poor and always dependent on the rich ;

Creed of a Christian Democrat. 361

that if there is a text in the Bible which says, "The poor ye have with you always," there is also another text which speaks of the time "when there shall be no poor among you."

29. We believe that the justification of Trades Unionism is to be found in the justice of the aim that "such as are in need and necessity have right," and that although the rough prosecution of this aim may often be irritating to those who inherit moods of feudal haughtiness, and may even interfere with and disturb the process of making money, yet still the postpone-ment of the interest of an individual to the interest of the class to which he belongs is a nobler, a more Christian thing than the desire to drive a large trade, or to scheme for personal enrichment.

30. We believe, however, that Justice is not always on the weaker side, and that never does organized oppression wear so ugly a look as when it is practised by those who inscribe "Liberty" and "Fraternity" on their banner, and that never does the contemptible cry, "Every man for himself," sound so forbiddingly as when it is uttered by those who have not hesitated to infringe personal liberty and to imperil social order.

31. We believe that society exists not for the sake of private property, but private property for the sake of society.

32. We believe that the right use of property must be insisted upon as a religious duty ; that as capital arises from common labour, so in justice it should be made to minister to common wants.

33. We believe that wealth does not release the rich man from his obligation to work, but only enables him to do unpaid work for society ; the only difference, indeed, according to Christian Ethics, between the rich man and the poor man seeming to be this—that the poor man receives his wages at the end of the week, and does not get them unless his work is first done, whereas the wealthy man receives his wages first, and is bound, as a matter of honour, to earn them afterwards.

34. We believe that life, labourous life, self-denying life, must be graced with beauty and filled with many pleasures, but that the highest pleasure is the pleasure of helpful life itself, the joy of love, of fellow-help, of comradeship, and that, therefore, no luxury, in fact, is culpable, no wealth is wasted, which serves to make its consumer a more useful, a more loving, a more helpful member of the community.

35. We believe that it is not the equalization of Capital that is needed, but its moralization.

36. We believe that as all life is of the kingdom of God; and the Church of Christ is concerned in the

ways of His disciples, however secular they may seem
to be, it is the duty of the Christian citizen to build
up, as far as his influence extends, the life of the great
civic brotherhood to which he belongs, and of every
sphere of action which it contains, in justice, righteousness, and the fear of God.

37. We believe, therefore, that it is the duty of the
Christian city, in the interests of its citizens, to provide,
first, for the three essentials of physical life—pure air,
pure water, pure food; and, secondly, for the three
essentials of spiritual life—admiration, hope, and love;
and with these objects in view we believe that such
a city will take legal measures to prevent the pollution
of air, water, food; will preserve open spaces and town
gardens, will provide playing fields and gymnasiums
and baths in connection with all Elementary Public
Schools, will pass not only a Sunday Closing Act for
public-houses, but a Sunday Opening Act for public
libraries, museums, art galleries, and other drawing-
rooms of the people.

38. We believe that in such a city the citizens will
have full control over the regulation and licence of
all trades, and that the drink traffic, as at present
organized, standing condemned by Christian principles,
will, if not suppressed altogether, be very largely cur-
tailed, and in the meantime compelled to compensate

the rate payers of the city for the increase of poor-rate and police-rate directly traceable to its influence.

39. We believe that in any truly Christian city there would undoubtedly be a by-law of the council suppressing the scandalous indecencies of the Divorce Court, and the brutalizing horrors of the police court, in the public prints, and prohibiting the publication in any newspaper of all betting lists, the odds on sporting events, and any information likely to stimulate gambling, whether on the Turf or the Stock Exchange.

40. We believe that the conception of family life is not only human but Divine, and that therefore it is the duty of the Church of Christ to unite men in actively opposing the corruption of national and social life, which springs from neglect of the principle that personal purity is of universal obligation upon man and woman alike, and when necessary to co-operate with the civil and municipal authorities in police efforts for the repression of prostitution and the degradation of women and children.

41. We believe not only in Progress, but in man's solidarity in Progress. We believe that the glory of a nation, like the glory of a citizen or a class, lies not in supremacy but in service, and that therefore the ruling principle of International Policy should be not to secure the conquest or the weakness of other nations

through War or Diplomacy, but the betterment of all nations through the co-operation of all, the progress and full development of each, for the benefit and the widest good of all.

42. We believe, finally, that Christ's whole earthly life is a direct command to His Church to spend a large part of her time and energy in fighting against all circumstances and conditions of living which foster disease and hinder health, in delivering people from evil environment and fatal heredity; that, in fact, the whole secular history of the Church should be an endeavour to realize in act the daily petition of her dominical prayer, "Father! Thy Kingdom come, Thy will be done, *on* EARTH!"

CHARLES W. STUBBS.

PRINTED BY WILLIAM CLOWES AND SONS, LIMITED, LONDON AND BECCLES.

www.ingramcontent.com/pod-product-compliance
Lightning Source LLC
Chambersburg PA
CBHW021711110726
47902CB00005B/1139